APR 0 2 2015

Where You Go
Is Not
Who You'll Be

An Antidote to the
College Admissions Mania

FRANK BRUNI

GRAND CENTRAL
PUBLISHING

NEW YORK   BOSTON

Grand Central Publishing
Hachette Book Group
1290 Avenue of the Americas
New York, NY 10104

www.HachetteBookGroup.com

Printed in the United States of America

RRD-C

First Edition: March 2015

10 9 8 7 6 5 4 3 2 1

Grand Central Publishing is a division of Hachette Book Group, Inc. The Grand Central Publishing name and logo is a trademark of Hachette Book Group, Inc.

The Hachette Speakers Bureau provides a wide range of authors for speaking events. To find out more, go to www.hachettespeakersbureau.com or call (866) 376-6591.

The publisher is not responsible for websites (or their content) that are not owned by the publisher.

Library of Congress Cataloging-in-Publication Data has been applied for.

ISBN: 978-1-455-53270-4

To all the high school kids in this country who are dreading the crossroads of college admissions and to all the young adults who felt ravaged by it. We owe you and the whole country a better, more constructive way.

Contents

INTRODUCTION

Peter Hart didn't try for Harvard, Princeton or any of the Ivies. That wasn't the kind of student he'd been at New Trier High School, which serves several affluent suburbs north of Chicago. Nearly all of its roughly one thousand graduating seniors each year go on to higher education, and nearly all of them know, from where they stand among their peers and from the forecasts of guidance counselors, what sort of college they can hope to attend. A friend of Peter's was ranked in the top five of their class; she set her sights on Yale—and ended up there. Peter was ranked somewhere around 300: not great but wholly respectable considering the caliber of students at New Trier. He aimed for the University of Michigan or maybe the special undergraduate business school at the University of Illinois.

Both rejected him.

He went to Indiana University instead, and arrived there feeling neither defeated nor exhilarated. He was simply determined to make the most of the place and to begin plotting a career and planning an adult life.

Right away he noticed a difference. At New Trier, a public school posh enough to pass for private, he'd always had a sense of himself as someone somewhat ordinary, at least in terms of his studies. He lacked his peers' swagger and ready-made eloquence. He wasn't especially quick to raise his hand, to offer an opinion, to seize a position of leadership. At Indiana, though, the students in his freshman dorm and in his freshman classes weren't as uniformly poised and showily gifted as the New Trier kids had been, and his self-image went through a transformation.

"I really felt like I was a competent person," he told me when I interviewed him in June 2014, shortly after he'd turned twenty-eight. "It was confidence-building." He thrived during that first year, getting a 3.95 grade point average, which earned him admission into an honors program for undergraduate business majors. And he thrived during the rest of his time at Indiana, drawing the attention of professors, becoming vice president of a business fraternity on campus, cobbling together the capital to start his own tiny real estate enterprise—he bought, fixed up and rented small houses to fellow students—and finagling a way, off-campus, to get interviews with several of the top-drawer consulting firms that trawled for recruits at the Ivies but often bypassed schools like Indiana. Upon graduation, he took a plum job in the Chicago office of the Boston Consulting Group, where he recognized one of the other new hires: the friend from New Trier who'd gone to Yale. Traveling a more gilded path, she'd arrived at the very same destination.

Peter worked for three years with the Boston Consulting Group and another two with a private equity firm in Manhattan. When I talked with him, he was between his first and second year at Harvard's graduate business school. Yes, he said, many of his Harvard classmates had undergraduate degrees fancier than his; no, he said, he didn't feel that his Indiana education put him at any disadvantage. Besides which, he and most of the others in the Harvard MBA program had been out of college for as long as they'd been in it. What they'd learned in the workplace since graduation had more bearing on their assurance and performance at Harvard than did anything picked up in any class, let alone the name of their alma mater.

The main, lasting relevance of Indiana, he told me, was the way it had turned him into a bolder, surer person, allowing him to discover and nurture a mettle that hadn't been teased out before. "I got to be the big fish in a small pond," he said. Now, if he wanted to, he could swim with the sharks.

Jenna Leahy, twenty-six, went through the college admissions process two years after Peter did. She, too, was applying from a charmed school: in her case, Phillips Exeter Academy, which was less than a mile from her family's New Hampshire home and which she attended as a day student. She wasn't at the very top of her class but she had as many A's as B's. At Exeter, one of the most storied prep schools in America, that was nothing to sneeze at. She was also a captain of the cross-country team and active in so many campus organizations that when graduation day rolled around, she received one of the most coveted prizes, given to a student who'd brought special distinction to the academy.

Jenna had one conspicuous flaw: a score on the math portion of the SAT that was in the low 600s. Many selective colleges cared more than ever about making sure that each new freshman class had high SAT scores, because that was one of the criteria by which *U.S. News & World Report* ranked schools in its annual survey, the influence of which had risen exponentially since its dawn in the 1980s. In fact, the college on which Jenna set her sights, Claremont McKenna, cared so much that its dean of admissions would later be exposed for fabricating and inflating that statistic.

Jenna applied early to Claremont McKenna. And was turned down.

She was stunned. She couldn't quite believe it. And partly because of that, she didn't sink into a funk but moved quickly to tweak her dreams and widen her net, sending applications to Georgetown University, Emory University, the University of Virginia and Pomona College, which is one of Claremont McKenna's sister schools. She threw in a few more, to have some insurance, though she was relatively certain that she wouldn't need it.

In early spring the news came. Georgetown said no. Emory said no. No from Virginia. No from Pomona. She felt like some kind of magnet for rejection: Earlier that semester, her first serious boyfriend had broken up with her. He was a sophomore at Stanford, the sort of school she was now being told she simply wasn't good enough for. What *was* she good enough for? What in the world was going on? Many of her Exeter classmates were bound for the Ivies and their ilk, and they didn't seem to her any more capable than she. Was it because they were legacy cases, from families with more money than hers?

All she knew was that they had made the cut and she hadn't.

"I felt so worthless," she told me. "It was a very, very depressing time."

As she remembers it, she was left essentially with two

options. One was Scripps College: another of Claremont McKenna's sister schools, though not quite as desired as Pomona. The other was the University of South Carolina. It wanted her badly enough that it offered her a significant scholarship. "But that wasn't enough for me," she said. "I wanted a name. I wanted some prestige." That was the immediate legacy of the application process. She was determined to grab whatever bragging rights she could.

But there was another, better legacy, which came later. Once she got through the summer, crossed the country to Southern California, beheld how gorgeous the Scripps campus was and saw how well she fit in there, she realized not only that the most crushing chapter of her life was in the past but that it hadn't crushed her. Not even close. Actually, it had helped her separate the approval that others did or didn't give her from what she believed—no, *knew*—about herself.

One day she happened to sign up for a day trip from Scripps to Tijuana, Mexico, to help do some painting and other charitable work in an especially impoverished neighborhood. When she got there, she recalled, "I held a baby who could barely breathe, and the mother didn't have the money to take the baby to the doctor, and you could literally see the United States on the other side of the border. I was just blown away." The moment stayed with her, and during her sophomore year, she applied for a grant that would give her the funds necessary to live in Tijuana for the summer and work with indigent children there. She got it.

A pattern emerged. "I applied for things fearlessly," she said, "because I knew now that I was worth something even if I wasn't accepted." Rejection was arbitrary. Rejection was survivable.

She entered a contest at her school to spend a weekend among the Mexican poor with Jimmy Carter, and she was chosen. She put in a request to study abroad in Senegal and then in Paris, and was permitted to do both. After graduation she went to work for Teach for America and, toward the end of her time with the organization, she sought a special fellowship in school administration that was typically given only to educators with more experience. She nonetheless received it, and later got a federal grant to write the three-hundred-plus pages of the charter for a public elementary school she was proposing to start in Phoenix, where she now lives. That school, serving children from low-income families, opened in August 2014. Jenna is its cofounder and its director of students and operations.

"I never would have had the strength, drive or fearlessness to take such a risk if I hadn't been rejected so intensely before," she told me. "There's a beauty to that kind of rejection, because it allows you to find the strength within."

Is Peter's example so remarkable? I don't think so. People bloom at various stages of life, and different individuals flourish in different climates. The hothouse of secondary school favors only some.

And Jenna's arc isn't unusual in the least. The specific details, the proper nouns: Those are hers and hers alone. But for every person whose contentment and fulfillment come from faithfully executing a predetermined script, there are at least ten if not a hundred who had to rearrange the pages and play a part they hadn't expected to, in a theater they hadn't envisioned. Life is defined by little snags and big setbacks; success is determined by the ability to distinguish between the two and rebound from either. And there's no single juncture, no one crossroads, on which everything hinges.

So why do so many Americans—anxious parents, addled children—treat the college admissions process as if it were precisely that?

This book was born during the annual height of that process, as another March ended and the chatter among many of the adults around me grew predictably heavy with the words *acceptance, rejection, safety school* and such. Their children had been waiting three months or longer to find out whether the applications they'd submitted to their dream schools would do the trick. The notices would come in any day. The suspense was at its peak.

I was familiar with it from the previous March and the March before that, because to live among Americans affluent enough to give their kids a certain kind of grounding and gilding is to recognize a particular rhythm to the year and specific mile markers on the calendar. November 1 is the deadline for many early-admission applications, January 1 for general-admission applications. In the days just before April 1, the school's decisions dribble out, and I'll watch the parents in my orbit exult like they rarely exult or reel like they seldom reel. The intensity of these reactions always stops me short, because it attaches a make-or-break importance to a finite circle of exalted institutions—and to private colleges and universities over public ones—that isn't supported by the evidence, by countless stories like Peter's and Jenna's, by the careers and the examples all around me, by common sense. A sort of mania has taken hold, and its grip seems to grow tighter and tighter.

I'm describing the psychology of a minority of American families; the majority of them are focused on making sure that their kids simply attend a decent college—any decent college— and on finding a way to help them pay for it. (Note: In this book I'll often use "college" as a catchall term, and interchangeably with "university," but only in reference to the undergraduate portion and years of an institution, like the University of Michigan or Stanford, that also has graduate schools and doctoral programs.) When I asked Alice Kleeman, the college adviser at Menlo-Atherton High School in the Bay Area of California, about the most significant changes in the admissions landscape over the twenty years that she has inhabited it, the lust for elite schools and the fixation on them was only the third dynamic she mentioned. The first? "More students are unable to attend their college of first choice because of money," she said, alluding to the country's economic doldrums over the last decade and the high cost of higher education. Second, she brought up what she saw as the positive development of colleges being willing to admit and extend financial aid to undocumented immigrants. Her answers were crucial reminders that an obsession with the Ivies and other colleges of their perceived caliber is far more privilege than curse.

But the number of parents and students who succumb to it is by no means small, and that's clear in the escalation of applications to elite schools and in the dizzying expansion and expense of college admissions coaching. There's a whole industry devoted to prepping and packaging students, to festooning them with all the right ribbons and all the prettiest bows. For too many parents and their children, getting into a highly selective school isn't just another challenge, just another goal. A yes or no from Amherst or Dartmouth or Duke or Northwestern is seen as the conclusive measure of a young person's worth, a binding verdict on the life that he or she has led up until that point, an uncontestable harbinger of the successes or disappointments to come. Winner or loser: This is when the judgment is made. This is the great, brutal culling.

What madness. And what nonsense.

For one thing, the admissions game is too flawed and too rigged to be given so much credit. For another, the nature of a student's college experience—the work that he or she puts into it, the skills that he or she picks up, the self-examination that's undertaken, the resourcefulness that's honed—matters more than the name of the institution attended. In fact students at institutions with less hallowed names sometimes demand more of those places and of themselves, convinced that they have ground to make up, a disadvantage to compensate for. Or, freed somewhat from a focus on the packaging of their education, they get to the meat of it. In any case, there's only so much living and learning that take place inside a lecture hall, a science lab or a dormitory. Education is indeed everything, but it happens across a spectrum of settings and in infinite ways. It starts well before college. It continues long after college. College has no monopoly on the ingredients for professional success or for a life well lived.

I know many wildly accomplished people who attended Ivy League schools and other highly selective private colleges and benefited in precisely the ways that alumni of these institutions are supposed to. I know more who attended public universities and schools without major reputations, and in this book I'll introduce some of them, describing their paths, letting them reflect on their achievements and putting college in a saner, healthier, more accurate perspective. I even know a fair number of distinguished overachievers who never graduated from college. I wouldn't recommend that last route, but my reasons aren't solely practical. They're intellectual, philosophical, spiritual. College is a singular opportunity to rummage through and luxuriate in ideas, to give your brain a vigorous workout and your soul a thorough investigation, to realize how very large the world is and to contemplate your desired place in it. And that's being lost in the admissions mania, which sends the message that college is a sanctum to be breached—a border to be crossed—rather than a land to be inhabited and tilled for all that it's worth.

This mania has many roots, a few of which I'll look at in the pages to come. But it can't be divorced from a chapter of American life and a corrosion of American discourse in which not just Chevrolet and Cartier but everyday people worry about their "brands," and in which everything imaginable is subdivided into microclimates of privilege and validation. At the amusement park, you can do general admission or a special pass or an even fancier package that puts you instantly at the front of every line. At the Equinox fitness chain, trainers are designated by numbers—Tiers 1, 2 and 3—that signal their experience and hourly rate, and there are deluxe hideaways within certain Equinox clubs, which use eye-scanning technology to figure out who belongs. In the plane, it's no longer just first class and coach. For a surcharge, there's extra legroom. For frequent-fliers, there are exit-row seats, early boarding and first dibs on the overhead bins. You ascend and cling to a designated stratum with designated perks: gold, silver, platinum, diamond. In the United States circa 2015, it's not just shoes, handbags and SUVs that signal your status and how enviable you are. It's a whole lot else, and colleges have climbed higher and higher up the list—against all reason, and with needlessly hurtful consequences.

"The demand for elite institutions is through the roof," Anthony Carnevale sighed to me one day. Carnevale is the director of Georgetown University's Center on Education and the Workforce, which studies their relationship and interplay, and I've gone to him repeatedly when working on columns for the *New York Times* about higher education. He's informed. He's wise. And he's flummoxed and deeply frustrated by the premium that so many families place on the supposed luster of a first-choice college and by the breathlessness with which kids approach the admissions process.

"Life is something that happens slowly, and whether or not they go to their first choice isn't that important," he noted. "It's not the difference between Yale and jail. It's the difference between Yale and the University of Wisconsin or some other school where they can get an excellent education.

"They should be thinking more about what they're going to *do* with their lives," he continued. "And what college is supposed to do is to allow you to live more fully in your time." It's supposed to prime you for the next chapter of learning, and for the chapter beyond that. It's supposed to put you in touch with yourself, so that you know more about your strengths, weaknesses and values and can use that information as your mooring and compass in a tumultuous, unpredictable world. It's supposed to set you on your way, and if you expect it to be a guarantee forevermore of smooth sailing, then you've got trouble infinitely greater than any rejection notice.

In March 2014, just before Matt Levin was due to start hearing from the schools to which he'd applied, his parents, Craig and Diana, handed him a letter. They didn't care whether he read it right away, but they wanted him to know that it had been written before they found out how he fared. It was their response to the outsize yearning and dread that they saw in him and in so many of the college-bound kids at Cold Spring Harbor High School, in a Long Island suburb of New York City. It was their bid for some sanity.

Matt, like many of his peers, was shooting for the Ivies: in his case, Yale, Princeton or Brown. He had laid the groundwork. He had punched all the necessary holes. Good SAT scores? After studying with a private tutor, which was pro forma for kids in his upper-middle-class community, he had scored close to the median for students at the Ivies in his sights. Sports? He was on Cold Spring Harbor's varsity baseball team, toggling between the positions of second baseman and shortstop. Music? He played alto sax in several of Cold Spring Harbor's bands. Academics? He was the recipient of a special prize for junior-year students with the highest grade point averages, and he was a member of pretty much every honor society at the school. Character? He had logged more than one hundred hours of community service.

For Yale, Princeton and Brown, that wasn't enough. Matt's top three choices all turned him down.

His mother, Diana, told me that on the day he got that news, "He shut me out for the first time in seventeen years. He barely looked at me. Said, 'Don't talk to me and don't touch me.' Then he disappeared to take a shower and literally drowned his sorrows for the next forty-five minutes." He kept to himself all that evening as he tried to summon the energy to study for a physics test. He went to bed after midnight—still mute, still withdrawn.

The next morning he rallied and left the house wearing a sweatshirt with the name of the school that had been his fourth choice and had accepted him: Lehigh University. By then he had read his parents' letter, more than once. That they felt compelled to write it says as much about our society's warped obsession with elite colleges as it does about the Levins' warmth, wisdom and generosity. I share the following parts of it because the message in them is one that many kids in addition to their son need to hear:

Dear Matt,

On the night before you receive your first college response, we wanted to let you know that we could not be any prouder of you than we are today. Whether or not you get accepted does not determine how proud we are of everything you have accomplished and the wonderful person you have become. That will not change based on what admissions officers decide about your future. We will celebrate with joy wherever you get accepted—and the happier you are with those responses, the happier we will be. But your worth as a person, a student and our son is not diminished or influenced in the least by what these colleges have decided.

If it does not go your way, you'll take a different route to get where you want. There is not a single college in this country that would not be lucky to have you, and you are capable of succeeding at any of them.

We love you as deep as the ocean, as high as the sky, all the way around the world and back again—and to wherever you are headed.

Mom and Dad

ONE

THE UNSUNG ALMA MATERS

"My wife really wanted to go to the University of Virginia and didn't get in. I really wanted to go to Georgetown and didn't get in. So we both ended up at Delaware. It was a place where all of us felt that if we worked hard, we could do well. I never felt like the school wasn't going to give me the tools to be successful."

— Chris Christie, the governor of New Jersey and
a 1984 graduate of the University of Delaware

There's a widespread conviction, spoken and unspoken, that the road to riches is trimmed in Ivy and the reins of power held by those who've donned Harvard's crimson, Yale's blue and Princeton's orange, not just on their chests but in their souls.

No one told that to the Fortune 500.

They're the American corporations with the highest gross revenues. The list is revised yearly. As I write this paragraph in the summer of 2014, the top ten are, in order, Wal-Mart,

Exxon Mobil, Chevron, Berkshire Hathaway, Apple, Phillips 66, General Motors, Ford Motor, General Electric and Valero Energy. And here's the list, in the same order, of schools where their chief executives got their undergraduate degrees: the University of Arkansas; the University of Texas; the University of California, Davis; the University of Nebraska; Auburn; Texas A&M; the General Motors Institute (now called Kettering University); the University of Kansas; Dartmouth College and the University of Missouri–St. Louis. Just one Ivy League school shows up.

The chief executive of Wal-Mart, Doug McMillon, went on from the University of Arkansas to get a master's in business administration. That was at the University of Tulsa. Likewise, Joe Gorder, the chief executive of Valero, didn't end his education with his undergraduate degree, from the University of Missouri–St. Louis. He, too, acquired an MBA—from Our Lady of the Lake University.

When I look just a few notches farther down the list of the Fortune 500 chief executives and take in the top thirty, I spy the University of Central Oklahoma, the University of Pittsburgh, the University of Minnesota, Fordham and Penn State—along with Cornell, Princeton, Brown, Northwestern and Tufts. It's a profoundly diverse collection, reflecting the myriad routes to a corner office.

Among the American-born chief executives of the top one hundred corporations on the list, about thirty went to college in the Ivy League or at a dozen or so schools, from MIT to Bowdoin, with similarly selective admissions practices. A handful did their undergraduate work at the most widely and traditionally revered public schools—the University of Texas, for example, and the University of Michigan. But forty or so went to public schools of considerably less luster, at least in the eyes of many college-bound kids and their parents; never finished school; or were educated outside the United States. The remaining quarter went to a mix of selective and less selective private colleges and to schools that exist in narrow niches or are overtly religious in nature.

In other words there's no pattern. None at all. But in so many of our conversations about success and so many of the portraits that those of us in the media paint of accomplished individuals, we insist on divining one. And we often go with the obvious, equating achievement later in life with time spent earlier in rarefied enclaves. It's a cleaner narrative than saying that anything goes. It's a more potent mythology: There are the round table's gleaming knights, chosen young and charmed forevermore, and then there are the vassals who make do on the other side of the moat.

The discussion about the fortune-kissed denizens of 1600 Pennsylvania Avenue is a case in point. We've heard repeatedly in recent years that elite schools have a stranglehold on the White House, because the last four presidents are draped in Ivy. Barack Obama got his undergraduate degree from Columbia, his law degree from Harvard. George W. Bush went from Yale to Harvard Business School. Bill Clinton: Georgetown and then Yale Law. George H. W. Bush: a bachelor's from Yale.

But that's only a fraction of the fuller story, whose moral is not the magic that happened the moment these men were accepted by the most exclusive clubhouses of higher education. For starters, Obama didn't *begin* college in the Ivy League. Where he headed right after high school was to Occidental College in Los Angeles. Columbia came later, via a transfer, proving that the initial culling isn't the last word.

As for the Bushes, they were both legacy cases at Yale. Prescott Bush, a United States senator, had studied there before them, paving the way for his son and grandson. For the two Georges, getting into Yale was less a seal of approval and a springboard to greatness than an inevitability, and their life trajectories arguably had more to do with their bloodlines — with networks independent of Yale — than with anything that the Yale admissions committee thrilled to or with anything they gleaned in a lecture hall on the New Haven campus. I don't say that as an insult, nor am I belittling their talents. I'm just describing how the world works.

But let's look beyond the Bushes, Clinton and Obama. Let's expand the ring of political heavyweights, first by reaching farther back in history. Ronald Reagan? He attended Eureka College, a tiny school in Illinois that, in 2014, was ranked only 31st among "Regional Colleges (Midwest)" on the infernal *U.S. News & World Report* survey. Jimmy Carter? He moved around during his undergraduate and graduate years, landing not just at the U.S. Naval Academy but also at Georgia Southwestern College and Georgia Tech. Richard Nixon got his bachelor's from Whittier College in Southern California. Lyndon Baines Johnson got his from Southwest Texas State Teachers College.

And if we consider running mates and politicians who didn't make it all the way to the White House but got as far as their party's presidential nomination, the collection of colleges is similarly diverse. Vice President Joe Biden went to the University of Delaware (and then to Syracuse University's law school). Paul Ryan, the Republican vice presidential nominee in 2012, went to Miami University of Ohio. John Edwards, the Democratic vice presidential nominee in 2004, got his undergraduate degree from North Carolina State University and his law degree from the University of North Carolina at Chapel Hill.

I hesitate to mention anything about the education of Dan Quayle, the country's vice president from 1989 to 1993, given that he became known in no small part for his inability to spell the word *potato*. (He gave it a bonus vowel, dangling an *e* on the end.) But he *was* a mere heartbeat away from the presidency, and he traveled to that position by way of DePauw University in Indiana and law school at Indiana University. Biden's schooling in Delaware, Edwards's in North Carolina, Quayle's in Indiana and Carter's in Georgia illuminate something important: If a person is making a career that's closely tied to a particular geographic area, a school in and of that area may be more relevant and helpful than a highly selective institution elsewhere. And Biden, Edwards, Quayle and Carter all made such careers. The first three won election to the U.S. Senate from the states in which they had studied. Carter's stepping-stone to the White House was the governor's office in Atlanta.

Among the 100 men and women in the United States Senate in mid-2014, fewer than 30 got their college degrees in the Ivy League or in the slightly larger circle of schools widely deemed Ivy-caliber. Nearly 50 of them went to public and private colleges well below the top 25 in the sorts of conventional rankings to which so many Americans pay so much heed. And among the fifty governors in the same time period, the picture is similar. A quarter of them went to the most selective private and public colleges. Almost as many went to private colleges that don't cause applicants' hearts to go pitter-patter, and more than a third went to public schools that aren't remarkably selective.

Nikki Haley, a South Carolina Republican, is in the latter group. When she assumed office in January 2011, she was just thirty-eight years old, not to mention a woman and an ethnic minority (she has Indian ancestry) in charge of a conservative southern state. Her college degree is from Clemson University, whose regard in South Carolina far eclipses its national reputation, and she exemplifies politicians whose higher educations deepened their roots in—and their claims on—the states they'd eventually lead or represent. She told me that if you're going to make your career in South Carolina, there's no better badge than Clemson's. I suspect that someone in Alabama might make the same boast of Auburn's impact there and someone in Dallas would testify to Southern Methodist University's sway over that city. Geography plays such a key part in which college provides the best professional launch.

Haley told me that in South Carolina, "If you look at the graduates of Clemson, the network we have is absolutely amazing. It immediately takes away barriers, immediately allows transactions to take place that wouldn't normally happen. If you come to South Carolina and you went to a school out of state, you lose that entire network. And it's a huge resume booster if you're running for office to say that you're from one of the state's schools."

Even more important, she said, Clemson gave her an entirely new footing in the world. She grew up in a tiny South Carolina town where almost no one else had her family's skin color or looked like them. She needed to feel less isolated, and she needed exposure to all sorts of arts and sports and vocations that didn't exist in her community, but she also needed some sense of continuity and familiarity: a transition she could handle. Clemson, a big university in her home state, threaded that needle. "I was a small-town girl and it had this small-town feel but it was big enough that you could grow," she said. She started out majoring in textile management; switched to accounting; worked on the side as a chiropractor's assistant to help pay for school; graduated into a job for a waste management company and didn't enter politics for several years. When I spoke with her, the eldest of her two children had just begun to think seriously about colleges, but not about the Ivy League or the Northeast. "She wants to look at Clemson," Haley said.

Let's stay with politicians and politics a bit longer and examine the men and women who, in the fall of 2014, were most frequently discussed as potential candidates for the presidency in 2016. The field included many contenders without fancy undergraduate diplomas. Yes, the leader of the pack was Hillary Clinton, who got her bachelor's degree at Wellesley and then went to law school at Yale, where her partnership with Bill was forged. But Maryland governor Martin O'Malley, itching to take her on or to take her place if she teetered, did his undergraduate work at Catholic University and then got his law degree from the University of Maryland. Another potential contender, Elizabeth Warren, U.S. senator from Massachusetts, was once on the faculty of Harvard but went to college at the University of Houston and law school at Rutgers. New York governor Andrew Cuomo, lurking on the edges of the race, did his undergraduate work at Fordham, followed by the Albany Law School.

On the Republican side, Governor Chris Christie of New Jersey went to the University of Delaware, and then got his law degree at Seton Hall; Jeb Bush to the University of Texas; Rand Paul, the Kentucky senator, to Baylor University, which he left before actually graduating to move on to medical school at Duke; Marco Rubio to the University of Florida (undergraduate) and then the University of Miami (law); and Wisconsin governor Scott Walker to Marquette University, from which he never graduated. The Ivies were represented only by Louisiana governor Bobby Jindal, who got his bachelor's from Brown, and by Ted Cruz, the Texas senator, who went to Princeton as an undergraduate and then Harvard as a law student.

Most profiles of Cruz mention his alma maters, the way early profiles of Obama harped on Harvard Law. Many profiles of Christie leave out Delaware and Seton Hall. One that didn't, in the *National Review*, felt the need to characterize them as "respectable but middling schools." And this was in a *flattering* story that was praising the New Jersey governor as a victor in "a war for fiscal sanity." It certainly didn't note that Christie and Biden, who were then two of the most prominent figures on the national political landscape, *both* went to Delaware, and it didn't wonder about the dawn of a new power school. Good luck finding a magazine, newspaper or television report that did.

I asked Christie if he'd noticed, as I had, a greater tendency to mention the Ivy League pedigrees of some politicians than to note the Ivy-less pedigrees of others, and what he made of it.

"I think there's a bias toward thinking that if they went to Princeton, Harvard or Yale, then that's a significant fact," he said. "But if they went to Rutgers or the University of Delaware or a school like that, it's less significant. It's the bias that we all feel that somehow the education at those places is better.

"It's interesting," he added, "because our oldest son goes to Princeton, and I remember when he was applying, he said, 'If I get in, do you want me to go?' I said, 'Sure.' He said, 'But you went to Delaware and turned out okay.' I said, 'You're absolutely right, but I had to work a lot harder.' That's the difference. There's this assumption that if you went to Princeton, you're smarter than the next guy."

Was the assumption a fair one? "I don't think it is," Christie said. "There are a lot of things that happen when you're fifteen and seventeen that affect your ability to get into a school like that." Those last years of high school are just one short stretch of a life with many passages before it and many to come, plenty of ups and plenty of downs, and intelligence is only part of what enables you, at that time, to walk through certain doors.

Christie, who graduated from high school in 1980, said that he'd applied to a mix of public and private schools, including Georgetown, his first choice, which rejected him. He went to Delaware primarily because it "offered me a good amount of scholarship and grant money," he said. "My family was not affluent at all, and it made a huge difference.

"The second reason was, I went down there and visited—it's strange the way you make decisions when you're seventeen or eighteen—and everybody seemed happy and everybody seemed to be enjoying themselves," he added. "The campus was nice and it was relatively close to home. It wasn't a whole lot more complicated than that."

When I asked him if, once he'd arrived on campus for good, Delaware felt like the right decision, his answer wasn't about his dorm or initial group of friends or classes he'd signed up for or any of that, and it underscored that in college as in everything else, messy, unplanned stuff intrudes. He was immediately grateful for Delaware, he said, because it was close to his New Jersey home and he winded up wanting and needing to return there frequently during his freshman year, just before which his mother had been diagnosed with breast cancer.

He's grateful still. He met his wife, Mary Pat, there. He majored in political science, with a minor in history, and whether it was a function of Delaware or of his personality, professors were readily accessible and several became lifelong friends, including one who volunteered to work the phone banks when Christie first ran for governor in 2009. And there were attributes of a state university that aren't shared in full by most elite private schools. "What I got out of being at a place like Delaware was a real diversity in terms of the economic and social strata of the people who went there. I met lots of different people who had lots of different life experiences." Although that's especially beneficial for a politician, it's obviously useful in most other jobs as well.

"I look back at those four years so fondly," he said. "I had an amazingly good time and great experience. There's nothing I would change." Through his four children, the second oldest of whom is a freshman at Notre Dame, he has noticed an awareness and veneration of elite schools that's much more pronounced than in the past; it was especially intense, he said, at the Delbarton School, in Morristown, New Jersey, from which his son Andrew, the one at Princeton, graduated in 2012. In Andrew's class at Delbarton, ten kids headed off to Princeton, more than went to any other college, and another sixteen went elsewhere in the Ivy League. Only one went to Delaware. I know this because the school breaks it all down for students and parents on its website, listing several years' worth of information about how Delbarton graduates fared.

Referring to both himself and his wife, Christie said, "The thing that really disturbed us was the extraordinary pressure that some parents were putting on their kids from the seventh or eighth grade. That's something that we don't quite yet know what effect it's going to have on kids over the long haul. My fear is that these kids are always going to be evaluating their self-worth in terms of whether they hit the next rung society has placed in front of them at exactly the time that society has placed it. And that's dangerous, because you're going to slip and fall in your life."

Christie said that he went to Seton Hall after Delaware because he didn't have the grades for one of the most prestigious law schools and felt that if he wasn't going to be in the top tier, he should be in New Jersey, where he planned to practice law and pursue his career. It was interesting to hear him mention academic shortcomings, because whatever else you make of Christie—whether you find him bold or bullying, a refreshing truth-teller or an egomaniacal schemer—he's an unusually nimble thinker, with a striking verbal dexterity. Once, at a charter school fund-raiser, I heard him deliver a half-hour keynote speech without a teleprompter or any notes, and every sentence, every paragraph, was impeccable. There's no equivalence between straight A's in school and sharp professional tools, and that's one of the many reasons to question the obsession with colleges that admit only students with the highest GPAs.

More than a few of the political masterminds behind recent presidents and presidential campaigns honed their intellects at schools of relatively modest repute. Donna Brazile, whose stewardship of Al Gore's 2000 race made her the first African American to manage a major presidential bid, graduated from Louisiana State University. Maggie Williams, who managed Hillary Clinton's 2008 race, graduated from Trinity Washington University, a small Catholic women's college. Karl Rove, a longtime aide to George W. Bush who was sometimes referred to as "Bush's brain," zigzagged from the University of Utah to the University of Maryland to George Mason University. He never got a diploma.

Steve Schmidt, the senior strategist for John McCain's ill-fated 2008 presidential campaign, went to—here it comes again!—the University of Delaware, which is *also* the alma mater of David Plouffe, who managed Obama's triumphant, history-making presidential campaign that same year. In 2012, the job of managing Obama's campaign fell to Jim Messina. He's a graduate of the University of Montana.

Both Schmidt and Plouffe left Delaware without diplomas. Neither had accrued enough credits to graduate. But when they returned to the campus in the spring of 2009 for a joint discussion of the 2008 campaign, the university president asked to see them and said, in Schmidt's recollection: "Guys, you're killing us, you've got to finish this." Delaware wanted to count them as honest-to-goodness graduates, so the president laid out for each of them what they had to do. Plouffe said he needed to do a nutrition, a human development and a math course. Schmidt just needed a math course: the one that Plouffe needed as well. They were assigned the same math professor, Kay Biondi, who was supposed to monitor and help them online.

"She was picked to deal with us psychologically, with our math phobia," Schmidt said with a laugh. He said that he sometimes conversed with her on Saturday mornings, from a bar near the ski slopes in Vermont, with a Bloody Mary in his hand. And he sometimes called Plouffe, his former adversary, to commiserate about being students again all these years later.

"Good memories," Plouffe told me in an email, maybe sarcastically, maybe not. He added that he and Schmidt "went from vicious adversaries to good friends." Plouffe quickly finished his courses and got his diploma in 2010. Schmidt dallied, getting his in 2013.

Schmidt said that while many of the policy advisers in campaigns and government went to elite colleges, "I don't think there's a tremendous amount of people at the top level of running campaigns who have Ivy League degrees." I asked if he had any theories about why. "I think part of the reason is that campaign politics is a rough business, a tough business emotionally," he said. "I think it carries a fair degree of common sense and a blending of emotional intelligence and IQ intelligence, which isn't necessarily a virtue of the people coming out of the most elite universities if you were to make generalizations and stereotypes."

In May 2014, the sociologist D. Michael Lindsay published the results of something he called the Platinum Study, which involved interviews with 550 American leaders, including more than 250 chief executives of corporations, more than 100 leaders of major nonprofit groups, a few former presidents and many government officials. Lindsay's aims were to see where they came from, how they reached their destinations and how they thought and behaved once they arrived.

"I fully expected that we would see that a large percentage of people had gone to highly selective schools both for secondary and higher education," he told me. He learned differently, as he spells out in the book that grew out of the study, *A View from the Top: An Inside Look at How People in Power See and Shape the World*. He writes that "while we often assume that the most direct path to national influence goes through major academic universities (such as Ivy League schools), nearly two-thirds of the leaders I interviewed attended schools that are not considered elite institutions."

The reputations of the colleges that they attended, he discovered, seemed to matter much less than the reputations of the graduate schools that they moved on to, and they weren't shut out of these graduate schools on the basis of where they'd applied from. "Nearly two-thirds of the leaders who received graduate degrees went to a top 10 graduate school in their field," Lindsay writes.

But the belief in the primacy of a person's undergraduate pedigree is stubborn in many quarters, as I've learned when I've used my column in the *New York Times* to challenge that thinking and to argue that education is so much more than brand. "Oh yeah?" one reader wrote to me. "Tell me where you and your colleagues went to college. I bet it was the Ivy League."

In many cases, yes. In just as many, no. My own undergraduate degree is from the University of North Carolina, and there's a story about how I ended up there that I'll tell later. When I became an op-ed columnist for the *Times* in

June 2011, I joined a group of accomplished writers that includes Maureen Dowd, who got her bachelor's from Catholic University, and Gail Collins, who got hers from Marquette. Nicholas Kristof and Ross Douthat indeed went to Harvard and David Brooks to the University of Chicago. But Joe Nocera is an alumnus of Boston University, Charles Blow of Grambling State. Tom Friedman spent his first years in college at the University of Minnesota, after which he transferred to Brandeis.

Because I've reported extensively on candidates, campaigns and public office holders, the newspaper's leading political correspondents are among my close friends. They come from a spectrum of colleges. You won't find a saucier or more sophisticated chronicler of the nation's capital than Jennifer Steinhauer, who was previously the newspaper's Los Angeles bureau chief. She went to college at the School of Visual Arts in Manhattan. You won't find a wiser political analyst than Adam Nagourney, who has had a major hand in covering five presidential races for the *Times*. He went to the State University of New York at Purchase. Carl Hulse, perhaps the *Times'* most trusted interpreter of Congress, studied at Illinois State University.

Jim Rutenberg, who was the newspaper's chief political correspondent during the 2012 presidential race and now has a prized writing slot on the *Times'* Sunday magazine, attended New York University back when it was significantly less selective but never actually got his diploma. He had financial and family challenges that sidelined him, but he wasn't, in the end, set back by that, because he had and has something better that any degree: a cunning, a drive and a grace in dealing with other people that are shared, to varying extents, by all of the journalists I just mentioned. Their careers weren't built on the names of their colleges. They were built on carefully honed skills, ferocious work ethics and good attitudes.

The *Times* is no aberration. After the winners of the Pulitzer Prizes in journalism were announced in 2014, I looked to see where they'd gone to college. The American schools on that list were the University of Richmond, Syracuse University, Boston College, the University of South Carolina, Middlebury College, the University of Michigan, the University of Minnesota, Boston University and Stanford. I rewound a year, to the Pulitzers in journalism for 2013. I found Northwestern, the University of St. Thomas, the University of Georgia, Boston University, the University of Colorado-Boulder, Yale, Indiana University, the University of Chicago, Gannon University and the University of Minnesota.

And I rewound once more. The 2012 Pulitzer winners did their undergraduate work at Colby College, the University of Maryland, Villanova, Bowling Green State University, Purdue, Penn State, Cornell, Columbia, Pomona, Yale, the Rhode Island School of Photography, Lewis & Clark College and the State University of New York at Binghamton. The journalist who went to that last school is my friend and *Times* colleague David Kocieniewski. He won for explanatory reporting.

In the spring of 2014, he and I each taught a seminar as visiting faculty members at Princeton. He reveled in the irony of that. About three decades earlier, Princeton had rejected him. So had Harvard. Brown, too. SUNY Binghamton was one of his fallbacks, and he told me that because its students fancied themselves freer spirits than most, "They used to call themselves the Brown of public universities, though I've never heard anyone at Brown call it the SUNY Binghamton of the Ivies."

He said that going there was a mercy of sorts, as he would have had trouble affording a private college. But even with the in-state tuition break he got, he had to work his way through school, and for the first two years, he put in fifteen hours a week as a janitor. It was one of many unglamorous gigs over the years, including a stint in his early twenties as the driver of a Mister Softee ice cream truck in Buffalo. "Ah, the summer of Softee," he said. "It's the worst job ever. You work every sunny day. You're off when it rains. And you have no idea how many impotence jokes there are until you've driven a Mister Softee truck."

Journalism, of course, isn't representative. (Then again, no profession is.) So I cast my gaze in an unrelated direction, toward the world of science, and examined the alma maters of the 102 men and women, most of them in their thirties and forties, who had been invited to the White House as recipients of the 2014 Presidential Early Career Award for Scientists and Engineers (PECASE). I couldn't track down the college information for eight of the 102 winners; among the rest, 72 did their undergraduate work in the United States, and the list of schools they attended is by no means dominated by the likes of Stanford and the Massachusetts Institute of Technology, though both appear on it more than once.

But then so do Rutgers, the University of Arizona and North Carolina State. Public schools, including those three, represented just under half of the list. When you also took into account private and niche schools well outside the Ivy League—and I don't mean Stanford, MIT, Wellesley and

Smith, but institutions like Adelphi University, Linfield College and Augustana College—nearly two-thirds of the list was covered. The dubious importance of precisely where a driven, able person goes to college was underscored by something else. When I was hunting down the educational pedigrees of these distinguished scientists and engineers, it was usually easy to find the names of the schools where they'd done their graduate work. Their employers were sure to put that in their online profiles. It was less easy to identify the colleges they'd attended, which often weren't even mentioned. Those four years were clearly seen as the staging area, not the actual operation; as the throat clearing, not the aria. College wasn't considered the most rigorous or targeted work that these scientists and engineers had done, nor was it the place from which they'd been plucked for their enduring employment. With each year that they had moved beyond it, its relevance to who they were and how they'd been schooled waned.

The diversity of colleges at which PECASE recipients had studied was not unlike what I encountered when I researched recent winners of MacArthur Foundation "genius grants." The undergraduate alma maters of the two dozen geniuses anointed in 2013 included SUNY Purchase, SUNY Albany, Louisiana State, Villanova, DePaul and the University of California, Santa Barbara. And the alma maters of the twenty-one geniuses in 2014 included the University of Kansas, the University of Cincinnati, Coker College, the University of Illinois, Columbus State University and the University of Maryland. My analysis of the winners in 2009 through 2014 showed that more than half of MacArthur's geniuses got their undergraduate educations at public and private schools that aren't typically placed in the highest echelon.

*   *   *

Of course all of those sample sets generally reflect people who have been out of college for more—in most cases, much more—than a decade. They don't say much about the fates of relatively recent graduates. But a website named the 60second Recap waded into that topic with a brilliant, hilarious post by Peter Osterlund that responded to the "30 Under 30" list of promising young Americans that *Forbes* magazine has begun to put out every year. The list actually names thirty people in each of fifteen categories—law, media, tech, finance, etc.—so it encompasses 450 honorees in all. Osterlund's post happened to deconstruct the group of honorees for 2013.

And it poked fun at the very Ivy mythologizing that I mentioned above, observing that *Forbes* made sure to mention "Harvard, Stanford, Princeton, Princeton, Princeton" in the profiles of 30 Under 30 honorees who had graduated from those schools. *Forbes* simply omitted information about alma maters in profiles of nominees who hadn't.

"Well," Osterlund wrote, "we dug." And the discoveries? "*Forbes* tells us of one 30 Under 30 honoree's experiences as an undergraduate at Duke, but doesn't mention the Arizona State University undergraduate degrees carried by three of its young stars." In terms of the number of a school's graduates on the *Forbes* list, ASU actually beat out Duke, the post determined. "And it beats Dartmouth. And Cornell. And Johns Hopkins. And…you get the idea.

"We found that most *Forbes* 30 Under 30 honorees attended, well, ordinary colleges—in some cases, obscure places, in other cases, state schools like the University of Where-They-Just-So-Happened-To-Live-At-The-Time." For instance Isaac Kinde, who was an honoree in the category of science and health care, did his undergraduate work at the University of Maryland, Baltimore County (UMBC), which accepts more than 60 percent of its applicants. *Forbes* didn't identify that school. It did, however, make clear that Isaac was doing a combined MD and PhD program at Johns Hopkins.

I reached out to Isaac, now thirty-one, to learn more about how he ended up at UMBC. Our conversation was a reminder that there are many families and communities in which the mania over college admissions is an exotic and unthinkable luxury. They're either unable or loath to participate in it. And they don't necessarily suffer for taking a pass.

Isaac grew up near San Bernardino, California, and went to a parochial school where the college chatter wasn't all that constant or intense, he said. He was a standout who knew that he wanted a career in the sciences, almost certainly in medicine, and felt that he should probably not stray too far geographically from his home and his parents. So he applied to several schools in the University of California system and to Stanford. And got in everywhere.

He also applied to UMBC, specifically to its Meyerhoff Scholars Program, not because he'd learned about it through extensive research but because a family friend had happened to mention it. It gives free rides to minority students with promise in the fields of science, technology and engineering. To get the scholarship, Isaac had to travel east one weekend for a series of interviews, and during that trip he got to see the UMBC campus and meet some of the Meyerhoff students and administrators. "What I remember is the immediate feeling of comfort that both my father and I had," he said. But the Meyerhoff promised more than just comfort: It was a tightly knit community within UMBC that existed for, and was dedicated to, the nurturing and advancement of its scholars. It was a ready-made support system, a guaranteed network. He felt that it would help him stay focused on his work and avoid the many distractions of college life. "I hadn't realized it was out there, but as I soon as I was exposed to it, I thought, 'This makes sense. This seems right. Now that I see it, I want it.'"

The education he ended up getting at UMBC, he told me, was sufficiently excellent to give him his pick of many top medical schools and to provide him with the foundation he needed for success at Hopkins, where his research over the last ten years, which is how long it takes to get both an MD and the doctorate he chose, has focused on improving DNA sequencing in a way that may help detect certain cancers. But he said that he did have one big regret about UMBC. "It would have been nice to have a football team," he said. "I would have liked that. Now I don't feel as connected to college football as many of my colleagues are. That would be my only thing. Would I change anything else in hindsight? Absolutely not.

"I thought that it was a unique place to be," he said. "I never have been the kind of person to care about the reputation of a particular program or school, in terms of, 'Is it Top Five?' I just think that that preoccupation is a little misguided." What matters, he said, is what you do in the classroom and in the laboratory, not the school banner that flutters over you, not the school colors in which you're dressed.

"I think you can get what you need out of college at most colleges," Isaac said. "The biggest thing that varies from college to college is the location and the price." For him the price at UMBC was right. So was the price at the University of

California, Los Angeles, a more widely respected school that had also offered him a large scholarship. But UCLA, which he visited and liked, wasn't likely to give him the personal attention and have the investment in his future that the Meyerhoff did, or at least that was his strong sense of things. That was what his careful survey of his options and his gut both told him. Plus the Meyerhoff, on the other side of the country from where he'd grown up, was sure to be a different kind of adventure, and an expansion of his world. He went with the greater, longer journey.

Four years after he made that decision, his younger brother, Benyam, followed suit, also going to UMBC on a Meyerhoff. And Benyam, twenty-seven, is now doing a combined MD and PhD program of his own—at Harvard.

UMBC appeared in a pointedly jokey "15 Over 50" honor roll on Osterlund's *Forbes* takedown, which catalogued and lionized fifteen alma maters of 30 Under 30 designees that accept more than 50 percent of applicants, proving that more exclusive schools don't enjoy any monopoly on present talent and future glory. The other fourteen schools on the 15 Over 50 included the American River College, Westminster College (that's in Utah, not Britain) and Santa Fe College (that's in Florida, not New Mexico). American River and Santa Fe take 100 percent of their applicants. You knock; the door swings wide.

The 60second Recap didn't follow up in 2014 and examine the next batch of honorees. So I reviewed it, and again found no shortage of graduates of schools that aren't especially selective. There were several alumni of Penn State. One, Josh Blackman, was a law professor who had written a book about the constitutional challenge to Obamacare and had founded

FantasySCOTUS, a popular Supreme Court online fantasy league and prediction market.

Another, Carryn McLaughlin, was a vice president at J.P. Morgan in charge of managing a $2.7 billion portfolio for real estate moguls and their families. McLaughlin appeared in the finance category, as did graduates of the City University of New York and of the University of Miami. I learned that by digging into just a small patch of the 30 Under 30.

It was clear that with the 2014 list, I could ask the same question that Osterlund had asked at the end of his analysis of the 2013 honorees. "Take a look and you tell us," he wrote. "Does a prestigious college make you successful in life? Or do you do that for yourself?"

TWO

THROWING DARTS

"When I went to college thirty or forty years ago, I said to my dad, 'What's the Ivy League?' And he said, 'That's just a bunch of snooty girls, you don't want to go there.' Today he would say, 'We absolutely must visit the Ivy League.' It's become a whole different thing."

—Jennifer Delahunty, former dean of admissions at Kenyon College and a 1980 graduate of the University of Arizona

Determined to get into one of the dozen or so most selective institutions of higher learning in America? No problem—as long as you're the winner of a national science contest, the winner of a national singing competition, a Bolshoi-ready dancer, a Carnegie-caliber harpsichordist, a chess prodigy, a surfing legend, a defensive lineman who led his region in tackles, a striker who scored a record number of goals in her soccer league, a published author and I don't mean blogger, a precocious chef and I do mean molecular gastronomy, a stoic political refugee from a country that we really loathe, a heroic political scion from a country that we really love, a Roosevelt of proper vintage, a Rockefeller of sufficient relevance, or Malia or Sasha Obama. If none of those descriptions fit and you don't have perfect scores on every standardized test since the second grade, your visions of Stanford would more correctly be termed hallucinations.

Of course I'm exaggerating, but not by all that much. And I'm singling out Stanford on purpose: In the spring of 2014, it established a new extreme in exclusiveness, offering admission to a lower share of supplicants than any school ever had. For the class of 2018, Stanford received 42,167 applications. It sent acceptance notices to the authors of just 2,138 of them. That's roughly one aspirant of every 20, and those 20 weren't slackers, stumblebums, unhinged gamblers or delusional narcissists. At least not most of them. They were, generally speaking, accomplished secondary school students for whom Stanford wasn't and shouldn't have been a completely ludicrous wish. Yet Stanford took just 5.1 percent of that pool.

The arithmetic was nowhere near as merciless for previous generations. It's important to emphasize that, to keep in mind that a kid today angling for acceptance to the kind of super-elite school that a parent attended is not trying to replicate that accomplishment but, in fact, to one-up it. Unless the child is applying to the exact *same* school that a parent attended (and, better yet, that a parent recently gave copious sums of money to), his or her challenge is significantly greater. At Yale, roughly 20 percent of applicants were offered admission back in the late 1980s. A quarter century later, in 2014, just over 6 percent were.

That trajectory is mirrored at dozens of the most desired American colleges. At Northwestern University in Evanston, Illinois, for example, the acceptance rate fell from over 40 percent a quarter century ago to under 13 percent in 2014. And the sharpest declines in acceptance rates at these schools have occurred for the most part over the last fifteen years and especially the last ten, according to data from Noodle, a company that compiles education statistics that are meant to guide both consumers and policy makers. Researchers at Noodle took an ambitious look back at the last thirty years of admissions information from schools that *U.S. News* routinely ranked in its top 100, and Noodle shared those results with me. They show that between 1984 and 1994, many of these schools' acceptance rates were unchanged or even went *up* slightly. But those rates began to drop between 1994 and 2004. And since 2004, they've declined sharply. The acceptance rate at Tufts University went down only seven percentage points, from 34 to 27, between 1984 and 2004, but it has since gone down another six. Bowdoin's 2004 rate was roughly the same as its 1984 one—about 24 percent—but it's now closer to 15. Amherst's held relatively steady at about 21 percent for the two decades leading up to 2004, but over the last decade, it's plummeted to 13.

And while major public universities haven't reached nearly that degree of selectiveness, they, too, have become much more difficult to get into. The University of Michigan's rate fell from 56 percent in 1984 to 32 percent in 2014, and that's a combined figure for in-state students, who get the bulk of the spots in each class, and out-of-state students, who compete for fewer slots and face odds much worse than one in three. The University of California, Berkeley's rate fell over the same period from 48 percent to 17 (again, for in-state and out-of-state students combined).

The declining rates across the board have continued well past what anyone once thought possible. As the *New York Times* noted in a front-page story in April 2014 that was headlined "Best, Brightest and Rejected," "In 2003, Harvard and Princeton drew exclamations of dismay (from prospective applicants), envy (from other colleges) and satisfaction (from those they accepted) when they became the first top universities to have their acceptance rates dip below 10 percent. Since then, at least a dozen have gone below that threshold." And there are at least another dozen with acceptances rates not much higher than 10 percent.

What's happened at these schools is straightforward: The number of slots for incoming students either hasn't expanded significantly or hasn't risen nearly as much as the number of young people applying for them, and that surge in applications reflects a confluence of developments. One is that more and more students from outside the United States have been applying. More and more of them have been gaining acceptance, too, and that means fewer spots at some of the most fiercely competitive schools for American kids. I talked to many college admission consultants—the kind who charge lofty fees to advise families on packaging high school students to the liking of the gods of admission—and while I was primarily curious about the stratagems deployed, the consultants kept mentioning something else: the steady rise over the last five years in clients from Europe and Asia.

David Leonhardt, a colleague of mine at the *Times*, frequently analyzes data from different sources to get an accurate picture of college students and the college experience today, and in the spring of 2014, just as Stanford hit its milestone of selectivity, he reported that at elite colleges, international applicants now represented nearly 10 percent of the student bodies, and that at five of those schools, the percentage of slots available to American teenagers had dropped by more than 20 percent from 1994 to 2012. (The five were Carleton, Dartmouth, Harvard, Yale and Boston College.)

"Colleges have globalized," Leonhardt wrote, suggesting two motivations for a more international student body: It diversifies campuses in a way that's consistent with the borderless nature of business today, and students from overseas tend to come from affluent families who can pay full freight.

But it's not just globalization that has plumped up the numbers of applicants to highly selective schools. More American kids are trying to get in as well. The Internet has made it easier for all kinds of students in all kinds of places to research and home in on schools that they might not have become as easily excited about before, and the ease and relative economy of long-distance travel mean that many students no longer feel as bound by geography to schools nearest them. For the most coveted colleges, this has meant many more comers. And while these schools are still attended predominantly by children of privilege—according to one widely cited estimate, roughly 75 percent of the students at the two hundred most highly rated colleges come from families in the top quartile of income in the United States—the funnel from top-drawer prep schools to the Ivy League doesn't function the way it did once upon a time, and there is a broader and more diverse network of secondary schools channeling students toward elite institutions. This is good. This is also an engine of

increasingly cutthroat competition, which the schools themselves take great pains to encourage.

Somewhere along the way, a school's selectiveness—measured
in large part by its acceptance rate—became synonymous with
its worth. Part of the blame can be placed on *U.S. News &
World Report*'s annual rankings of American colleges, which
began in the 1980s and have grown in influence since. The
rankings factor acceptance rates into their evaluation of
schools—the lower the rate, the loftier the evaluation—and
many schools have inevitably responded with efforts to bring
their rates down by ratcheting up the number of young people
who apply. Colleges bang the drums like never before. From
the organization that administers the SAT, they buy the names
of students who have scored above a certain mark and are
at least remotely plausible, persuadable applicants, then they
send those students pamphlets and literature that grow
glossier and more alluring—*that leafy quadrangle! those
gleaming microscopes!*—by the year. The college admissions
office is no longer a mere screening committee. It's a ruth-
lessly efficient purveyor of Ivory Tower porn.

"Colleges really go overboard," Ted O'Neill, the dean of
admissions at the University of Chicago for several decades
until 2009, told me, explaining that a surfeit of applications
"became a way to promote your college, and the admissions
office became, in effect, a public-relations arm of the university." Bruce Poch, a former dean of admissions at Pomona
College, said that to an extent unheard-of decades ago, emissaries from colleges will fan out across the country, extolling
the magic of their schools and exhorting students to come
aboard even as those very exhortations lengthen the odds

against any one student getting in. The emissaries are ginning up desire in order to frustrate it, instilling hope only to quash it. In other words, their come-on is successful if it sows more failure.

Admissions officers even pay travel expenses to fly college placement counselors from high-profile secondary schools to their campuses and to give them a painstakingly choreographed pitch, so that these counselors might go back to the students they advise and promote the colleges that just treated them to such a polished song-and-dance.

"We did it at Pomona," said Poch, who left there in 2010. He now works in college guidance at Chadwick, a tony private school in the Los Angeles area that educates children from kindergarten through twelfth grade, and he noted: "The staff at Chadwick has been flown around."

When the American economy turned sharply downward around 2008, the flying let up a bit, but it has since come back with a vengeance. Lauren Gersick, a college placement counselor at the Urban School of San Francisco, told me that from the fall of 2013 through the summer of 2014, she was flown to the College of Charleston; to the University of Southern California; to Smith College, in Northampton, Massachusetts; and to the College of the Atlantic, in Bar Harbor, Maine. It was her first year on the job.

There's yet another factor in all of this: the sheer ease of applying in the digital age. Students aren't dealing with paperwork per se and envelopes and stamps, the way someone like me did back in the early 1980s, which might as well be the Mesozoic era in terms of how much has changed. They aren't typing each application individually. They have the word-processing wonders of cut-and-paste, and beyond that they have the Common

Application, a single electronic form that they can submit, along with specific supplements requested by particular schools, to most if not all of the colleges in their sights.

While the Common Application made its debut in 1975, decades went by before it took firm hold, and its currency and prevalence have increased with particular speed recently. During the 2008–2009 academic year, about 416,500 college-bound students used it. That number almost doubled over the next five years, and during the 2013–2014 academic year, about 809,000 students used the Common Application, according to the organization that drafts and promotes it. Its popularity with applicants tracks its popularity with colleges themselves, 517 of which accepted it during the 2013–2014 academic year. Scott Anderson, the senior director of policy for the Common Application, told me that for the 2014–2015 academic year, 550 colleges were on board.

The Common Application, or "Common App," renders it relatively painless for students to add another two or three or six schools to the list of ones that they're primarily interested in. So individual kids are applying to more schools than ever before—and individual schools are in turn seeing unprecedented numbers of applicants. A quarter century ago, only one in ten college-bound students applied to seven or more colleges. Now, more than one in four do.

Many of the college placement counselors, students and parents with whom I spoke told me that it's not at all unusual, in communities where a fee of $35 to $90 per application isn't considered prohibitive, for someone to apply to at least twelve schools and as many as twenty and for the thinking to be, "If I throw enough darts at the board, maybe one will hit the bull's-eye."

"I applied to fourteen schools," said Katherine Gross, an eighteen-year-old from Newton, Massachusetts, who began her freshman year at Johns Hopkins University in the fall of 2014. "I had friends who applied to twenty. I'm completely serious." Judah Axelrod, an eighteen-year-old from Fanwood, New Jersey, who began at Rutgers University in the fall of 2014, told me, "I know kids who applied to seventeen or eighteen schools." He was a model of restraint. He applied to ten.

Kids have become accustomed to applying to schools almost reflexively, without any real attachment to many of them, and schools have become invested in the sheer number of applications they receive, regardless of the seriousness of the applicants. When Swarthmore College noticed a 16 percent drop in applications in 2014, it investigated the reason, and concluded that its requirement of two five-hundred-word essays in addition to the standard one had turned away students. That finding was consistent with the experiences of several other schools that have seen applications rise or fall markedly based on essay requirements. So Swarthmore, whose acceptance rate rose to 17 percent from 14 percent, is substituting the two supplemental essays with only one, of just 250 words. It could have decided to stay the course, on the theory that applicants going the extra mile were applicants with a passion for Swarthmore. It didn't.

The acceptance rates at individual schools don't tell a complete story or at least a sufficiently nuanced one, not the way John Katzman figures it. He's the chief executive and founder of Noodle; previously, he founded the *Princeton Review*, which evaluates and provides information about colleges. And he has a dissenting take on the admissions hysteria, which he sees as just that: hysteria.

"The process is much *less* selective today," he told me, adding that any contention to the contrary is "smoke and mirrors."

But he wasn't looking at Stanford, or for that matter at any given school in the Ivy League. He was looking at a bigger picture, by which I mean a broader group of colleges and universities that may not be ranked in the top 10 but are ranked in, say, the top 100 and regarded as superior. He noted that while the Ivy League perhaps hasn't seen any remarkable expansion in the number of undergraduates it can accommodate, many of these other schools—for example, the University of Michigan, the University of California, Berkeley and Boston University—have indeed grown significantly over the last thirty years. And during that time, many large schools like New York University and the University of Southern California have upgraded themselves enough to join the ranks of colleges generally considered elite. Katzman said that those two trends together mean that it's statistically easier today than it was thirty years ago for an American high school senior who seeks admission to one of the 100 or even 50 most highly regarded colleges to gain it.

Then he made a crucial clarification: He was talking about the odds of getting into *one or another* of those schools, not of getting into *the* one, two or four that your heart was set on. He was saying that if you apply widely within the universe of selective colleges, you're in better shape than you were decades ago to find a school that takes you, because that's the mathematical reality of the overall number of available slots per Americans your age who are applying to college.

"So why is everybody getting so worked up?" he asked.

There are several reasons. One is that the ratio of available slots per college-bound Americans doesn't take into account the intensity with which a greater cross section of those Americans are pursuing those slots: a fervor that translates into perfect, painstakingly constructed high school resumes and, in turn, a surfeit of overachieving students in the hunt. At some schools, the admissions bar has been lifted higher than it was before. Additionally, those of us in the media find the hunt so transfixing that we accord it ever more coverage, which further raises the anxiety levels of college-focused families, who get drawn further into the admissions mania, generating behaviors and statistics that justify another crop of news stories. With education as with politics, we're drawn to competition and mad for winners. As Katzman noted in a column that he wrote for the *Washington Post* in September 2014, "The *New York Times* wrote more about Harvard last year than about all community colleges combined."

And rightly or wrongly, sanely or insanely, most students aren't merely interested in going to *a* top school; they have strong preferences within that category. For more and more of them, those preferences are the top 20 or even the top 10 schools, where gaining admission is certainly more difficult than in the past.

The difficulty isn't even fully captured by those breathtakingly low acceptance rates, which don't represent the odds confronting a random candidate who's only generically outstanding. (How's that for an oxymoron?) No, that candidate faces even worse odds, because there are other applicants who belong to one of several preferred groups and thus have a leg up. Princeton may be taking 7.3 percent of all comers, but it's taking significantly more than 7.3 percent of so-called legacies, or kids with a parent or other relative who attended the school, and it's taking significantly more than 7.3 percent of star athletes. So it's taking significantly less than 7.3 percent of brainy klutzes whose ancestors went to public colleges.

In 2011 Michael Hurwitz, who was then a doctoral candidate at Harvard University's Graduate School of Education, published the results of his research into just how much of an edge legacies enjoyed. He looked at more than 130,000 students who'd applied in the 2006–2007 academic year to be admitted as freshmen to one or more of thirty highly selective colleges. And he found that among students with seemingly equivalent grades, test scores and other qualifications, legacies had a 23.3 percent better chance of admission than nonlegacies.

If students were "primary legacies," meaning that a parent rather than an aunt or a grandparent had gone to the college in question, they had a 45.1 percent better chance. Put another way, if a given applicant who wasn't a legacy of any kind had a 15 percent chance of getting into a given school, a roughly identical applicant who was a primary legacy had a 60 percent chance. That's a profound difference, one that shocked many people when Hurwitz laid it out and one that students who are applying to top schools *without* any family connection should keep in mind. These schools may talk expansively about, and with a genuine belief in, diversity. These schools may advertise, and on some level desire, student bodies of exhilarating eclecticism. But these schools are unequivocally prioritizing alumni's progeny, who will be represented in abundance on campus. And that's because these schools are businesses as well as laboratories of learning—and maybe businesses *before* laboratories of learning—and children of alumni are equivalent to loyalty club members.

You can see that in Hurwitz's research or you can see it in a Pulitzer Prize–winning series of stories that the journalist Daniel Golden wrote for the *Wall Street Journal* eight years earlier, in 2003. Chronicling case after case in which some of the most revered colleges lowered their standards for affluent applicants, including legacies, he documented the power of social privilege, and of money in particular, in the admissions contest. He then updated and expanded that reporting for a 2006 book, *The Price of Admission*, whose subtitle pointedly summarizes his conclusions and makes clear that an advantage given to some applicants means a disadvantage endured by others. It reads: "How America's Ruling Class Buys Its Way into Elite Colleges—and Who Gets Left Outside the Gates."

In *The Price of Admission*, Golden writes that Duke University "accepted at least one hundred non-alumni children each year due to family wealth or connections." In these cases, the university wasn't rewarding past donors but panning for future ones. Golden also looks at the fate of Harrison Frist, who applied during the 2001–2002 academic year for early admission to Princeton University in the fall of 2002. "Admissions officers were taken aback: His grades and test scores fell far below university standards," writes Golden, who got someone on the inside to spill the beans. "On Princeton's 1 (best) to 5 (worst) academic scale for applicants, he was rated a 5. On its parallel nonacademic scale, he was a 3 or 4, signifying extracurricular leadership in his school but not talent of a state or national scope."

No matter. Harrison Frist was the son of Bill Frist, a Princeton alumnus who was then an important United States senator, representing Tennessee. And the Frist family, perhaps foreseeing the day when Harrison might need a boost, had pledged $25 million of their vast wealth to renovate and re-purpose a former physics building at Princeton. It was also rechristened—as the Frist Campus Center.

Princeton opened its arms wide to Harrison Frist. It also did something else during that early-admissions cycle that Golden found especially fascinating. It admitted four class-mates of Frist's from St. Albans, an exclusive private school near Washington, D.C., who had also applied; who possessed much better academic records than Frist did; and whose re-jections would have made Frist's acceptance look even odder, perhaps generating chatter that Princeton didn't want. Golden writes that in the years just before and after, applicants from St. Albans hadn't enjoyed this magnitude of success with Princeton, which, he suggests, was trying to camouflage the favoritism they were showing Frist.

That favoritism endures. It flourishes. Over recent years, Harvard has acknowledged that children of alumni constitute 12 to 13 percent of a typical class. That percentage presumably ticks up a bit higher for all legacies, not just primary ones. Harvard has also acknowledged that the acceptance rate for primary legacies is in the vicinity of 30 percent—or roughly five times what it is for the overall applicant pool.

A post that appeared on the website of the *Nation* in 2011 asserted that the situation at Yale wasn't much different. Ac-cording to the magazine, 13.5 percent of the freshmen arriving at Yale in the fall of 2011 had a parent who'd gone there as an undergraduate or a graduate student. And so it goes through-out the Ivy League. Among children of Princeton alumni who sought to begin as freshmen at that school in the fall of 2011, about 35 percent gained admission, according to a story in the *Times*. Two years later, Cornell conceded that children of alumni accounted for about 15 percent of its student body.

So it's good to be a legacy. But it may be better still to be an athlete who is superior enough, or plays a sport that's obscure enough, to be of instant and sure use to a school. Cornell may not have a football team on a par with Auburn's and swimming at Georgetown may not be anything like swimming at the University of Florida, but both Cornell and Georgetown care about a broad, rich palette of activity on campus. Both schools also care about a winner's aura, in all arenas. And both schools have alumni who participated in those sports, enjoy following them or both. Their feelings about their alma maters—and the size and frequency of their financial contributions—can be influenced by the teams' performances, so the schools want the teams to perform well. Athletics, in other words, affect the business. And there are no athletics without the right athletes.

In the spring of 2014, I taught a journalism class at Princeton and lived there for four days a week, mingling not only with the sixteen seniors, juniors and sophomores in my seminar but also with other students. And I was surprised by how often I brushed up against kids for whom sports had in some way been their entrance ramp to the school. One student I came to know told me that she had ended up at Princeton because just as she was entering her senior year of prep school, Princeton's coach for women's crew had identified her as a potentially valuable rower. Learning that she was also an excellent student, the coach ardently wooed her, and Princeton's admissions committee gratefully accepted her.

Another student came from the kind of neighborhood and private school in Manhattan that harbor an infinity of Ivy League aspirants and potentially lengthen the odds of admission: All those children of doctors, lawyers and Wall Street titans blur, and accepting too many of them runs counter to a diverse campus. But this student was an ace fencer. Princeton has a fencing team. And ace fencers aren't a dime a dozen.

Athletes are so prized and sports accorded such precedence that college coaches begin courting high school kids as early as the ninth grade and, soon thereafter, making them promises of admission if they keep their GPA above a 3.5 and get an SAT score that's not *too* far below the median for the given college's student body. I'm talking about coaches everywhere, not just at the huge Southern and Midwestern state schools whose football games are televised and whose basketball teams go to the NCAA semifinals. I'm talking about coaches at most of the colleges whose pride is rooted in academics, and I'm talking about sports in addition to football and basketball. For example, lacrosse and ice hockey coaches are especially aggressive about recruiting. They have fewer players to pick among, because not every secondary school fields teams in those sports.

But it's not just athletes and legacies who get preferential treatment. In *The Price of Admission*, Golden estimates that at elite schools, minorities make up 10 to 15 percent of students; recruited athletes, 10 to 25 percent; legacies, 10 to 25 percent; children of people who are likely to become generous donors, 2 to 5 percent; children of celebrities and politicians, 1 to 2 percent; and children of faculty, 1 to 3 percent. If you take the middle figure in each of those ranges, you're looking at as many as 55 percent of students who were probably given special consideration at admissions. I hedge because an applicant can be both a minority and a legacy, or both a legacy and an athlete, and so on. And I hasten to note that some legacies would have gained admission without that designation, and that athletic accomplishment is indeed accomplishment, something that often reflects discipline and character and warrants no less respect than academic glory.

Fifty-five percent, though, could also be a *conservative* guess. I'm using the middles of Golden's ranges, not the tops, and his breakdown doesn't take into account applicants who aren't legacies and aren't faculty children but are connected in some other way or have used their and their families' social networks to pave an inside track. Maybe they have a relative who knows a trustee of the university. Maybe they have a neighbor who knows the university president. Maybe their best friend's parent or Mom's fellow partner at the law firm or Dad's colleague at the hospital is a hugely influential graduate of the college. Someone somewhere can make a call or write a letter that will be heard above the din.

"I see that a lot," said Joie Jager-Hyman, the founder and president of College Prep 360, a Brooklyn-based firm that provides private tutoring and college admissions guidance. She told me that when a family swears to her that they have a connection that's going to make the difference at their child's top choice, they're right more often than they're wrong. "They'll say, 'Don't worry, don't worry,' and I'll say, 'Okay, but let's do six or seven safety schools,' and then the kid gets in," she said.

There's no straightforward, unbiased assessment of worth being made. For one thing, such an assessment is impossible, because worth is wholly subjective. For another, a given school may be using its applicant pool to microcast its student body. It may want some kids but not too many who dabble in amateur filmmaking, an oboe player for an orchestra that's been hankering for one, somebody from Idaho and somebody from Alaska, a few Farsi and Hindi speakers to complement all those kids fluent in Spanish and Mandarin. The wish list changes from school to school and year to year.

"Maybe they need a volleyball player, they need a squash player, they need someone who's worked with orphans but not five people like that," said Tim Levin, the founder and chief executive of Bespoke Education, a tutoring and counseling service that's based in New York but has offices and clients around the country and world. "You can take cooking classes, become a great high school chef. And then Yale will turn you down because they took three chefs in that class and they don't want a fourth."

Is the institution concerned about dwindling student interest in, and support of, a particular department? If so and the department is philosophy or art history, a kid who has demonstrated a strong interest in studying that subject has an edge—maybe without even knowing or having planned it. And after all is said and done, admissions officers are in some cases playing a hunch, exercising a whim—whatever. "I think the admission committees are thoughtful, but they're human and they're fickle and they're often reading these applications at ten p.m. at night," said Gersick. "What's their mood when they're reading? Who knows what's going to happen?"

I go through all of this because if you're a parent who's pushing your kids relentlessly and narrowly toward one of the most prized schools in the country and you think that you're doing them a favor, you're not. You're in all probability setting them up for heartbreak, and you're imparting a questionable set of values that I'll talk about later in this book.

If you're a kid becoming desperately attached to a handful of those schools, you need to pull back and think about how quixotic your quest is, recognizing the roles that patronage and pure luck play. You're going to get into a college that's more than able to provide a superb education to anyone who insists on one and who takes firm charge of his or her time there. But your chances of getting into *the* school of your dreams are slim. Your control over the outcome is very, very limited, and that outcome says nothing definitive about your talent or potential. To lose sight of that is to buy into, and essentially endorse, a game that's spun wildly out of control.

THREE

OBSESSIVES AT THE GATE

*"What is merit anymore? There are a million ways that
people get into college that may not seem fair or right."*

— *Tara Dowling, a college counselor at the Choate
Rosemary Hall school*

If you maintain even a shred of doubt about how nutty this
has all become, peek inside the office of an Ivy League professor I know and eavesdrop on a recent conversation he
recounted to me.

He's being visited by some relatives. He knows them a
bit—enough to make time to greet them—but not all that
well. There are three of them: mother, father, daughter. And
the daughter is getting ready to apply to college, though "getting ready" is a woefully inadequate phrase. It implies something relatively casual, something that she's just turning her
attention to, rather than the full-on siege that has been under
way for years as she, like many of her frantic and frazzled
peers, aims for ever better board scores, ever dizzier heights of
accomplishment, ever richer fodder for her applications. She

and her parents know how fierce the competition is. The professor can see that in their faces, which communicate more than mere nervousness, more than garden-variety hope. What these three tremulous pilgrims seem to be feeling is closer to desperation.

They're in his office and on this campus not just or even mainly to acquaint themselves with the school. They're here to genuflect and prostrate themselves before it. To grovel. To preen. They're trying to recruit the professor to their cause, to impress him with their pitch, so that after they leave, he'll perhaps pick up the phone or peck out an email and tell someone in the admissions office that he just met the most fabulous girl. That the school could really use someone like her. That she's a keeper.

So she and her parents tell the professor about her grades. They tell him about her tests. They tell him about her extracurricular activities. And as the girls' parents wonder if they've exhausted the treasure chest of her charms, they realize that there's yet one more bauble they haven't retrieved, one more gem they haven't flaunted.

"Tell him," they say to their daughter, "about how you're president of your school's survivors-of-bulimia group."

I would have doubted that story if, around the time that he told it to me, I wasn't hearing so many similar tales about kids so keyed up about getting into colleges with low acceptance rates that they'd examined every facet of their personalities and scoured every byway of their biographies for admissions bait, willing to repurpose any and all oddities, humiliations, hardships.

When I met with Michael Motto, a former admissions officer at Yale who screened applicants there from 2001 to

2003 and then again from 2007 to 2008, he recalled leafing through an application from a young woman whose grades, test scores and all else were hugely impressive. He was poised to recommend her to the wider committee.

Then he got to her essay. As he remembers it, she mentioned a French teacher she greatly admired. She described their one-on-one conversation at the end of a school day. And then, this detail: During their talk, when an urge to go to the bathroom could no longer be denied, she decided not to interrupt the teacher or exit the room. She simply urinated on herself.

"Her point was that she was not going to pull herself away from an intellectually stimulating conversation just to meet a physical need," Motto told me, shaking his head. He called the college guidance counselor at her school to express his bafflement with the girl's choice of subject matter and to make sure the school knew about it, in case it reflected some self-sabotaging instinct or emotional trouble. The counselor knew about the essay, had also been baffled by it and wasn't sure what it all meant.

The girl was rejected at Yale, and so was a boy whose essay Motto also mentioned to me as an example of how disturbingly eager kids seem to be to stand out or curry sympathy in any way possible. "He wrote about his genitalia, and how he was under-endowed," Motto said. "He was going for something about masculinity and manhood, and how he had to get over certain things."

I ran those anecdotes by Marilee Jones, who was the dean of admissions at MIT from 1997 to 2007. They didn't shock her. "Kids would talk about the 911 calls because their father was beating their mother up," she told me. "Or anorexia. Or terrible, wrenching things about siblings with problems." She recalled at least one essay describing the author's struggle with the form of self-mutilation known as "delicate cutting." "And there are some things where I just feel like: Don't write that," Jones said. "Please. Don't expose yourselves."

Yearning and scheming have long been a part of applying to colleges, but they've turned into something darker. There's a swell of panic, a surrender of principle, a spreading cynicism and a disturbing gallows humor in stories I heard from students, parents, counselors, consultants and admissions officers, and in stories I read about:

- A kid who isn't gay writes an essay about the difficulty of coming out to his Asian-American family and community, then brags to classmates about his cunning subterfuge.
- A couple becomes the primary funders of an African orphanage so that it can be named after their kids, who then visit it a few times, do some token work and talk and write about their munificence during the college application process.
- A mother storms into the home of another mother in her affluent northeastern suburb in a fit of accusatory rage, blaming her own daughter's rejection from MIT on the fact that the other woman's daughter applied and got in without having any real intention of going there.
- A boy at a northeastern prep school studies the directory of students in his class, circling the pictures of the ones he thinks he'll be competing against for admission to Stanford and Harvard. He wants to keep an eye on them.
- A group of students at a private school in Manhattan start

a sort of fantasy league for odds and predictions about where different kids will be accepted or rejected.

- A group of students gathered in the library at a public school in an affluent suburb of New York note that the high-achieving kids in the Model United Nations club are away on a trip and joke that it would be a blessing if the bus crashed, because it would free up room in the "cum laude" society, reserved for the top 10 percent of the class.

- A mother in Westchester County screeches at an SAT tutor because her son's scores rose only 200 points, from the mid-1500s to the mid-1700s (out of a possible 2400), between the first time he took the test, in March of his junior year of high school, and the second time, in May. She decides that he must take it again in two weeks, in June, and puts him on a grueling ten-day schedule of additional preparation, including three full practice exams of more than three hours each.

- A parent trying to get his child off the "wait list" for Union College calls the director of admissions and yells, "I can't believe this happened! This is a horrible thing!" The parent calls again minutes later to apologize. Then the parent calls a third time: "I know you don't like me. I'm being a complete pest."

Motto recalled that an applicant eager to get off the wait list at Yale once sent him a box full of cookies arranged so that they spelled out Motto's name. (The applicant didn't ultimately get in.) Motto moved on from Yale and, a few years ago, founded Apply High, a Manhattan-based business that guides students through the college admissions process. It has given him a new vantage point on the determination and deviousness of people intent on the most exclusive schools.

He told me about a client whose parents thrust themselves into the crafting of his applications—if an outside coach was going to augment their son's efforts, why not Mom and Dad, too?—and came up with an idea for what they felt was the perfect college essay. It had struggle, suspense and a happy ending, describing their son as the product of "an exceptionally difficult pregnancy, with many ups and downs, trips to the hospital, various doctor visits," Motto said.

"The parents drafted a sketch of the essay and thought it was terrific," he told me. Then they showed it to their son, "and he pointed out that everything mentioned happened before he was born." He ended up choosing a topic that spoke to his *post*-utero life as a math lover who found a way to use those skills to help patients at a physical rehabilitation center.

Another student called Motto at eleven thirty at night because she'd changed a few punctuation marks in a letter to a college admissions office, which letter Motto had already reviewed and endorsed. She told him that she couldn't get to sleep until he'd reviewed her revisions and assured her that they were okay.

"It wasn't even an essay," Motto said. "It was a piece of correspondence."

The mother of a student in Europe who was between his junior and senior years of high school called Motto in a frantic state. She had just read somewhere that college admissions offices looked for kids who had spent their summers in enriching ways, ideally doing charity work, and her son was due to be on vacation with the rest of the family in August.

"Should we ditch our plans," she asked Motto, "and have him build dirt roads?"

Motto reminded her that she lived in a well-paved European capital. "Where would these dirt roads be?" he said.

"India?" she suggested. "Africa?" She hadn't worked it out. But if Yale might be impressed by an image of her son with a small spade, large shovel, rake or jackhammer in his chafed hands, she was poised to find a third-world setting that would produce that sweaty and ennobling tableau.

This magnitude of hysteria certainly isn't the norm. Nor are the rich, addled clients of Motto and other private consultants whose work centers around the supercharged environments of New York and other cities with concentrations of powerful, self-consciously influential people who are convinced that they can rig the system in their children's favor and are determined to. But they and their antics are extreme manifestations of a broader anxiety that permeates a bigger, more economically diverse world of families gearing up for the college admissions. And they open a window onto an industrialization of the college admission process that extends well beyond the wealthiest Americans.

New York is undoubtedly ground zero of the great race, which begins for some kids when they're mere toddlers. Susan Bodnar, a Manhattan psychologist, told me that about fifteen years ago, she took her son, Ronen, then three, to an interview of sorts at the Hollingworth Preschool, which all the parents in her Upper West Side neighborhood told her was a must, the start of a track that led straight to the Ivies. Currently its website boasts of "a hybrid program, influenced by a range of educational theories and approaches, as well as progressive beliefs in pedagogy."

Bodnar remembers arriving there, looking around at the other kids and getting the sense that they'd already somehow been prepped for what was happening, which was that a school administrator was walking around and asking them, one by one, to tell her stories related to the castles they were building or the figurines they were holding. "The three-year-olds were talking about the knight and the princess and all that," she said. "My son had a plastic frog in his hand, and she said, 'What's your frog doing?' And he said, 'Hopping.' And that was the end of his story."

"It was over," Bodnar said. "He didn't get in. His frog was only hopping. It had to be involved in a drama or a narrative, and his frog was only hopping. He was three."

Before Anthony Marx began his eight-year chapter as the president of Amherst College in 2003, he lived in New York. His children were then very young, and when his son was ready to start school, he told me, "I went to a parent orientation for admissions into Hunter [College Elementary School] kindergarten. I walked into that room and you could cut the adrenaline with a knife. You could physically feel it: 'Look at all these people we have to kill to get our six-year-old into Hunter.'"

Small wonder that in 2009, a former investment banker who had done her undergraduate work at MIT before getting an MBA at Columbia started the Aristotle Circle, which provides, for up to $450 an hour, guidance and test preparation for kids vying for admission to selective grammar schools, kindergartens and even preschools. The Aristotle Circle—the name is worth repeating—belonged to a growing business in tutoring for tykes, and in 2012 the *Times* reported a noticeable increase in the scores of four-year-olds and five-year-olds trying to qualify for spots in space-limited programs for gifted children in New York City's public schools. These programs were able to accommodate fewer than a sixth of the students whose test scores made them eligible, and the *Times* floated the unanswerable question of whether the hand of private tutoring was being seen.

A subsequent story in the *Times* provided an even better example of how early and enormously parents can get worked up about the scholastic track that their children are on. It examined the "implicit belief that a premier prekindergarten program guarantees an early leg up in a nearly 14-year battle to gain admission to the country's most competitive colleges." Note the use of the word *battle*. Note the battle's estimated duration: *nearly fourteen years.* The *Times* then did a lengthy, deadpan, utterly earnest analysis of various paths, public versus private, from the crib to the fearful, white-knuckle crossroads of college admissions, providing the pros and cons of expenditures of hundreds of thousands of dollars. Over the course of this analysis, the reader learned that the acceptance rate for the kindergarten at the Trinity School in Manhattan is 2.4 percent for kids without some family connection to the school, that half of Trinity's graduating high school class in a given year are students who've been there *since* kindergarten, and that a full year of full-day nursery school at Horace Mann in Manhattan costs roughly the same as any other grade at Horace Mann, Trinity, Riverdale, Fieldston and other members of a New York City group that calls itself the "Ivy Preparatory School League." That price tag is more than forty thousand dollars.

And many parents pay for private tutoring on top of that, especially as college looms closer. Tim Levin, the Bespoke Education president, said that while some families contract with his firm for only SAT preparation and spend perhaps $5,000 on that, others contract for different tutors in multiple subject areas and for mentors who help kids prioritize their time and complete their homework. These families may wind up spending $30,000 a year.

Michele Hernández, a longtime college admissions consultant, charges in the vicinity of $50,000 to families who sign their kids up in the eighth or ninth grade for ongoing guidance through the college application process five or four years later. She gets them ready for it by advising them on which courses to take, which summer programs to enter, and how to prioritize or reconfigure their extracurricular activities. Or families can pay $14,000 to enroll a kid in the Application Boot Camp that she stages every summer. For each of several sessions of the camp, twenty-five to thirty kids between their junior and senior years are tucked away for four days in a hotel to work with a team of about eight editors on what Hernández told me are as many as ten drafts each of three to five different essays. The fee they pay doesn't include travel to the camp, which in recent summers has been held in Cambridge, Massachusetts, or the hotel bill, breakfasts and dinners. It does include lunch and a range of guidance in addition to essay editing.

The very name of IvyWise, a college consulting firm in Manhattan, telegraphs the promise it's making, the reward it's dangling in front of salivating parents. Its founder, Katherine Cohen, whose diplomas come from Brown and Yale, sells a "platinum package" of twenty-four guidance sessions and an hour of weekly phone time during the junior and senior years of high school, for a price of about $30,000. Most years she cannot accommodate the number of people who want to go the platinum route. "I've got to clone myself," she told *New York* magazine, whose profile of her was like that of a movie star, replete with flattering appraisals of her furniture, clothes and even body.

But the type of professional who came to mind as I read about Cohen and spoke with people like Motto and Hernández wasn't an actor. It was the beauty-queen whisperer who studies the swimsuits and strides of past victors to make sure that current contenders have the most eye-pleasing jiggle, the most ear-tickling giggle. Just do your hair the right way and murmur "world peace" whenever possible and the crown could be yours. College consultants insist that they try to steer the parents and kids who come through their doors away from any belief in a surefire script and toward a healthier investigation of colleges that merely match their interests and goals, but that's not exactly what their come-ons communicate.

"Let us help you rise above the rest!" says Hernández College Consulting's home page, where you can click on "Ivy League Stats." The message in large type on the homepage of Apply High reads: "It's harder than ever to get into the top universities. Let Apply High give you a competitive edge." The homepage for Jager-Hyman's College Prep 360, to its credit, talks instead about filling educational gaps and positioning kids for the most rewarding college experiences possible, but when I clicked on "About Us," I was led to a page rife with testimonials like one in which the parent of a former client said that there was "no way my son would have gotten into Yale Early Action without Joie. She encouraged him and helped through every step of the way." It was signed by "a proud mother," a phrase that struck me as odd, coming as it did from someone who'd just attributed the difference between acceptance and rejection to a hired gun.

You can find even more exhaustive and elaborate coaching outside New York, but you have to go to China. Tara Dowling did, and what she saw floored her. Dowling has worked in college guidance for more than three decades and is currently the associate director of college counseling at Choate Rosemary Hall, a renowned private boarding school in Connecticut. But from 2010 to 2012, she was involved in a venture to create an Americanized high school program for Chinese kids that would lead to a virtual diploma recognizable to admissions offices in the United States. It ultimately didn't take root, but Dowling got a glimpse of how Chinese students applying to American colleges approach the process.

"They hire someone to create a profile and, if they can get away with it, take tests for them," she said. "Nobody submits an essay that isn't sanitized or ghostwritten. There are these crazy agents who make people believe that they can guarantee them admission. Virtually no transcripts seen in the U.S. are authentic, because they don't have transcripts like we do, so they have to Americanize what they have. It doesn't mean there aren't brilliant, amazing kids. But they're so different, that most of them have to submit something doctored just to fit into the American system."

And some of them, she told me, do get into the elite schools that they're set on. I asked her if that enraged or disillusioned her. Her answer was surprising, revealing and, I think, quite wise. "I think it's unfortunate when people cheat their way into anything," she said. "But that includes American kids. That includes people who buy their kids places at American high schools."

*   *   *

Just how well does all the fluffing work? People who are familiar with the admissions process and aren't financially invested in believing that you can buy a meaningful advantage say that the screeners of applications have grown savvy to, and cynical about, all the flamboyant charity work; all the leadership positions in self-started organizations with memberships of three; all the summers spent learning Swahili; all the soul-bearing essays about family melodramas as fulcrums for personal growth.

But it's impossible to know. And it's hard not to wonder if a statistic mentioned in the previous chapter—that roughly 75 percent of the students at the two hundred most highly rated colleges come from families in the top quartile of income in the United States—isn't influenced somewhat by all the high-priced prepping and primping. At the least, a kid whose parents can afford elementary and secondary schools with more expansive and rigorous programs has a better-than-average shot at the kinds of grades, Advanced Placement classes, extracurricular activities and SAT and ACT scores that are the very foundation of a potentially successful application to one of the most selective colleges. There's in fact a proven correlation between high SAT scores and high family income, and this surely reflects the sustained investment being made in a fortunate subset of kids. It also suggests that admission to an Ivy is in many cases a badge of privilege as much as of any intrinsic or earned mettle.

And while the Application Boot Camp and the "platinum package" are used by a small minority of the wealthiest families, some form of help in addition to the input of high school guidance counselors may not be all that rare. In 2009, a national survey of more than 1,250 high school seniors who scored in the top third of all students on the SAT or the ACT found that 26 percent of them had used the services of a paid college placement consultant.

Mark Sklarow, the chief executive of the Independent Educational Consultants Association, told me that he thinks that number is high, or at least was at the time. His own estimates as of July 2014 were that 25 percent of kids bound for private four-year colleges and 10 to 15 percent bound for public universities paid for at least some outside advice, and he said that the numbers of advisers grow continuously and have gone up with particular speed of late. A decade ago, he said, there were maybe 1,500 professionals working full-time as independent college consultants, meaning that they weren't paid by, or affiliated with, any school that gave students their services for free. In 2009, he said, there were perhaps 2,500, and by 2014, about 7,500: a tripling of the ranks in just five years.

Meanwhile, the test prep industry—special camps, special classes, targeted publications—is a multi-billion dollar behemoth, underscoring its insinuation into the lives of kids across a fairly broad economic spectrum. With differing intensities and strategies on different rungs of the economic ladder, kids are trying to boost their odds of admission, and there's no way it doesn't queer the process somewhat, favoring certain aspirants over others. Do the kids getting into their top-choice schools have greater potential? Or do they just have a better understanding of the system and how to work it?

An obsession with its workings is pervasive, and is evident in Internet traffic and in the volume of books that promise help. The College Confidential website, which is devoted to the admissions process, attracts tens of millions of unique visitors annually. It has its own insider shorthand, its own insider vocabulary. Often visitors, saving themselves keystrokes, don't bother to spell out Harvard, Yale and Princeton, which are simply "HYP." "HYPS" signals the inclusion of Stanford as well and "HYPSM" the addition of MIT. And "chance me" is the command for a popular game that visitors play; one of them describes his or her transcript and which school he or she dreams of attending, then others weigh in with predictions. The College Confidential chatter revolves largely around admissions odds and admissions tips.

As for books, well, Hernández is the author of *A Is for Admission: The Insider's Guide to Getting into the Ivy League and Other Top Colleges.* Jager-Hyman wrote *Fat Envelope Frenzy: One Year, Five Promising Students, and the Pursuit of the Ivy League Prize,* followed a few years later by *B+ Grades, A+ College Application.*

The creative titles of these overlapping manuals suggest how many are out there and how carefully and energetically each must try to distinguish itself from the others. You can choose among *Going Geek: What Every Smart Kid (and Every Smart Parent) Should Know About College Admissions, Crazy U: One Dad's Crash Course in Getting His Kid into College, How to Be a High School Superstar: A Revolutionary Plan to Get into College by Standing Out,* and *How to Make Colleges Want You: Insider Secrets for Tipping the Admissions Odds in Your Favor,* to name just a few.

For writing tips, there are *Escape Essay Hell! A Step-by-Step Guide to Writing Narrative College Application Essays* and *Conquering the College Admissions Essay in 10 Steps* and *The Art of the College Essay* and *100 Successful College Appli-*

cation Essays and *50 Successful Ivy League Application Essays* and *50 Successful Harvard Application Essays*. That's not to mention the pages upon pages of study guides for standardized tests. For the sake of college admissions, vast forests have died and whole continents could be denuded.

Shelves of books like that weren't around when Dick Parsons was finishing high school in the early 1960s, and he wouldn't have read them if they had been. He didn't sweat anything about the application process, not even the schools he set his sights on—all *three* of them. His approach was improvisatory, whimsical, accidental, leading him to Honolulu and the University of Hawaii. It wasn't exactly a likely destination for an African-American teen who was born in the Bedford-Stuyvesant section of Brooklyn, who grew up in South Ozone Park, Queens, and whose parents had both attended historically black colleges. And it isn't the alma mater you expect on the resume of a man who went on to become the chairman and chief executive of Time Warner, then the chairman of Citigroup. A trailblazer and a titan, Parsons was once rumored to succeed Michael Bloomberg as mayor of New York, and when President Obama took office, he put Parsons on an economic advisory team alongside Warren Buffett, Robert Rubin, Robert Reich and Google's Eric Schmidt. In 2014, he drew a messier appointment and was chosen as the interim chief executive of the Los Angeles Clippers basketball team, charged with cleaning up the mess made by Donald Sterling.

His own three children grew up in more affluent circumstances and in an environment where the competition to get into highly selective colleges was keen and out in the open. And sometimes, he told me, his wife would present him and his educational background to the anxious fellow parents around them as a reality check and calmative. "She would have people talk to me as a kind of confidence-building exercise: If this idiot can end up on the right side of the ledger, you can," Parsons said with a laugh.

Against the backdrop of the current obsession with college admissions, it's funny to be reminded of just how little thought many spectacularly successful people put into where they went to school—and of just how unremarkable that was in an earlier (and, admittedly, different) era. But it's also important. Instructive. And that's not because such heedlessness is worth emulating, a strategy superior to all the fretting that occurs now. No, a story like Parsons's simply puts the relevance and predictive power of a fancy diploma in context. And it underscores that many of the talents and strengths that wind up fueling someone's achievements don't necessarily emerge or play a part in the college application process, and aren't honed in the classrooms of exclusive schools.

Parsons did dream of the Ivy League—or, rather, of Princeton. Growing up, he knew he was supposed to aim for, and go to, college—his parents drilled that into him and his four siblings—and when he was in the seventh grade, his class took a trip to Princeton to see a football game.

"And I was gobsmacked," he said. "Those ivy-covered walls, the archways: It was what college was supposed to be. If you grow up in the Northeast, you have an ideal of college, and Princeton just looked like it." Its quadrangles had the right aura of authority, its spires the right air of enchantment.

So that was that. It was settled. "Whenever anybody would say, 'Where are you going,' I'd say, 'I'm going to

Princeton,' as if it were a rite of passage," he recalled. He was certainly a fine student; he'd even skipped two grades. And he reliably aced standardized tests. But he could also be lazy and inattentive, and there were plenty of B's on his transcript. A few of the adults around him advised him not to pin all of his hopes on his Princeton application. His parents insisted that he apply to City College of New York as an insurance policy and more affordable alternative. He was sure he wouldn't need a fallback, but, even so, he was determined that CCNY not be his only one, as he was eager to travel farther from home. So he filed a third application to a place *very* far away: the University of Hawaii. It had popped into his head in part because a pretty high school classmate of his was from Hawaii.

"It was a lark," he said.

That is, until he didn't get into Princeton and had to pick either CCNY or Hawaii. He went for the Pacific and the palms, and began to cast it as a considered choice. "They had this very exciting astrophysics department," he said, explaining that it had something to do with mountaintop telescopes and a sky unsullied by pollution and excessive light. In his mind he dwelled on how wonderfully exotic his adventure would be.

When he headed west, it wasn't just to school but to an unprecedented kind of independence, a degree of self-reliance unlike anything he had experienced before. With five kids, his parents couldn't contribute much to his education and he didn't have a scholarship, so he had to pay for his tuition and living expenses himself and took a sequence of jobs, putting in enough hours at some to qualify as nearly full-time.

His first year, he worked at a biomedical research center,

and while he had a title that smacked of seriousness and pleased him—"lab assistant"—he had duties less vaunted. "I washed test tubes," he said. He might as well have been dealing with dirty dishes in a restaurant kitchen.

Later he worked as an attendant in a parking garage, and for his last year he laid pipes for a local gas company. Along the way he played some school basketball and went to his classes, though he wasn't an intensely dedicated student. He started out as a physics major but found the coursework grueling and switched to history. Even so, he was six credits shy of what he needed for a diploma by the time graduation rolled around. He never bothered to get those credits or that diploma, because he'd aced yet another exam—the one for law school applicants—and Albany Law School was willing to enroll him despite his shortfall of credits. To help with his bills there, he worked part-time as a janitor.

Although his college days don't read like the prelude to professional greatness, he said that they actually were pivotal, as was the University of Hawaii. "I cannot remember a single thing I learned in college," Parsons told me. "But it worked for me because what I learned was that I could make it in this world." He had traveled five thousand miles from his home, and was able to circle back to Queens to visit his family only once a year, during the summer. He had been sixteen when he arrived in Honolulu. He didn't have local relatives, local connections, any kind of ready safety net. He was utterly on his own. And the magnitude of that dislocation had forced on him a maturity and poise that another, different college experience might not have.

"At the end of four years, I was still standing," he said. "Maybe wavering a bit, but still standing. I learned that surviving and prospering—with a small *p*—was something that I could do." Back in elementary and middle and high school, when he'd been skipping grades and prophesying Princeton and was blissfully unaware that the boldest plans have a way of being thwarted, he'd had arrogance. Now he had something less gaudy but infinitely more useful.

"Confidence," he said. "And for me, that was an essential part of the equation of success."

Parsons doesn't think that his particular trajectory would be right for everybody. No single trajectory is—and that includes one that takes a student to and through an exclusive, brand-name college. "You should try to find a school that fits you," he said. "You should ask yourself where are you going to develop those other important life skills.

"By the time I got out of law school," he added, "nobody asked me where I went to college. They didn't care. Everybody goes to college, and with the exception of maybe a few brands, you don't really know what that means, wherever they went." The source of an MBA or JD can have significant impact, he said, but even then, the degree is no substitute for abilities nurtured outside the classroom.

I asked him which abilities those were, what "important life skills" he'd been referring to. "The ability to relate to people," he said. "To be comfortable with risk. To manage ambiguity and to be resilient."

"Are you prepared to bet on yourself?" he asked. "Are you prepared to show up?" In going to Hawaii, he'd taken an enormous bet on himself. And maybe that set him up to take a sequence of additional bets—to reach high—as the years went by.

✻   ✻   ✻

I would have chalked up the way that Parsons chose the University of Hawaii as some anomalously superficial oddity had I not spoken just a few days earlier with Bobbi Brown. She's the founder and chief creative officer of Bobbi Brown Cosmetics, one of those companies that divined an unoccupied niche and an untapped market in a business that seemed utterly saturated with competitors. And she's been hailed as a savvy entrepreneur because of that.

I reached out to her because I was intrigued by where she'd received her degree: Emerson College in Boston, which specializes not in business but in communications and the arts. And when I spoke with her, I learned that her adventures in college were even more surprising than that. Emerson was the third institution of higher learning that she attended. And while it was chosen in a thoughtful fashion, the first two weren't.

Brown grew up and went to a public high school in the mid-1970s in an affluent suburb of Chicago. While many of the kids around her were acutely concerned about where they'd be going to college, she and the other girls in her crowd weren't. She graduated a semester early—not, she says, because she was such a great student, but because she'd dutifully finished all her requirements—and enrolled for the spring semester at the University of Wisconsin Oshkosh. She had one and only one reason for doing that. Her boyfriend at the time was older than she was and was already a student there.

After that semester, she convinced him to pack up and move on with her, to a destination that she deemed more exciting, but it wasn't a highly selective school picked for its specific programs or academic boasts. "The only consideration in where I went was, honestly, where my friends were going," Brown told me. And that turned out to be the University of Arizona.

"We knew we could get in there, it wouldn't be a big deal, it was far enough from Chicago, it was fun," she said, explaining that among her peers in that place at that time, you headed to school in Colorado if you wanted skiing and Arizona if you wanted sun. Her friends chose sun.

She completed only one year at the University of Arizona, after which she announced to her mother: "School's not for me." Her parents were supportive but insistent: A college education—some kind of college education—was a must. Her mother asked her what she was really passionate about. The honest answer: makeup. And rather than dismiss that as irrelevant, mother and daughter actually sought to incorporate it into a plan. Makeup was important in theater and movies, the world of which included professional makeup artists. So maybe Brown should look for a school that trained people for theater and movies.

Emerson qualified, though Brown told me that what really hooked her was her visit to the school. She spotted a bunch of people at an outdoor café, and instantly liked the look of it and them. She had a feeling.

At that time, she said, Emerson was aggressively wooing students and trying to establish itself as an institution uniquely responsive to their creative impulses, so they let her design a concentration that didn't exist. "I told them, 'I want to study makeup,'" she recalled. "I thought I wanted to do theater makeup. They had one makeup class. They said, 'You can work with the director of the school play, you can work with the TV department.'" So that's what she did: She journeyed through genres—theater, TV, film—that were a part of the curriculum, and in each, she focused as much as possible on foundation and powder, chins and cheekbones, shadow and light.

"I left with a bachelor of fine arts in makeup with a minor in photography, but what I really left with was the knowledge that it was all up to me," she said. Emerson had cast her as the captain of her fate, a role she continued to play from then on. "Everything in life—everything—is what you put into it. It's not just Harvard, Stanford or Yale that gets you a foot in the door. There are so many options for how you can live your life and make a career for yourself."

But there's one guideline she finds unfailingly reliable: If you can identify and stick with something you're genuinely passionate about, you're ahead of the game. "Often kids say they want to be a lawyer or go into marketing or go into business and make a lot of money," she said. "That's the wrong answer. You'll figure out how to make money *once* you figure out what you love to do."

Emerson turned out to be the right school for her but not because she'd had to beat out her peers for the privilege of studying there, just as that dynamic wasn't what made the University of Hawaii work, in its way, for Parsons. She and Parsons connected with their colleges in other fashions. They're hardly alone in that, or in wandering to those schools in fashions that didn't include nighttime sweats, daytime tutors, four stabs at the SAT, essays that veritably bled on the page and a jittery conviction that absolutely everything was on the line.

FOUR

RANKINGS AND WRONGS

"I think U.S. News & World Report *will go down as one of the most destructive things that ever happened to higher education."*

—*Adam Weinberg, the president of Denison University*

What's troubling about the fixation on a small cluster of colleges to the exclusion of others isn't just the panic that it promotes in the people clamoring at the gates, the unwarranted feelings of failure that it creates in the kids who don't make it through and the pessimism that it suggests about America's fortunes. It's the number of rickety assumptions that it's built on, and chief among them is that rankings of schools—in particular, the rankings revised annually by *U.S. News & World Report*—have enormous meaning.

They don't. In the case of *U.S. News*, they're largely subjective. They're easily manipulated. They rely on metrics and optics of dubious relevance. They're about vestigial reputation and institutional wealth as much as any evidence that the children at a given school are getting an extraordinary education and graduating with a sturdy grip on the future and the society around them. They're an attention-getting, money-making enterprise for *U.S. News*, not an actual service to the college-bound. They don a somber gray suit of authority, but it's a hustler's threads.

And yet the *U.S. News* rankings maintain their quasi-biblical power, year after year, exploiting people's insecurities about their own judgments and indulging our love of tidy and digestible lists, preferably numbered ones with scores attached, in a digital world of so much random information. We use such lists and scores for cars, for dishwashers, for restaurants, for hotels. And, with four years and a king's ransom on the line, secondary school students and their parents use them for colleges, which have indeed become more and more like products, albeit expensive ones. The assumption is that the No. 5 school must somehow be better, and more likely to yield returns, than the No. 25 school, which in turn must be an infinitely safer bet and more enviable boast than anything below 50. And that belief is unshakable, surviving countless attempts to shake it.

"We might as well rail against Cheetos, soft drinks, lotteries, or articles about the Kardashians," wrote John Tierney, in a spirited post for the *Atlantic*'s website in late 2013 that did a masterful job of capturing many observers' frustration with the rankings. "You can bash people over the head with information about how empty, useless, or bad-for-you some things are, yet lots of folks will still want to consume them. Each of us has some kind of tripe that sustains us. For many, it's the *U.S. News* college rankings." The paradox of pervasive contempt for them and yet widespread obeisance to them was underscored by the title of Tierney's post. "Your Annual Reminder to Ignore the *U.S. News & World Report* College Rankings," it read, with a subtitle that asserted that their "real purpose is to exacerbate the status anxiety of prospective students and parents."

I refuse to accept that the bashing is fruitless. I'll proceed to bash, because I believe passionately that the college experience can't be reduced in this fashion, nor can an individual college's merits be evaluated by this formula. I also worry, despite all the bashing, that many parents and kids still don't understand how questionable the *U.S. News* approach is and how much contempt many of the people *in* higher education, including those whose schools benefit from the rankings, have for it.

Nearly all of the current and former educators I know cite the *U.S. News* rankings as a major culprit in the admissions mania, and nearly all of them disparage the criteria behind the rankings as fatally flawed. One of the most thoughtful laments that I've heard or seen came from Jeffrey Brenzel, who spent eight years, ending in 2013, as the dean of admissions at Yale, a school that routinely appears at or near the top of various rankings, including the ones by *U.S. News.* Brenzel posted it on Yale's website after he stepped down from that job. "Make no mistake," he wrote. "The publication of college rankings is a business enterprise that capitalizes on anxiety about college admissions."

He said that while choosing a college is indisputably more important than buying a household appliance, "College rankings systems all take a far *less* thorough and scientific approach than *Consumer Reports* does when testing vacuum cleaners. Another problem with rankings is that they allow the dominant player—*U.S. News & World Report*, a magazine that has actually gone defunct and exists now only as a purveyor of rankings—to exert undue influence."

He then relayed the story of a former Yale admissions colleague who went on to work as a college placement counselor at a high school. Time and again, she watched students jettison carefully constructed lists of colleges that might be right for them in favor of lists with a familiar cast of schools. "These new lists always seem to correlate with the rankings in *U.S. News*," Brenzel wrote. "Students tend to discard excellent and appropriate colleges ranked lower in *U.S. News* and to add 'stretch' schools that are unlikely to offer them admission."

"The simplicity and clarity that ranking systems seem to offer are not only misleading, but can also be harmful," he continued, adding, "Rankings tend to ignore the very criteria that may be most important to an applicant, such as specific academic offerings, intellectual and social climate, ease of access to faculty, international opportunities and placement rates for careers or for graduate and professional school."

International opportunities are not part of the *U.S. News* survey. Nor are job-placement rates (which, to be fair, would be awfully difficult to define and measure) or any assessment of the distinction that graduates of a given school go on to achieve. Do those graduates feel that the school gave them the grounding in the world and the launching into adulthood that it should have? The only part of the *U.S. News* scoring formula that comes close to getting at that is the percentage of alumni who give money to the school, and that's a fuzzy yardstick with an additional problem that I'll explain in a bit.

But the SAT scores of admitted students? These are important to *U.S. News*; in fact, their impact on a school's ranking has increased in recent years, to 8.125 percent for the rankings published in the fall of 2014. "It's like what Einstein said about measurements," said Hiram Chodosh, the president of Claremont McKenna College, when I asked him about *U.S. News.* "You measure what you can count easily, and then often fail to measure what really counts."

U.S. News rightly and smartly divides schools into a few categories, the two most prominent of which are "national universities"—which is where you find big state schools, the Ivies, and other doctorate-granting research institutions like the California Institute of Technology, Emory, Notre Dame, Carnegie Mellon and Howard—and "national liberal arts colleges," which is where you find smaller schools like Williams, Reed and Colorado College. Beyond that its decisions grow more and more debatable.

More than a fifth of the score that *U.S. News* assigns a school reflects what high school guidance counselors think of it and the regard in which presidents, provosts and admissions deans at other colleges hold it. But most of these people, when surveyed, aren't likely to be weighing in with deep and continuously updated knowledge of the entire higher education landscape. They haven't been in the classrooms of the colleges they're grading. They've met only a few, if any, of most colleges' current students and recent graduates.

"I don't know how to rank Sewanee College," said Jennifer Delahunty, the admissions dean at Kenyon College. She's one of three people at Kenyon, along with the president and the provost, who are annually mailed a form by *U.S. News* that asks them, in an absurdly superficial manner, to give each college on a list of more than one hundred a grade of distinguished, strong, good, adequate, marginal or "don't know" by checking the relevant box. The scoring is no more nuanced than that. And she was using Sewanee as a somewhat random example. "I have a good friend who's a dean there, so should I rank it high?" she said. "Should I just go through and make Kenyon excellent and everybody else good? Would that be the thing to do?"

In the end, she said, "I just throw it in the trash." Year after year. And she's pretty sure she's not the only one in academia who takes that approach.

Those who dutifully check the boxes and size up their peer institutions are often going by reputation. And because one of the principal engines of reputation is, well, the *U.S. News* rankings, there's a self-fulfilling prophecy at work. Schools are rated highly because they've been rated highly before.

"It's a teenage thing," Marilee Jones, the former admissions dean for MIT, told me. "We're a bunch of lemmings. There is no best. *There is no best.*"

Schools are also judged by both their graduation rates and the way those rates stack up against what would be expected in terms of the school's demographic and socioeconomic profile. But in an era of rampant grade inflation, how trustworthy are those barometers?

And schools are judged by how much they spend per student. But where that money goes isn't determinable, and one of the distinct trends of the last decade has been for schools, in their competition for top students and for those who can pay full freight, to upgrade the fitness facilities, beautify the communal spaces, multiply the amenities and add layers of nonacademic services. As Matthew Segal wrote in an online column for *Fortune* magazine in late 2013, George

Washington University "built a new $130 million 'super dorm' and $33 million textile museum.

"It is not alone," added Segal, now twenty-nine, one of the cofounders of OurTime.org, a nonprofit that does political advocacy for young Americans. "The University of Pennsylvania's gym recently underwent a $10 million renovation to include an Olympic-sized swimming pool, co-ed sauna, juice bar, golf simulator, and climbing wall." Segal noted that Kenyon "has a $70 million athletic center with similar country club features."

Dollars don't equal learning. Nor do they equal teaching, and yet the *U.S. News* scoring formula rewards schools that pay higher faculty salaries, as if professors getting bigger checks are somehow going to be giving better instruction.

"As I understood it, there's nothing in there, directly, about the quality of education," said Anthony Marx, the former Amherst president, referring to the *U.S. News* formula. His assessment wasn't sour grapes: Amherst has traditionally fared as well as Yale in the rankings. "Basically," he continued, "the driver is how much money does an institution have and therefore how much money does it spend. And how many kids can you turn away. The incentives of the rankings are to raise the price and fund-raise so as to spend more, and make it more crazy-selective, not for any measured educational outcome."

One of the most disturbing wrinkles of the *U.S. News* rankings is that they have a potentially adverse effect on keeping the cost of college down. Why would rankings-cognizant administrators, eager to see their schools rise on the list and attract more applicants, look for economies and limit tuition increases when *U.S. News* rewards schools that have a whole lot of money sloshing around but not those that are seemingly concerned with affordability?

U.S. News endorses selectiveness in several ways. A part of a school's score is determined by its acceptance rate, with lower being better. Other parts are determined by the SAT or ACT scores of the students it admits and by their class rank. All in all, the harder a school is to get into, the more worthy it's deemed. Why?

Sure, its selectiveness may confer some immediate professional advantage on some graduates, inasmuch as there are job recruiters, looking for a shortcut to outstanding students, who assume that the University of Pennsylvania or Northwestern has done the heavy-duty screening for them and that they can now limit their own canvass to those schools and others like them. And, yes, high scores and class ranks often connote smarts and a seriousness of purpose, which an ideal student body would be brimming with. But while a campus full of kids in the upper 3 percent of SAT scorers can boast about that and find an impressed audience at *U.S. News*, is it truly more attractive than, and superior to, a campus full of kids in the upper 15 percent?

"I have long believed that below a 30 percent acceptance rate, a class is not really getting better," wrote William M. Shain when he was the dean of admissions at Vanderbilt University. "Rather, test scores rise from the very high to the stratospheric, and more valedictorians are denied admission. To my knowledge, no one has ever documented that this brings any improvement in the quality of intellectual discourse on campus. Institutions do not change as rapidly as do guidebook ratings."

This assessment was made a decade ago, since which acceptance rates have plummeted even further, and it was echoed by Todd Martinez, a professor of chemistry at Stanford University. He told me that the sorts of distinctions being drawn between applicants to a school that's accepting only 5 or 10 or 20 percent of them are almost inherently meaningless and subjective. "All that human beings can do is triage—good, bad, mediocre," he said. "That's about the limit of our ability to divide things up. When it gets below thirty percent or twenty percent, it's just a lot of noise."

Selectiveness is hardly a straightforward proxy for desirability. It's in some cases a decision a school makes, principally by drumming up applications. It can be fudged, prettied up. Bruce Poch, the former admissions dean at Pomona, said that when *U.S. News* revises its rankings yearly, in part to take into account the fresh group of students who have arrived at a school, it looks only at freshmen who enter in the fall. As a result, he said, some schools, which he declined to name, will accept the sorts of lower-scoring students who won't impress *U.S. News* for enrollment in the spring semester, making them wait to come to campus, or will offer them a guaranteed place as transfers into the sophomore class.

Schools also throw around lucrative merit scholarships to woo the high scorers who elevate a student body's statistical profile, though they do this with more than just *U.S. News* in mind. Whatever the motive, this practice appears to be significantly more prevalent than it was decades earlier, and much of the money involved is going to kids who don't really need it instead of kids who sorely do. A 2008 study by the Institute for College Access & Success found that in the 2005–2006 academic year, 30 percent of the roughly $11 billion in financial aid that institutions of higher education provided was "non-need-based."

"It's odious, it's wrong, but at your peril, you don't participate," said Kenyon's Jennifer Delahunty. "I am so lucky. I am the envy of my peers. No trustee here ever said, 'Drive up those SAT scores.' But the truth of the matter is, I'm evaluated on those benchmarks. If our test scores drop, people are going to get very concerned."

Ted O'Neill, the former dean of admissions at the University of Chicago, said that schools monkey around with more than just how distinguished their student body appears. *U.S. News* smiles, understandably, on colleges with smaller class sizes, so administrators will try to schedule such seminars and tutorials "in the fall quarter, which is what *U.S. News* cares about," he said. *U.S. News* also smiles on alumni generosity—specifically, as I mentioned before, what percentage of a school's alumni is donating money—and this metric, too, is corruptible: Just launch a fund-raising campaign that stresses that full participation is paramount and that $1 is as appreciated as $100. "There's been a lot of pretty blatant manipulation of alumni giving numbers," O'Neill said.

His verdict on the *U.S. News* rankings wasn't any kinder than that of others who spoke with me about them. "They seem to imply a kind of scientific evaluation of quality," he said, "and they're really not talking about quality at all. That's an illusion. They're doing a profile of a college's power."

It is hard, maybe even impossible, to engage anyone in higher education about the college admissions frenzy, its causes and its negative consequences without *U.S. News* coming up. And, sure enough, Condoleezza Rice alluded to it relatively soon into my conversation with her.

She currently teaches at Stanford, where she served as

provost just before her years in George W. Bush's administration, first as his national security adviser and then as his secretary of state. And she has no gripes with Stanford's standing: In the *U.S. News* rankings released in September 2014, it tied with Columbia for fourth place among national universities, behind Princeton, Harvard and Yale, in that order.

"I think Stanford is unbelievable," she said, her voice brimming with an enthusiasm that seemed genuine. "But there are other places that are also great to go: big state universities that have a different character; research universities; small liberal arts colleges; regional colleges that are very good and maybe there's a reason a particular student would be better off close to home." And one of her chief problems with the *U.S. News* rankings—and with the kind of attention accorded them—is the phenomenon that Yale's Jeffrey Brenzel mentioned in relation to the college placement counselor he knows: They unnecessarily shrink the pool of schools that kids consider. In constructing a hierarchy of colleges, they give short shrift to the multitude and diversity of them, and they imply that certain schools are better for everyone, when they may only be better for particular students with particular dispositions. "I think we end up limiting students' horizons too early," she said. Certainly few students would be prodded by the *U.S. News* rankings to attend Rice's alma mater, which placed 88th among national universities in the fall of 2014 and has come *up* in the world since she graduated from it. It's the University of Denver.

She went there because it was close to home and because her father worked there, which meant that she got a financial break on tuition. In 1968, John Rice had moved her and her mother from Alabama to Colorado to take a job as an assistant dean of admissions at the University of Denver, where he would subsequently rise to other, higher posts. He enrolled her at a private, Catholic all-girls school whose graduates were expected to go off to college, though she told me that few set their sights on the Ivy League or, for that matter, schools outside the state. The message she got from her parents was that she should attend either the University of Denver or Colorado College.

That's partly because she, like Dick Parsons, had zipped through school quickly and would be starting college younger than most other kids—in her case, at the age of fifteen. Her parents, understandably, didn't want her going too far away just yet. She lived at home for her first years at the University of Denver, and she initially majored in piano at the university's Lamont School of Music. She'd been studying the instrument since she was a little girl, and she'd often been hailed as a piano prodigy.

At the University of Denver, she learned that she wasn't. She was good, not great, or maybe great, but not quite great enough. And so, about midway through her time there, she went on the hunt for a new field of study. She flirted briefly with English, but it didn't feel quite right. Then she happened across something that did. As my *Times* colleague Elisabeth Bumiller writes in *Condoleezza Rice: An American Life:* "In the spring of 1973 Rice wandered into a course called 'Introduction to International Politics,' taught by Josef Korbel, a sixty-three-year-old Czech refugee who had founded Denver's Graduate School of International Studies and was a university elder statesman. In one of the great coincidences and complications of modern American diplomatic history, Korbel also happened to be the father of Madeleine Albright, who would become the only other woman secretary of state." (Bumiller's book preceded Hillary Clinton's appointment to the job.)

"For Rice, like Albright, Korbel would be one of the great influences of her life," Bumiller writes. "Until she met him, Rice had shown almost no interest in foreign policy....But when she heard Korbel speak to her class on Stalin, she 'fell in love'—the phrase she has used in virtually every interview she has given about this moment in her life."

During my conversation with Rice, years after all those other interviews, she was still marveling at the hand of happenstance in her academic trajectory, something that she emphasizes to the young men and women at Stanford who turn to her for guidance. "My students will come in and say, 'How do I do what you do?' which means they want to be secretary of state," she told me. "I say, 'So here's how you do it—you start as a failed piano major.' They're stunned. But what I'm trying to get them to see is that you have some time to recognize that special combination of what you love and what you're also good at. Taking the time to do that is very important." Rice noted that a college admissions process that focuses on selectiveness and heated competition doesn't properly stress that. If anything it encourages methodical planning, blind conformity.

Rice also said that there's a transcendent importance—all too frequently overlooked—in how fully students throw themselves into the college experience and how much they demand and extract from whichever institutions they wind up at. Great educations aren't passive experiences; they're active ones. At the University of Denver, she got involved in student government and, for a short stint, with the student newspaper, though she quickly decided that journalism wasn't for her. For a while she ran the university's speakers bureau: a great way to meet and mingle with prominent visitors to the campus and a good motivation for keeping up on current events. She remembers an episode from her time in that job that made her feel as if she were in the middle of history (a place she'd later grow accustomed to inhabiting). Bob Woodward, one of the *Washington Post* writers who broke the Watergate story, was supposed to come to the campus for an appearance. Just beforehand, she recalled, "I got a panicked phone call that he had canceled. They said, 'Something's come up.' This was 1974. It was the tapes." She was referring to the public release, in the spring of 1974, of transcripts from audio recordings that President Nixon had made in the White House. "I had to hustle and get notices that Woodward had canceled and that ticket prices would be refunded," Rice told me. "You don't get that kind of organizational experience and skill just in your classes."

But with classes, too, "I was very aggressive," she said. "I was very assertive in getting to know faculty. I was always the first kid to make an appointment during office hours the first week of class. And then I'd go in knowing how I wanted to talk to faculty, how I wanted to use it.

"I tell students: If you're taking a class and you see a faculty member that you're interested in, read something the faculty member's written, then go see them. Faculty are vain. They'll love that. And then they'll remember you. No matter what university you're in, you'll find this across the board. I've had friends who've taught at San Diego State, at Hamilton College. Across the board, the student who shows initiative in a way that captures the imagination of that faculty member is going to get more time."

And, she added, "You will find faculty at almost every college who are vibrant and exciting. I found Josef Korbel at the University of Denver, and it changed my life." Although she got her master's in political science at Notre Dame, she returned to the University of Denver—and to Korbel—for her PhD. It was a decision that had nothing to do with rankings or with any hierarchy of esteem. It had to do only with a relationship that she'd forged, through her own initiative, and with a plan that made sense to and for her.

I asked Rice if her perch at Stanford affords her a perspective of how much hope and work many kids today invest in getting into a school of its altitude. She said she knows the score simply from listening to friends' children talk. (Rice herself isn't a parent.) She recalled a recent conversation with the son of someone she knows well. "I said to him, 'Are you going to look at Stanford? Where do you want to look?' And he said, 'Well, I'd never get in there.' And then he could recite, for the last five years, who in his high school class *had* gotten in.

"Now that seems to me a little extreme," she said.

U.S. News isn't alone in the rankings racket. Over recent years, there's been an uptick in attention to the annual "College Salary Report" by PayScale, a website that lists schools in accordance with the "median mid-career salary" of their graduates. Budding plutocrats, take note: These are the institutions that will supposedly help you maximize your earning potential. Emphasis on *supposedly*.

For starters, PayScale doesn't randomly survey alumni

across a broad spectrum of schools. It doesn't conduct a scientific poll along the lines of Pew, Gallup or Quinnipiac. Instead it requires visitors to its website, which is a resource for employers and employees who are trying to figure out the usual compensation for various positions in an array of fields, to fill out questionnaires that ask where they attended college and what they're making.

So PayScale is entirely reliant on the people who happen to come to it, and there's no way they're going to be a representative cross section of the population of college graduates. They're going to be people more concerned with matters of compensation, in professions where such matters are central. For some colleges, PayScale has thousands of completed surveys; for others, a statistically dubious fraction of that.

The surveys rely to some extent on respondents' honesty. And the results for a given school have more to do with which majors and career tracks are most popular there—and, thus, the kinds of students the school attracts—than with the quality of instruction or timbre of campus life. Accordingly, schools that specialize in engineering or send legions of students to Wall Street tend to fare well in PayScale's rankings.

Flawed as the information that PayScale rounds up is, it's what *Forbes* leans on for *its* annual rankings, which use earnings along with an array of other factors, including how positively students speak of their teachers on the entirely voluntary, entirely unscientific website RateMyProfessors.com. The PayScale information is also used by *Money* magazine, which joined the college rankings party in 2014. For its list of top colleges, *Money* combined graduates' earnings with the "quality" and "affordability" of the school.

The metrics that *Money* used for a school's quality—SAT

scores, graduation rates—mirrored those employed by *U.S. News*, and were equally debatable. But in considering affordability, which *Money* determined based not only on tuition but also on the amount of aid available to students and how many years they were taking to complete school, the magazine in some sense improved on both *U.S. News* and PayScale. It also guaranteed findings that would be original and would thus garner some attention from the news media. On *Money*'s top 10, Harvard, Princeton, Stanford and MIT made predictable appearances. But Babson College (No. 1), Webb Institute (No. 2), Cooper Union (No. 8) and Brigham Young University (No. 9) made unpredictable ones.

Part of what's so frustrating about the *Money*, *Forbes*, PayScale and *U.S. News* rankings is that there are all sorts of other lists and all manner of other measurements that get little attention and that, in some cases, communicate information that's equally or more relevant. You can look, for example, at which schools are producing the most Fulbright Scholars, and in October 2013, the *Chronicle of Higher Education* did. It found that among small colleges, the top 10 performers recently were, in order, Pitzer, Smith, Oberlin, Pomona, College of the Holy Cross, Williams, Occidental, Vassar, Bates and Bowdoin. Only three of those schools—Williams, Bowdoin and Pomona—are on the list of top 10 national liberal arts colleges published by *U.S. News* in the fall of 2014.

Among what Fulbright classifies as "doctoral/research institutions," which corresponds with "national universities" in *U.S. News*, the ten schools that recently produced the most Fulbright recipients included the University of Michigan (No. 2), Arizona State (No. 3), Rutgers (No. 5) and the University of Texas (No. 7). Only one of those public schools, Michigan, ranks in the *U.S. News* top 50 national universities. And yet all of them, on the Fulbright list, beat Yale, Columbia, Cornell, Duke and Stanford. Stanford tied with Ohio State, even though more Stanford students applied for Fulbrights than did Ohio State students.

Why not look at which schools have the most students who do at least some study abroad? These kids presumably come back to campus with stories and perspectives that will enrich the entire study body, and the popularity of studying abroad may well say something about an institution's signals to students and about their intellectual curiosity. *U.S. News* in fact compiles this data, which it doesn't use in its rankings.

But for what it's worth, the ten schools with the greatest percentage of students who had ventured outside the country for part of their studies, at least according to information released by *U.S. News* in the fall of 2014, were Goucher College, Soka University of America, Thomas More College of Liberal Arts, Centre College, Goshen College, Kalamazoo College, Pitzer College, Susquehanna University, Carleton College and Elon University. Along with those institutions, a dozen others sent a greater percentage of their students abroad than any Ivy League school did.

Global university assessments are done by several organizations, which tend to focus on the output of an institution's graduates, as measured by prizes, publications, patents. And there are schools in the United States that shine much brighter on these lists than they do in the eyes of American students fixated on certain brands. Among them: the University of California, San Diego; University of California, San Francisco; the University of Wisconsin–Madison; the University of Washington and the University of Illinois.

These institutions don't soar in the *U.S. News* rankings in part because of their sheer size and the big gap between their highest-achieving students and their lowest-achieving ones. They're less exclusive. But what's clear in the global rankings is that at each of them, there's no shortage of top-notch scholars who find everything they're looking for and more. And if the people around those standouts aren't the survivors of a screening process as intimidating as Stanford's, is that really a minus? With exclusivity often comes sameness, and there's an argument that college shouldn't take you out of the real world but thrust you into it, exposing you to places unlike the ones you've already inhabited and people different from the ones who've surrounded you thus far. There's nothing in the formulas used by *U.S. News*, PayScale or most other organizations in the rankings racket that addresses that. And there's no way a formula really could, because a school that will be old hat to a student from one background will be eye-opening to a student from another.

The limited, dubious utility of rankings was summed up succinctly by the man who's been in charge of the *U.S. News* list for several decades now. His name is Bob Morse, and in September 2014 he gave an interview to the *Washington Post* in which he jovially acknowledged that his rankings are "like the 800-pound gorilla in higher education" and shared his own thoughts on the relevance of a college's reputation to a student's future.

"It's not where you went to school," he told the *Post.* "It's how hard you work." Morse got an undergraduate degree at the University of Cincinnati. His MBA is from Michigan State.

FIVE

BEYOND THE COMFORT ZONE

"Be as curious as you can. Put yourself in situations where you're not just yielding to what's familiar. I came out of college with a level of confidence and self-understanding that I don't think I could have possibly gotten from an East Coast school, where I would have been among the kind of people I grew up with and lived near."

—*Howard Schultz, the chairman and chief executive of Starbucks and a 1975 graduate of Northern Michigan University*

From the tenth through twelfth grades, I attended a private school, Loomis Chaffee, in the suburbs of Hartford, Connecticut. Before then my siblings and I had always gone to public schools, but my parents grew nervous, as college neared, about whether they were giving us the very best chance of admission to the most selective colleges. Loomis was supposed to help. Most of the students there belonged to families in the upper-middle class or above. Most set their sights on one of several dozen elite private colleges in the Northeast. And those colleges, despite earnest stabs at diversity, tended to have disproportionate numbers of kids much like the ones at my private school. What these students found at college was a bigger theater and more intense work but not an unfamiliar milieu. College was an upsizing and extension of secondary school.

It was initially going to be that way for me as well. The elite northeastern colleges were the ones mentioned most frequently and admiringly around my house. They were our quarry, and my parents were ecstatic when my older brother, Mark, went from Loomis to Amherst. They were equally thrilled when I applied successfully the following year for early admission to Yale. But before I had to commit to Yale, I was nominated for, and then received, something called a Morehead Scholarship. Financed by a foundation affiliated with the University of North Carolina at Chapel Hill, it sought (and still seeks) to lure students away from private colleges and to Chapel Hill by paying all of their expenses there, giving them access to special seminars and even funding summer internships and experiences like Outward Bound.

I'd had my heart set on Yale, partly because it had always been held up as the point of my hard work at Loomis. It was the return on the investment, the validation. My parents were in a comfortable enough financial position to pay, without grave hardship, the bill for tuition, room and board, which would have been about $60,000 over four years. (Adjusted for inflation, that would be about $130,000 today.) But they weren't so well-off that the figure was utterly negligible. They told me, repeatedly, to forget about the money. They insisted on it. But a part of me refused to. I didn't want to be a person who could forget that so easily.

I had never thought about applying to Carolina. But when I gave it a close examination, I realized what a strong reputation it enjoyed and how many excellent professors and departments it harbored. I also realized something else: It might well be a greater challenge for someone like me, given where it was and where I was coming from. I'd spent my childhood in upper-middle-class suburbs in New York and Connecticut and, if I discounted one trip to Virginia and maybe two to Florida, was wholly unfamiliar with the South. Chapel Hill took 85 percent of its student body from North Carolina, and that meant that the look, accent and vibe of the place would be nothing like Loomis's—or Yale's—and would be new to me. Chapel Hill threatened to make me uncomfortable, at least briefly and at the start. I worried about that and simultaneously came to believe that my worry was the best reason to go.

So I went. Was it the right call? Would I be a more knowledgeable, happier, better person today if I'd made the opposite one? There's no answer to that. The road not taken can never be anything more than a guess, a hypothetical. So there's nothing solid to judge the road taken against.

I can tell you that I have many regrets. They're about the classes I didn't take at Chapel Hill because I didn't want to overburden myself; the classes I didn't take because they conflicted with the soap opera *All My Children*; the classes I didn't take because I didn't want to get up before 8 a.m.; the lectures I skipped because friends could be counted on to share their notes; the study-abroad opportunities I didn't seize; the people I didn't push myself to meet; the people I wasn't open or sufficiently kind to; the romantic relationships I cut short because I couldn't respect anyone who respected me too readily; the number of fried-chicken biscuits I ate; the number of egg-and-cheese biscuits I ate; the bulimia I fell prey to for a while; the excess of time I spent in front of a mirror; the paucity of time I spent trying to improve my Italian; the frequency with which I indulged my newfound fondness for bourbon; and the fact that after getting my scuba-diving certification, I used it only once. I'd go back and change all of that. And I'd finish *Middlemarch*, *An American Tragedy* and *Beowulf*, all of which I faked having read. On second thought, I'd leave *Beowulf* be.

But Chapel Hill? I wouldn't take that back. It's where I happened to learn that you could put blue cheese on a burger, which for me was like a first kiss. The sky in autumn and spring was the gentlest, rarest, most perfect of blues. I needed that solace, because I did initially feel out of place, but I also learned that out-of-place was endurable and that a person can play neat tricks with it in his or her mind, converting the dross to gold. I fancied myself an iconoclast. I fancied myself quirky. I took advantage of those times when I retreated from it all by reading and reading and reading, though not always what I was assigned.

English was my major, and more than a few of the professors in that department were extraordinary. One, who specialized in twentieth-century English and American drama, allowed me into two of his graduate seminars, where I marinated in Samuel Beckett and Harold Pinter and Tom Stoppard and Edward Albee and Sam Shepard. The school newspaper was an ambitious one, and once I found my way there, I also found an enduring posse. There and elsewhere at the university, I was among people who took much less for granted than the kids at Loomis had. And it wasn't just because all of us were now a few years older, a few years less reckless and naive. It was because the in-state kids at Chapel Hill hadn't, as a group, come from backgrounds as economically privileged as my prep school peers.

My younger brother, Harry, ended up going to Dartmouth. My sister, Adelle, the youngest of us four, went to Princeton. Mark's, Harry's and Adelle's closest college friends had second homes on Caribbean islands or the slopes of North America's prettiest mountains and had enough of a financial safety net under them to do things like follow the Grateful Dead around all summer long. My closest college friends had part-time jobs off-campus to help pay for their tuition or to pick up some of the spending money that their parents couldn't lavish on them. It wasn't that Chapel Hill had much grit to it; if anything, it had too little. But it seemed to hover closer to the earth than my siblings' schools did. And it gave me a perspective that I appreciated then and appreciate even more now.

I did wind up taking a spin through the Ivy League, attending Columbia for nine months in the service of a master's degree in journalism. The Columbia name, I concede, was part of what lured me, and a teacher I had there connected me with my first full-time position, at the *New York Post*. But the *Post* hired me only after, and because of, a four-week tryout, the success of which had less to do with the classes I'd taken at Columbia than with the writing I'd done at the UNC newspaper and on the side. And none of the people who hired me for subsequent jobs ever asked about or mentioned Columbia—or, for that matter, Chapel Hill.

*   *   *

Among the young men and women I interviewed for this book were a few Yale alumni, including Rebecca Fabbro, who graduated in 2009. She headed to Yale from the wealthy New York City suburb of Edgemont, which shares a zip code with Scarsdale, and from a high school whose college counselor was savvy enough to press her to get some high-level physics and computer science on her transcript, telling her that girls with those leanings stood out.

Rebecca said that her one qualm with Yale was how many other students there were like her, in the sense that their passages to Yale had been smoothed by the advantages of growing up in an affluent or relatively affluent family. That qualm has grown stronger over time, partly because Rebecca spent two years after Yale working for Teach For America in a public school in Marks, Mississippi, once the starting point of the "mule train," a 1967 trek to Washington to protest the poverty in which so many black Americans were mired. Rebecca said that when one of her seventh graders learned that she'd gone to Yale, the student said, "Oh, are you rich?"

She told me about an email that she'd received from Yale's president in the fall of 2013 about the class of 2017, whose members were starting just then. It praised their variety of backgrounds, noting proudly that "over half attended public schools." That boast stuck with Rebecca, because the more she thought about it, the odder and less boast-worthy it seemed. "Given that most students in this country (nearly 90%) attend public schools, I was surprised that having more than 50% of a Yale class coming from a public institution was a mark of diversity to celebrate (especially since many of those students who attend public schools attended affluent ones like

Edgemont and Scarsdale)," she wrote to me in a long shortly after we'd spoken.

As it happens, Yale had posted some information onlin about that very same incoming class, and I checked it, discovering that the percentage of public school kids was 57.6. From the same post I learned that 13.8 percent of the class of 2017 had some kind of legacy connection to the university, a situation that hardly abets diversity.

Rebecca said that she'd dug into some literature that Yale had sent her over time and had also done some other research, and she'd learned that 52 percent of students at Yale receive some level of need-based aid, a figure in which the university takes pride. But, she wrote in her email, "It concerns me that 48% of students at Yale are not on need-based aid. Given that nearly all families who make between $0 and $200,000 a year qualify for financial aid and that 'many families who make more than $200,000 a year receive some need-based aid,' that means (unless I'm reading the stats wrong) that nearly half of all Yale students who accept Yale's offer of admission are coming from families who make more than $200,000 per year. So, around 50 percent of Yale students are from families in the top 5 percent in this country."

Her deconstruction reminded me of a column written by a Harvard alumnus, Evan Mandery, that the *Times* published in April 2014. He, too, was troubled by what he saw as insufficient socioeconomic diversity at elite schools. "To be a 1 percenter," Mandery wrote, "a family needs an annual income of approximately $390,000. When the *Harvard Crimson* surveyed this year's freshman class, 14 percent of respondents reported annual family income above $500,000. Another 15 percent came from families making more than

$250,000 per year. Only 20 percent reported incomes less than $65,000. This is the amount below which Harvard will allow a student to go free of charge. It's also just above the national median family income. So, at least as many Harvard students come from families in the top 1 percent as the bottom 50 percent."

Rebecca's focus on figures like these wasn't motivated simply by questions of justice and fairness, though those concern her. She was wondering as well about the educational implications of a school so rife with children of wealth. "I have certainly learned more in more diverse environments than in others," she wrote.

"When I was making my college decision," she added, "I was concerned with prestige. Smart, successful people from my school went to places ranked highly by *U.S. News* and featured prominently in the *Times*'s wedding pages. I wanted to be like them. I also wanted to make my parents proud.

"But I had very little conception of the world outside the one in which I had grown up," she wrote. "And most students from the school I went to did not attend very socioeconomically diverse institutions."

They could have looked at a broader universe of schools. They also could have consulted rankings other than the ones by *U.S. News.* For instance, the magazine *Washington Monthly* does some of its own, which are devoted to the "contribution to the public good" that schools make, and these receive minimal attention. They try to gauge the promise of social mobility that schools offer, and they do this— imperfectly, I concede—by looking at the high percentages of poor kids admitted and how many of them are successfully ushered to diplomas. They also reward schools at which many kids do community service or go on to the Peace Corps or participate in ROTC.

By *those* measures, the top 10 national universities as of the fall of 2014 were, in order, UCSD, UC Riverside, UC Berkeley, Texas A&M, UCLA, Stanford, the University of Washington, the University of Texas at El Paso, Case Western Reserve University and Harvard. And the top 10 liberal arts colleges were Bryn Mawr, Carleton, Berea, Swarthmore, Harvey Mudd, Reed, Macalester, the New College of Florida, Williams and Oberlin. Needless to say, that lineup was a departure from the one showcased by *U.S. News.*

In the news media, I'm noticing more and more attention to the subject of how much colleges are (or aren't) doing to identify, recruit and retain students from poor and middle-class families. It's a clear and laudable outgrowth of the intensifying concern over income inequality in the United States. Along these lines, the *Times* crunched numbers and, in September 2014, published what it called a College Access Index, evaluating and ranking schools according to the percentage of students who qualified for federal Pell grants, which are reserved for low-income families, and the net price being paid by students whose families weren't affluent. The *Times* looked only at "top colleges," which it defined as those whose four-year graduation rate was at least 75 percent. The schools that scored highest on the index were, in order, Vassar, Grinnell, UNC Chapel Hill, Smith and, in a tie for fifth place, Amherst and, actually, Harvard.

Even more interesting were the discrepancies between schools. According to the index, Washington University in St. Louis has a remarkably less economically diverse student body than Pomona does, and Princeton—which held the top

U.S. News spot for national universities in 2013 and 2014—lags far behind Harvard and Columbia. Yale trails Princeton. Wake Forest does poorly; so does George Washington University.

I wonder how many prospective college students see this kind of information. I wonder if more than a few even go looking for it. They should, and I say that not out of some politically correct, reflexively liberal concern for the concept of diversity, though diversity has a whole lot going for it. I say it because a diverse campus is going to be truer to the grand, messy chaos of life and less like the deceptive nook into which the circumstances of your birth tucked you.

Vassar's president, Catharine Bond Hill, explained her push to recruit and admit low-income students—and to have a student body varied in all kinds of other ways as well—in terms of not just what's best for the kids trying to climb the ladder but what's best for every student at the school and what honors the mission of education. "If our students are going to make successful contributions to the future well-being of our society, they need to understand how to deal with diversity, and college campuses are a perfect place—an important place—to learn that," she told me.

Students from affluent families who attend a truly diverse school may be more likely to "understand that the rest of the United States hasn't grown up in the same circumstances that they have, and they might think about whether that's a fair society," she said. Whatever they conclude, it's an essential question to mull. Even from a purely careerist viewpoint, she added, there's an argument for diversity on campus. "I think that just about anything you're going to go on to do for the rest of your life—be a lawyer, a doctor or a teacher—you're going to be dealing with people very different from the kids you've gone to high school with, and understanding that is going to make you more successful when you go forward."

Those people invariably widen your frame of reference. Maybe they test you, too. Perhaps they even knock you off your stride. If so, that's a good thing.

Howard Schultz saw it that way.

He didn't go to a school that he knew to be especially diverse, and he wasn't looking to make sure that poor kids were in the mix: He *was* one of those poor kids. But he went to a college that was a complete, abrupt departure from his high school and from everything he'd known until that point. It unsettled and disoriented him, at least at first. And that was perhaps its greatest blessing, he said.

"Here's this Jewish kid from Brooklyn who lands in the Upper Peninsula of Michigan," Schultz, the chairman, president, and chief executive of Starbucks, said, recalling his journey in the early 1970s to Northern Michigan University. "I was the only Jewish kid in my dorm. I remember hearing so often, 'I've never met anyone who's Jewish.'" His tone of voice as he recounted this for me wasn't bitter or astonished. It was amused, fond, even grateful. While he often jokes that he might have *really* amounted to something if he'd gone to an Ivy League school, he of course doesn't believe that. Northern Michigan, he said, served him well, and in ways that aren't easily measurable and don't translate into catalogue-ready copy.

Simply going to college was an event and thrill for him, because neither of his parents had been able to take their education that far. As he was growing up, his father suffered through a sequence of jobs that he didn't like much and that didn't pay well, at one point driving a truck that delivered and picked up diapers, the smell of which made every work-day a misery. The family of five—Schultz has a sister and a brother—lived in the projects. Schultz remembers occasion-ally being told by his mother to answer the phone and to say that his parents weren't home, even though they were. They were trying to avoid a bill collector.

They wanted more for him and his two siblings, both younger. "My mother drilled in us that we were going to col-lege, come hell or high water," he told me. College was the way out, the ladder up. But there wasn't much chatter at home or among his friends at Canarsie High School about *where* to go to college. Nor was he sure how to pay for it. So when a football recruiter who had come to one of Schultz's high school games and had seen him play quarterback asked him if he'd be interested in a scholarship to Northern Michigan, he said a relieved yes and moved enthusiastically in that di-rection. In Schultz's autobiography, *Pour Your Heart Into It*, he writes that his family's road trip during his last semester of high school to see the campus in Marquette, Michigan, was his first time out of New York State.

At Northern Michigan he majored in communications. He joined a fraternity. He didn't, in the end, play football, at least not for long: An injury prevented him from making the kind of contribution that he'd hoped to. The scholarship went away, and he had to take out loans and work part-time. He tended bar. He even on occasion sold his blood for money. He put enough energy into his studies to maintain a B average, but not enough to do any better than that. His graduation, he said, was one of the happiest moments of his mother's life—

but she didn't attend the ceremony. The trip out would have cost more money than she and his father felt they could spend at the time.

In the end, he said, what mattered most about college was that he "came of age" there, getting a glimpse of a world far beyond Brooklyn and being forced to stand on his own two feet in it. In this sense he sounded a lot like Parsons—and he provided another reminder of how fundamentally different the college experience is for kids who can't count on Mom and Dad for frequent visits or generous handouts. That difference is often termed a disadvantage, a bit of nomenclature that should probably be revisited. It's a burden, no question. It's not something most parents would elect for their kids or most kids would volunteer for. But it winds up steeling some young people in ways that can actually prove advantageous. It's how their resolve is forged.

Schultz said that he drew particular strength from his success navigating terrain that was an adjustment, to say the least. "I was in farmland," he said. "All the kids I was meeting were from the Midwest: Michigan, Ohio, Illinois." And he was as exotic to them as they were to him. "If you are part of a very diverse background of young adults, both inside and outside the classroom, I think the experience adds significant value to the kind of person you're going to be," he said. "I'm not saying that that doesn't exist at an elite school, but when you go to a state school that doesn't perhaps have the same patina or reputation, the opportunities to expose yourself to things outside the classroom provide a different kind of education."

As I listened to Schultz, I longed more and more for a robust, sustained national conversation about the ways in which all college students, and in particular those at exclusive institutions, navigate their years of higher education and what they demand from that chapter of life. And I yearned for that largely because college has the potential to confront and challenge some of the most troubling political and social aspects of contemporary life; to muster a preemptive strike against them; to be a staging ground for behaving in a different, healthier way.

We live in a country of sharpening divisions, pronounced tribalism, corrosive polarization. We live in the era of the Internet, which has had a counterintuitive impact: While it opens up an infinite universe of information for exploration, people use it to stand still, bookmarking the websites that cater to their existing hobbies (and established hobbyhorses) and customizing their social media feeds so that their judgments are constantly reinforced, their opinions forever affirmed.

And college is indeed a "perfect place," as Catharine Bond Hill said, to push back at all of that, to rummage around in fresh outlooks, to bridge divides. For many students, it's not only an environment more populous than high school was; it's also one with more directions in which to turn. It gives them more agency over their calendars and allegiances. They can better construct their hours and days from scratch—and the clay hasn't yet dried on who they are.

But too many kids get to college and try to collapse it, to make it as comfortable and recognizable as possible. They replicate the friends and friendships they've previously enjoyed. They join groups that perpetuate their high school cliques. Concerned with establishing a "network," they seek out peers with aspirations identical to their own. In doing so, they frequently default to a clannishness that too easily becomes a lifelong habit.

If you spend any time on college campuses, you'll notice this. And you'll understand why one of my utopian fantasies is a student orientation period in which students are given these instructions, these exhortations: Open your laptops. Delete at least one of every four bookmarks. Replace it with something entirely different, even antithetical. Go to Twitter, Facebook, Instagram, Tumblr and such, and start following or connecting with publications, blogs and people whose views diverge from your own. Conduct your social lives along the same lines, mixing it up. Do not go only to the campus basketball games, or only to campus theatrical productions. Wander beyond the periphery of campus, and not to find equally enchanted realms—if you study abroad, don't choose the destination for its picturesqueness—but to see something else. Think about repaying your good fortune by mentoring kids in the area who aren't sure to get to college, or who don't have ready guidance for figuring it all out. In some American studies classes at Columbia University, this is a course requirement, and there are similar arrangements and programs at other schools. It's a trend that's worth tilling, a movement that should grow.

Now more than ever, college needs to be an expansive adventure, propelling students toward unplumbed territory and untested identities rather than indulging and flattering who they already are. And students, along with those of us who purport to have meaningful insights for them, need to insist on that.

SIX

FROM TEMPE TO WATERLOO

"I've had students who've had transformative experiences at schools that nobody's ever heard of."

—*Alice Kleeman, the college counselor at Menlo-Atherton High School in California*

With colleges as with so much else, we have an unfortunate tendency to peddle in stereotypes, and Arizona State University suffers from an especially negative one, which was captured by its description on the College Confidential website as "a party school and you will always be just a number there." That's what a student who identified herself only as AZseniorchick wrote not long ago. She also opined that Northern Arizona University was "for hippies and ugly people." What a shame that she didn't proceed, school by school and cactus by cactus, through the whole state. Her eye is as keen as her judgments are subtle.

Arizona State, better known as ASU, has long fought against a factory-like impression given by its size. With some 60,000 students enrolled at its main campus in Tempe and another 13,000 or so at nearby satellites, it's the largest single-administration university in the United States. (There are university *systems*, with different administrations for different branches, that are bigger.) It has also struggled against its location in "a place with bright sunshine and palm trees and beautiful weather," as Michael Crow, its president, described it in an on-camera interview for the 2014 documentary *Ivory Tower*, about higher education in America. There's a broad assumption that no one can really study when it's summertime almost all of the time. ASU's meteorological blessing is its reputational curse.

Ivory Tower includes footage of kids at ASU drinking and dancing. One of them shouts, "It's the party school! Come on, what are we doing right now?" Another exults, "It's paradise, baby! What's not to love?" There are also images of the annual "undie run" on the last day of classes, which looks like the kind of fitness regimen Hugh Hefner might prescribe, and there's an onscreen reminder of ASU's 2011 ranking by *Playboy* as the No. 3 party school in the nation. Over the last decade, it has toggled into, out of and around *Playboy*'s top 10.

The typical ASU student "comes to get drunk out of their minds and be in this sort of like vapid, hedonistic area," a senior identified as Brendan Arnold says in one scene in *Ivory Tower*. He's cut off by someone who approaches him and shouts something unintelligible. The impression is of beery bedlam in the desert. Bring Ray-Bans, Coppertone and Advil.

But that's not the ASU suggested by its multiple appearances on the *Forbes* 30 Under 30 list of young movers and shakers that I mentioned earlier in the book. And that's not the ASU that Wendy Zupac experienced.

Wendy, now twenty-seven, is the only child of two electrical engineers who immigrated to the United States from Serbia just before she was born. In their field, your actual skills and what you technically knew were more important than the source or even the fact of your diploma, and in Tempe, where they settled and raised Wendy, elite schools weren't mentioned as incessantly and anxiously as in the moneyed suburbs of New York, Boston, Washington and Los Angeles. Besides which, an elite college's yearly price tag of about fifty thousand dollars back when Wendy was in high school struck her parents, and her, as extravagant. Although Wendy was an A student who took many Advanced Placement classes and could have tried her luck with any number of colleges around the country, she wanted to go to ASU, where her in-state tuition would be around six thousand dollars a year and she could keep other expenses down by living at home.

"My plan was to go to a really good law school, and I felt I could get there through ASU," she said. "A lot of law schools will publish annual statistics of their incoming class, and one of the things that struck me was how the law schools I was looking at admitted kids from all kinds of undergraduate schools. I also knew that things like LSAT scores and undergraduate GPAs were important, and I knew I'd be focusing on that at any school I went to."

She worried somewhat about too many lectures in miniature auditoriums with hundreds of students, but she often found herself in seminars with fewer than twenty students, thanks in part to her admission into the Barrett honors college within ASU. Unbeknownst to kids who don't take a serious look at public universities, many of them have programs like

Barrett that enable the most academically accomplished students to take more advanced and adventurous courses. But Barrett wasn't the only reason Wendy encountered class sizes smaller than she'd expected. More than 40 percent of classes at ASU have fewer than 20 students; only 17 percent have 50 or more.

"If you were self-directed, you could do all kinds of things when you were there," Wendy said. "It was surprising how easy it was to find a group of people who were truly motivated, and professors responded really well to those students. I could walk into a professor's office at any time and they'd be happy to see me." She developed an especially close relationship with Jack Crittenden, who teaches political theory. He got his doctorate at Oxford, has won a National Endowment for the Humanities grant and has written three books that explore the confluence of politics and psychology, *Beyond Individualism*, *Democracy's Midwife* and *Wide as the World*. Wendy remembers taking at least four of his classes, including one or two at the graduate level.

She was also allowed into other graduate classes and into several classes at the law school. She took many more classes than she needed to and ended up completing three majors: political science, history and Spanish. The sun didn't distract or deter her. And she got into her first-choice law school, Yale, beginning there in the fall of 2009. She told me that she didn't find herself to be any less well prepared for Yale than kids who'd gone to smaller, more selective colleges. After her graduation from Yale in 2012, she clerked for a federal judge on the Ninth Circuit Court of Appeals in San Francisco, then took a job with a big, prestigious litigation firm in Washington, D.C. "I love it so far," she said.

A friend of hers from the honors college at ASU, Devin Mauney, twenty-eight, is clerking for a judge in the U.S. District Court for the District of Columbia. All four of his years at ASU were paid for by a Flinn scholarship, which is given to outstanding Arizona high school students who elect to stay in the state for college. Because of the Flinn, Devin did precisely that, though he'd been accepted at Yale and Brown, among other schools. He told me that while most of his peers endorsed his decision, one close friend thought it was cracked.

I asked Devin why.

"He just repeated the words *Yale* and *ASU* to me," Devin said. "He didn't have much more than that. It was mostly about prestige."

I asked Devin if he had any of his own misgivings or worries along those lines.

"My first semester of school, I certainly doubted my choice," he said. "I had set my sights on prestige in high school, and walking around school in my ASU shirt, I thought, 'What if I were at Yale?' And it seems silly now, because I'm happy with the way things worked out. And I wasn't unhappy then! And I didn't think I was getting a bad education. I was challenged. I had access to great opportunities and resources."

One aspect of his ASU education that he particularly appreciated was how permeable, even nonexistent, the barrier between the Tempe campus and the community around it was. The school wasn't just located in Tempe and in Arizona; it was entwined with them.

"I was involved in politics in Arizona during the entire time I was a student at ASU," he said. "I testified at the legislature a couple of times, one time about a bill aimed at limiting academic freedom. I ran a local campaign for a candidate running for county office. My friends who went to prestigious places weren't involved that way. These places that draw students from all over the country are islands."

He majored in economics, graduated in 2009 and, in the fall of 2010, began law school at Harvard. In terms of where his fellow Harvard students had done their undergraduate work, he said, "My class was extremely diverse: University of Georgia, *lots* of students from the UC system, lots of UT students, Michigan." I asked him whether he'd noticed much of a difference between them and classmates who'd gone to more selective schools. He said that it was difficult to generalize but that in a few cases, the alumni of elite institutions were less clear about why they were at Harvard and what they wanted from it. For them it was the next box in a series that they were dutifully checking over the course of their lives. They were also more likely to be from the Northeast, he said, and to have attended private schools before college.

ASU will never be a badge of exclusive honor, because its very composition, identity and mission work against that. It's *intended* to be accessible and to try to counter, and change, the fact that in the United States, according to one study from a few years ago, fewer than 10 percent of children from families in the bottom quartile of income are likely to get a college diploma by the age of twenty-four while more than 70 percent of children from families in the top quartile are. To that end, ASU basically admits any high school graduate in Arizona who maintains a B average or better in sixteen courses considered essential for college readiness. The average ASU student pays only about $3,800 a semester for tuition. And more than 40 percent of the school's students receive federal Pell grants, a form of tuition aid available only to lower-income families.

ASU sacrifices the kinds of attributes that impress prospective college students eager for a discerning club, and it throws in the towel on statistics that move the needle on rankings like those done by *U.S. News*. Its undergraduate acceptance rate is more than 80 percent, so it doesn't get points for selectivity. Its four-year graduation rate is below 40 percent and its six-year graduation rate is under 60 percent, both of which are similarly damning even though they're entirely understandable: Studies show a close correlation between low family income and the probability that a student who starts college doesn't complete it.

"We live in a country where the number one predictor of college success is not intelligence or hard work—it is student zip code," Michael Crow, the president of ASU, wrote to me in a letter in the summer of 2014, during which we had several exchanges, by mail and in person and over the phone. When I brought up *U.S. News* rankings, which in the fall of 2014 put ASU at No. 129 among national universities, he said, "They hammer us because of our graduation rate, and we're not able to be viewed as a top institution because we don't have these rising admissions standards."

But the school's emphasis on access and inclusivity means that it's potentially doing much more than any elite college to improve the social mobility that's central to our country's narrative, that's at the core of America's self-image and that's imperiled in this era of increasing income inequality. Who wouldn't want to go to a university with such laudable values? And while the student population at ASU may not be a model of geographic diversity, it's an exemplar of socioeconomic and ethnic diversity.

"If you come to ASU, you'll have the whole cross section of our society," Crow told me. "And you'll have them at scale, not just two Native American kids but several thousand. We make that case, but you've got to be a very sophisticated seventeen-year-old to grasp all of that."

And ASU, like many universities of its size, has no shortage of distinguished professors and programs for students who summon the initiative to connect with them. As of the summer of 2014, the school's faculty included two Nobel laureates, 10 members of the American Academy of Arts and Sciences, 11 members of the National Academy of Sciences, 25 Guggenheim Fellows and five Pulitzer Prize winners. Almost all began teaching there after 2002, an indication of the school's vigorous efforts to upgrade itself. But because of its party-school stereotype, you don't hear much about that.

In 2010, the *Wall Street Journal* did a survey of recruiters at 479 of the largest public and private companies, nonprofits and government agencies, asking them which schools they liked best and trusted most when they were looking for college graduates for entry-level jobs. ASU ranked fifth. But because of its party-school stereotype, you don't hear much about that, either. Or about its high rank among schools producing students who win Fulbright grants.

There are reasons to be envious, not suspicious, of ASU's size. "We don't limit what you can study," Crow said, noting that thousands of classes are offered annually. "The student has—I won't call it infinite—a menu of opportunity beyond any menu they can imagine." There are three hundred degree programs in fifteen colleges, "and in those micro-environments, you find your niche," he explained. For example, he said, "You can be in our opera program inside the school of music inside the Herberger Institute for Design and the Arts." And as Wendy Zupac and Devin Mauney attested, you can be completely satisfied with your education and what it leads to.

The difference between the negative image and the promising reality of ASU suggests just how perniciously superficial assumptions factor into the appraisal of schools and the esteem in which the general public, along with minimally informed applicants, holds them. Elite colleges don't have all the best teachers, students and facilities, though their endowments certainly help them attract or construct a disproportionate share. What elite colleges really have is a set of carefully maintained characteristics that are broadly accepted as synonyms for quality, along with a history of acclaim that it's easier for parents and children to buy into than to examine and question. What elite colleges have is a consensus, along with the benefit of the doubt.

Schools like ASU don't have that, and I've singled it out and dwelled on it for that reason, but also to illustrate just how ridiculously narrow the thinking about higher education can be, especially by parents and kids with enough resources and ambitions to be finicky about the schools they consider applying to. The same cast of colleges gets the same bounty of adulation year after predictable year, and students in certain geographic areas and socioeconomic groups draw up lists of target colleges that are comically redundant and sadly unimaginative.

There's so much more out there. There are big schools like ASU with pockets of moderately priced excellence less recognized than they should be. Texas A&M, for example, has a weekly business seminar unlike any other I've ever heard of. Every semester for about nine years now, it has been taught by Britt Harris, a wealthy financier who served as the chief executive of Bridgewater Associates when it was one of the world's largest hedge funds. He's not an academic, and the class, called Titans of Investing, wasn't put together, and isn't conducted, in a conventional fashion.

Although it covers market history and economic theory, it concerns itself just as much with questions of leadership, and of wisdom: recognizing it, acquiring it, using it. To that end, the seventeen participants in the class—juniors, seniors and graduate students—read and discuss an eclectic mix of books specifically suggested by American business bigwigs, including Wall Street giants, several of whom interact with the students by fielding and assessing their written analyses of those classics. One week, the class might dive into *Moby-Dick* or Tocqueville's *Democracy in America*. The next, it's on to a biography of Benjamin Franklin or Steve Jobs. Discussions are followed by long dinners promoting fellowship and sustained reflection, and the course's alumni aren't just encouraged, but pretty much required, to form an ongoing professional network.

A good friend of mine spent the fall semester of 2014 as a visiting professor at the University of Wyoming, with which she'd been wholly unfamiliar, and was blown away by the university's deep funds (thanks to the state's oil and gas wealth), the sophistication and training of its faculty, and the international diversity of its graduate students, most of whom interact extensively with undergraduates, sharing their world-views. My friend was teaching in the Global & Area Studies Program, and when she went to a retreat sponsored by the program at the start of classes, she found herself tangled in a back-and-forth between a professional soldier from India who was taking a break to get a master's degree and a graduate student from Kenya; they were debating and discussing marriage practices in their respective cultures. Three visiting scholars from Shanghai at the retreat were still getting accustomed to Wyoming's chill and altitude. One of two female students engaged in a game of checkers was blond, blue-eyed and from Wisconsin; the other was from Tunisia and wore a headscarf. Nearby, a Californian just back from several years in Taiwan chatted with a Moroccan who was teaching in the school's Arabic program.

At the University of Wyoming my friend also met two professors, a married couple, with doctorates from Cambridge University and a herd of wagyu cattle that they raised on their nearby ranch. She crossed paths with a sociologist from Sweden who'd begun her career as a detective with the Stockholm police department. And the class that my friend herself was teaching included a graduate student from Turkmenistan and another from Strasbourg, France.

"This is in Laramie, Wyoming!" my friend marveled—a city of about thirty-two thousand people in the least populous state in America. "Everyone I meet here is interesting. I hope these students understand how privileged they are." As she said that, I smiled. She'd invoked "privilege" in a way that it's too seldom used in conversations about college, but she'd done truer, fuller justice to the word.

There are also scores and scores of small institutions with distinctive strengths and one-of-a-kind wrinkles. But these colleges, like the University of Wyoming and ASU, are overshadowed and routinely overlooked as too many families chase the heralded brand, the envied address. They're looking for some imagined jackpot, and in their tunnel vision, they're not seeing any number of out-of-the-way opportunities and magical possibilities for four stimulating years that none of us ever gets back.

Did you know that there's a New Jersey school with a behavioral psychology course that takes place largely among the land and sea mammals at the Six Flags Great Adventure amusement and safari park? It's Monmouth University, in West Long Branch, and a few years ago a psychology professor there, Lisa Dinella, took her own children to the park and realized that the trainers' testimonials about animal behavior had significant overlap with her campus lectures. So she devised a new class at Monmouth that includes weekly meetings with trainers at Six Flags and fieldwork with the animals. It has been offered twice over the last three years.

Did you know that there's a New York school with a dormitory of yurts? Yes, yurts, those cylindrical Mongolian tents. The school is St. Lawrence University, in the upstate town of Canton, and I'm stretching by using the word *dormitory*, but not by much. St. Lawrence offers a program every fall called the "Adirondack Semester," and it's for a small group of students who elect to live in a yurt village in Adirondack Park, about an hour's drive from the campus. There's a lake and a thick canopy of pine trees, but no wireless. No electricity. No Chipotle. The students learn survival skills and make their own meals, largely with provisions from a nearby farm. And as they adapt to the wilderness, they contemplate its meaning and man's stewardship of it through a menu of courses on such topics as environmental philosophy and nature writing.

At Denison, in Granville, Ohio, there's an academic concentration in bluegrass music, designed by a professor with an upstairs-downstairs history of fiddling. He performs frequently with the Columbus Symphony; he has also repeatedly won the Georgia State Fiddle Championship. DeSales University, a Catholic school in Center Valley, Pennsylvania, has established an internship program with the Vatican that sends as many as six students to clerical and communications positions there every year.

St. Norbert College, in De Pere, Wisconsin, maintains a close relationship with the Green Bay Packers football team, including regular visits to the campus by players and internships with the Packers organization for students. Webster University, near St. Louis, emphasizes internationalism and has so many residential campuses in so many different countries, including Thailand and Ghana, that a student could study in a different place with a different language and culture almost every semester. It also had the top-ranked collegiate chess team in the United States in 2013 and 2014.

Oberlin College, in Oberlin, Ohio, is a veritable staging ground for doctorates and, since 1920, has had more graduates go on to earn PhDs than any other liberal arts college of its size. Speaking of which, the National Science Foundation ranks colleges by how high a percentage of their graduates go on to get PhDs in science in particular, and many of the top spots are claimed by small liberal arts colleges, including Reed (No. 4), Swarthmore (No. 5), Carleton (No. 6) and Grinnell (No. 7).

S. Georgia Nugent, who was the president of one such college, Kenyon, from 2003 to 2013, told me: "There would always be parents who would come with their prospective students and say, 'We love the college, but Billy really wants to major in science.' In fact, the small colleges are much more successful at producing STEM (science, engineering, technology and math) bachelor's graduates, and they're disproportionately successful at having those people go on to earn PhDs in the STEM fields."

Nugent's experience and perspective are interesting: She spent an earlier span of her career teaching at Cornell, at Brown and—for many years—at Princeton, where the jobs she held over time also included assistant to the president and associate provost. Kenyon exposed her to a more intimate academic environment, and she got an additional education into life well outside the Ivy League through her work, both at Kenyon and since then, with the Council of Independent Colleges. It includes Kenyon, Denison, St. Lawrence and more than 600 other small and midsize independent liberal-arts colleges and universities that are, in almost all cases, less widely venerated than Princeton, Brown and Cornell. And she has come around to the firm conviction that for undergraduates, they're ideal environments: especially approachable, uniquely nurturing. She said that each has a much greater bounty of programs than its size might lead an outsider to expect. And she noted that the colleges as a group present an extraordinary spectrum of options, with distinctive colors for individuals who take the time to notice.

For instance Luther College, a school in Decorah, Iowa, that's affiliated with the Evangelical Lutheran Church of America, has proven to be a surprisingly sturdy cradle for winners of some of the most prestigious academic prizes. Although it has an endowment of only $116 million and just 2,500 students at a time, it has produced eight Rhodes scholars and, since 2009, sixteen Fulbright scholars.

I could fill ten paragraphs this way. I could fill forty or four hundred or an entire book. Despite all the challenges facing higher education in America, from mounting student debt to grade inflation and erratic standards, our system is rightly the world's envy, and not just because our most revered universities remain on the cutting edge of research and attract talent from around the globe. We also have a plenitude and variety of settings for learning that are unrivaled. In light of that, the process of applying to college should and could be about ecstatically rummaging through those possibilities and feeling energized, even elated, by them. But for too many students, it's not, and financial constraints aren't the only reason. Failures of boldness and imagination by both students and parents bear some blame. The information is all out there. You just have to look.

These failures aren't anything new. There have long been schools that dominated the discourse and schools left inexplicably outside of it. I've marveled for some time over the fact that when I was in secondary school and people all around me spoke incessantly about the options beyond graduation and what some of the better or more interesting ones were, I never once heard anyone mention St. John's College. And while I've lived at least briefly in more than a half dozen states and interviewed thousands of people across scores of professions, I don't think I've met anyone who went there, or at least told me that he or she did, or brought it up as a school worth fantasizing about or prodding one's children toward.

Yet it's a fascinating, fierce, one-of-a-kind institution. At its two campuses, in Annapolis, Maryland, and Santa Fe, New Mexico, each with fewer than five hundred students, the relentless focus is on Great Books and great thinkers and the

Western canon: the Greek philosophers, the Bible, Milton, Shakespeare, Hobbes, Rousseau, the Declaration of Independence, Eliot, Twain. St. John's is about classic erudition, timeless discipline and rigorous thought. Students don't get formal grades but rather face-to-face oral appraisals, done on the basis of their participation in tiny classes and on their many written papers, which substitute for tests. In surveys, they say they adore the school and feel wholly satisfied.

Both the Annapolis and Santa Fe campuses have been mainstays on the list of Colleges That Change Lives, which originated with a 1996 book of that title that sought to showcase and exalt lesser-known schools outside the Ivy League. It embraced the idea that at a certain point of selectiveness, a college is corrupting its mission and skewing its identity in a manner that doesn't serve a true education. And it hinges on the belief that no one college, no matter how celebrated, is right for anyone and everyone who can gain admission there. A school, like a dress or a suit, has to have the contours and colors that work for the person choosing it. It has to fit.

When I spoke with guidance counselors, I often asked which colleges had proven to be spectacular experiences for the students sent off to them. I heard kind words about Stanford, about Brown, about Johns Hopkins. But I heard equally kind, if not kinder, words about the College of Wooster, in Wooster, Ohio, which requires students to do an ambitious independent study project in their senior year; about Butler University, in Indianapolis, whose theater program drew praise; about Indiana University, especially for music majors; about DePauw University, in Greencastle, Indiana, which has upgraded its campus significantly over recent years; about the University of Rochester, in upstate New York, which has strong science instruction.

Alice Kleeman, the Menlo-Atherton High School counselor, singled out Evergreen State College, in Olympia, Washington. It's somewhat famous as a progressive alternative to traditional schools, with narrative evaluations instead of grades, a pronounced attention to environmental issues and a student body of nonconformists. Kleeman said that when a boy from Menlo-Atherton who went there came back to visit her after his freshman year, "I almost didn't recognize him, because of the confidence that he'd gained, because he'd finally found a place where other students shared his interests and where people weren't judged in the same way they're judged in the college admissions process. He had friends. He stood up straighter. He had a whole new image of who he was, because he'd chosen a college that was a really great match for *him*. If you'd picked him up and dropped him into Harvard or Stanford, it just wouldn't have worked."

Each college-bound student has his or her own needs, and there are schools that are likely to meet them and schools that aren't. David Rusenko determined that Carnegie Mellon, which had accepted him, fell into the latter category. So he chose to go to Penn State instead.

He wanted the frat parties, the football games, the crowds. And that wasn't because he gravitated naturally to those. The opposite was true. But his goal was to change, to stretch, to become more, to become different. He'd had an unusual upbringing in an unusual world, and now was the time to round out the picture.

His parents, English teachers, had raised him abroad, first

in France and then, from the time he was seven years old, in Casablanca, Morocco. They'd actually started an English-language high school there. It was tiny, an island in an exotic sea. He was one of its students. In his graduating class in 2002, there were all of eleven others.

"At Carnegie Mellon," he said, "kids would be super-smart, I'd learn a lot and there was a computer science angle." All of which was good; computers were his strength and his interest. But he worried that he would emerge from Carnegie Mellon as "an unsociable nerd who wasn't going to have the people skills he needed to succeed.

"I was a quiet kid," he said, "and I figured it would be critical for me to pick up people skills. My thinking was that people skills, soft skills, play such a critical role if you're going to lead people. And it was always my desire to start a company."

So at Penn State he made it a point to stray from the classroom, to mingle, to get a taste of Greek life. And he indeed developed into a more outgoing, articulate, chattier guy. "Fraternities are a microcosm," he said. "You can learn a lot from them."

He benefited from his academic experiences, too. The school had just begun a special computer sciences major that focused not only on technology but on working in teams, giving presentations: the sorts of talents necessary for entrepreneurs who are trying to sell investors on their product and trying to rally employees toward a goal.

"The theory behind the program was to develop more well-rounded technologists," he said. "I probably gave more than sixty presentations over the years."

He benefited from Penn State in yet one more way, meeting and becoming friendly with two fellow students there who shared his ambitions. With them he developed Weebly, a service that guides people through the creation of websites. They started it in 2006. By 2009 it was profitable. And in 2014, it received a fresh infusion of $35 million from Sequoia, a venture capital firm that valued it at $455 million, according to Rusenko, twenty-nine, who is its chief executive officer and now lives in the tech utopia of San Francisco.

Rusenko said that Penn State had served him well, that fancier schools don't necessarily leave people in better stead, and that I should talk with Sam Altman, the president of Y Combinator, which is arguably Silicon Valley's most famous and influential source of first-step seed money for tech startups. Y Combinator had given Weebly its initial funding and has done the same for nearly 750 other young companies, out of thousands more who have developed and pitched ideas. Altman, Rusenko said, would have a sense of whether the graduates of elite schools were especially good at proposing and developing successful ventures.

So I called him. Altman, also twenty-nine, went to Stanford but never finished, because he and a classmate founded Y Combinator instead. He said that Stanford, by introducing the two of them, had blessed him, and he loved his time there, among what he described as "a density of smart people."

But, he added, "to my chagrin, Stanford has not had a really great track record." He meant that most of the proposals that Stanford students and grads had brought to Y Combinator didn't hold much promise and pan out. He noted that Y Combinator's biggest success, Airbnb, was started by graduates of the Rhode Island School of Design.

I asked him if any one school stood out as a source of

students and graduates whose ideas sparkled and winded up doing Y Combinator proud.

"Yes," he said, identifying an institution that hadn't sired supernovas like Airbnb but that had an unusually good track record of exciting ideas worth funding. "The University of Waterloo." It's a public school in the Canadian province of Ontario with more than thirty thousand students.

"I try not to travel very much, but I'm going to spend three days there this fall just to meet more students," Altman said when we spoke in July 2014. "They train really great engineers. Waterloo came up enough times that I thought: 'I really have to go there.'" He has paid visits to schools before, of course, but none, ever, for three whole days.

The list he gave me of successful startups that could be traced to Waterloo was eight ventures long: Thalmic Labs, BufferBox, Pebble, PagerDuty, Vidyard, PiinPoint, Reebee and Instacart.

Altman told me that in his opinion, the importance of attending an elite school "is going down, not up," because there are avenues to entrepreneurial success that don't involve submitting a transcript and flaunting your academic bona fides to a graduate school or a corporation. "Now a lot of the best people are not taking those paths out of college," he said. "They're doing a startup or doing something else."

And they're judged, he said, by the existing work that they can point to, the examples they can show. "Did you contribute to an open-source project? Did you create a video that did well on YouTube? Now you can answer how good you are with the Internet. It's a showcase for people. You can read about them on Twitter. You can look at what they've built.

"Writers get book deals based on the quality of their

blogs," he added. "Anyone can produce content. Anyone can make it available. And good work gets shared and then rises to the top. Before, there was no way for that to happen. Whoever had connections got their book published. Whoever had connections got their startup funded."

His vantage point is Silicon Valley, which isn't entirely representative. There are still plenty of freshly minted graduates hitting up companies for employment in a more old-fashioned way. But what those companies want isn't entirely predictable and may not be Stanford, which brings me back to that *Wall Street Journal* survey of employers, the one that ranked ASU fifth as a source for entry-level hires. The schools that ranked first through fourth were Penn State, Texas A&M, the University of Illinois and Purdue. Sixth through tenth were the University of Michigan, Georgia Tech, the University of Maryland, the University of Florida and Carnegie Mellon. The only Ivy in the top 25 was Cornell (No. 14).

SEVEN

AN ELITE EDGE?

"I think there's a conceit, a myth, that you can go and sit in a university and things will come to you. They don't. You have to go to them."

— *Condoleezza Rice*

The *Wall Street Journal* survey that lifted Penn State, Purdue and the University of Maryland so high isn't a full and accurate portrait. It requires a few qualifications and explanations, which the *Journal* story that accompanied it provided or at least suggested. Recruiters weren't exactly saying that students from the schools that they put at the top of the list were better educated and more intellectually nimble in some overarching sense, or that they had brighter careers ahead of them. The recruiters were saying that when it came to filling entry-level jobs that require discrete skills, state universities had proven more reliable pools of eager workers with specific, relevant training. In an uncertain era of unusually high unemployment for young men and women just out of college, that's worth noting and heeding. But so, in fairness, are a few other realities.

For example, certain firms are more likely to visit and interview students at highly selective schools than at the *Journal* survey's top five. A few of these firms may go to those highly selective schools alone. They're trying to put a cap on the amount of time, manpower and money that they devote to recruitment, and they're regarding and taking advantage of the rigorous admissions processes at elite colleges as a pre-screening that has whittled down an unwieldy universe of potential hires to a manageable group of finalists who can be presumed to possess some baseline of drive, poise and intelligence. To that end some of the richest banks and funds on Wall Street and some of the most highly paid consulting firms have developed close, sturdy relationships with Harvard, with Princeton, with the University of Pennsylvania.

And once a critical mass of people from an elite school set up shop somewhere, they tend to bring aboard yet more people from that school, because it's a place they have pride and faith in, because the compliment they're paying to the school is a form of self-validation and because they and their new hires all share points of reference, speak a common language and are products of the same culture. In rocky marriages, familiarity breeds contempt. In finance, law and other fields, it can breed comfort and job offers.

That's undeniable, and so is the disproportionate presence of alumni of highly selective colleges at revered graduate schools—in business, law, medicine and other disciplines—that can be magnets for recruiters and springboards to some of the best-paying jobs. Wendy Zupac, Devin Mauney, Peter

Hart and other interview subjects of mine who went from state universities to Ivy League law or business schools said that they met plenty of people there like them, but they also said that the fraction of their fellow students who'd been to the most selective undergraduate schools seemed to be at least slightly higher than the fraction who'd been to less selective public colleges.

The elite graduate schools don't routinely publicize information analyzing the undergraduate alma maters of their students, but the Yale Law School did precisely that in 2013 and again in 2014, looking at all of the hundreds of young men and women at various stages of study there. Just over 40 percent of them had gone to the eight schools in the Ivy League. Seven of those eight—all but Cornell—were among the ten colleges that had sent the most alumni to Yale Law. In contrast, graduates of state schools represented well under 20 percent of the student body—and that was even when you counted the many graduates of top-ranked public universities like UC Berkeley and UCLA at Yale Law.

My sense from scattered data is that the distribution of students at top business schools and in other graduate programs isn't nearly as flattering to the Ivy League as that snapshot from Yale Law. But whatever the case, there's a crucial caveat about how to interpret the composition of Yale Law and how to think about several studies that have suggested that graduates of elite colleges earn more across their lifetimes than graduates of less elite ones. It's obvious, and it's this: Did the elite college make the Yale lawyer and the robust breadwinner, or do the characteristics and priorities of a Yale lawyer and a robust breadwinner dovetail with the characteristics and priorities of a person who aims for the elite college and studiously and diligently succeeds in putting together the sort of high school resume that wins over the admissions committee there?

Because this question is ultimately unanswerable—how do you design a study that builds in the right controls?—it's too seldom asked whenever big, sweeping assertions about education and earnings are made. It's left on the curb.

Take the recent discussion and documentation of the enormous income gap between college graduates and others. There's no doubt that much if not most of that gap is attributable to skills picked up in college or the greater confidence an employer will have about a college graduate. Many employers won't look at someone without a college diploma, even if it's not specifically necessary for the position being filled. But some of the gap is almost certainly attributable to variables that aren't products of a college education but are merely associated with it. A person's odds of graduating from college rise exponentially if he or she comes from a family of means, and people from such families probably have more connections to draw on, greater confidence about their fitness for lofty jobs, bigger expectations and a host of privileged experiences throughout their youths that point them in a propitious direction. College graduates may have more discipline, or at least discipline of the right kind. College didn't create it, but getting to and through college reflected it, and that same discipline could be essential to hunting down a good job, keeping it and being promoted over time. And similar dynamics could well be at work in any discrepancy between the achievement levels of elite-college alumni and the achievement levels of graduates of less selective schools.

A 2011 study done by Alan Krueger, a Princeton economics professor who served for two years as the chairman of President Obama's Council of Economic Advisers, and Stacy Dale, an analyst with Mathematica Policy Research, tried to adjust for that sort of thing. Krueger and Dale examined sets of students who had started college in 1976 and in 1989; that way, they could get a sense of incomes both earlier and later in careers. And they determined that the graduates of more selective colleges could expect earnings 7 percent greater than graduates of less selective colleges, even if the graduates in that latter group had SAT scores and high school GPAs identical to those of their peers at more exclusive institutions.

But then Krueger and Dale made their adjustment. They looked specifically at graduates of less selective colleges who had applied to more exclusive ones even though they hadn't gone there. And they discovered that the difference in earnings pretty much disappeared. Someone with a given SAT score who had gone to Penn State but had also applied to the University of Pennsylvania, an Ivy League school with a much lower acceptance rate, generally made the same amount of money later on as someone with an equivalent SAT score who was an alumnus of UPenn.

It was a fascinating conclusion, suggesting that at a certain level of intelligence and competence, what drives earnings isn't the luster of the diploma but the type of person in possession of it. If he or she came from a background and a mindset that made an elite institution seem desirable and within reach, then he or she was more likely to have the tools and temperament for a high income down the road, whether an elite institution ultimately came into play or not. This was powerfully reflected in a related determination that Krueger and Dale made in their 2011 study: "The average SAT score of schools that rejected a student is more than twice as strong a predictor of the student's subsequent earnings as the average SAT score of the school the student attended."

When I interviewed Krueger, he explained: "The students are basically self-sorting when they apply to colleges, and the more ambitious students are applying to the most elite schools." The inclination to consider UPenn, not attendance *at* UPenn, is the key to future earnings. Or maybe it's the inclination coupled with assertiveness and confidence, two other attributes suggested by the fact of applying to a college or colleges where admissions are fiercely competitive.

"Another way to read my results is: A good student can get a good education just about anywhere, and a student who's not that serious about learning isn't going to get much benefit," Krueger told me.

There was, though, one wrinkle to the findings. Krueger and Dale found that even after their clever adjustment, minority students and those from disadvantaged backgrounds *still* seemed to make out better, in terms of income, if they'd gone to more selective colleges. The two researchers theorized that for these students, the networking opportunities at selective colleges were more important than for other students, who had access to fruitful networks apart from the one established in college.

I don't believe it's right or especially useful to view and evaluate colleges primarily as bridges to riches, but even a kid who is approaching higher education that way would be wise to look less at the names of institutions and concentrate more on what he or she plans to study. *Majors* make a greater difference. In one recent study, Georgetown University's Center on Education and the Workforce determined that the median annual earnings of college graduates who'd chosen the most lucrative major, petroleum engineering, was more than four times higher than the median of college graduates who'd chosen the least lucrative one, which was counseling/psychology. The likelihood of simply being employed varies just as greatly with major. Graduates who'd studied pharmacology had a 100 percent employment rate. Graduates who'd studied social psychology had a 16 percent one.

"It matters a lot less where you went to college than it used to," the Georgetown center's director, Anthony Carnevale, told me. "What really drives your earnings is your field of study. If you go to Harvard and become a schoolteacher, you're not going to make more than another schoolteacher who didn't go to Harvard."

But even your major recedes in importance once you've been out in the workforce for a while and have an actual performance to be judged by, a track record to be assessed. In early 2014, Gallup released the results of a nationwide poll in which business leaders were asked to characterize the importance of four different factors when making hiring decisions. Those factors were the amount of knowledge a job candidate had in a particular field, a candidate's "applied skills," a candidate's college major and where a candidate had received a college degree. They could characterize each as "very important," "somewhat important," "not very important" or "not at all important." Field-relevant knowledge was by far the employment criterion that business leaders most frequently called "very important." Nearly 85 percent of them described it that way. But where an applicant had gone to college? Only 9 percent of the leaders described *that* as "very important."

Interestingly, the same Gallup survey showed that average Americans' impressions of how business leaders made hiring decisions were different from what those leaders said. Nearly one in three respondents indicated a belief—erroneous, if the leaders' own answers were trustworthy—that where a job candidate had gone to college was very important.

As Rusenko's success and Altman's comments suggest, the tech world in general and Silicon Valley in particular may be the most vivid arenas in which ideas and know-how muscle educational pedigree out of the picture. This was captured in two 2014 columns in the *Times* by my colleague Tom Friedman that promptly went viral. Titled "How to Get a Job at Google" and "How to Get a Job at Google Part 2," they contained many insights and pieces of advice from Laszlo Bock, the supervisor of all of Google's hiring. As recounted by Friedman, Bock paid no particular heed to prestigious colleges.

"To sum up Bock's approach to hiring: Talent can come in so many different forms and be built in so many nontraditional ways today, hiring officers have to be alive to every one—besides brand-name colleges," Friedman wrote. "Because 'when you look at people who don't go to school and make their way in the world, those are exceptional human beings. And we should do everything we can to find those people.' Too many colleges, he added, 'don't deliver on what they promise. You generate a ton of debt, you don't learn the most useful things for your life.'

"Google attracts so much talent it can afford to look beyond traditional metrics, like GPA," Friedman continued, later adding: "Beware. Your degree is not a proxy for your ability to do any job. The world only cares about—and pays off on—what you can do with what you know (and it doesn't care how you learned it). And in an age when innovation is increasingly a group endeavor, it also cares about a lot of soft skills—leadership, humility, collaboration, adaptability and loving to learn and re-learn. This will be true no matter where you go to work."

I got that same message from Parisa Tabriz, whom I reached out to because she'd appeared on that 2013 list of 30 Under 30 in *Forbes*. She'd found her way to Google from the University of Illinois, where she received undergraduate and graduate degrees in computer science. Now thirty-one, she manages Google's Chrome Security Team and is involved in the hiring for it and for other security teams at Google.

"When I look at candidates' resumes, whether they have a degree or not is a data point, but I've never been especially interested in where they got a degree," Tabriz said. "I'm much more interested in what kinds of organizations they're involved in. I work in information security—finding security bugs, making software more secure—and I'm looking for experience doing that, which they wouldn't do in a classroom." They might do it, she said, in their free time, as a hobby. Or maybe while they were at school, they participated in some special, outside-of-class research project along those lines. That's what matters to her. That's what moves her.

"My experience at Google has really made me question how necessary a university degree is in the first place," she said. "If you have access to the Internet, you can teach a lot of this stuff to yourself. I have a Polish engineer—he's brilliant—who taught himself English by reading engineering manuals and participating in community forums and panels on the Internet. A degree in computer science isn't worthless, but getting an A in computer science doesn't mean you're a good programmer."

Well beyond Silicon Valley, many employers talk about trying to size up potential employees in ways that get beyond the window dressing of diplomas. Stuart Ruderfer, who runs a large marketing agency in Manhattan, told me that he's less concerned with the prestige of an applicant's college than with his or her GPA, which is often a barometer of how goal-oriented and hardworking someone is. He's also impressed when he sees or hears about aspects of an applicant's involvement in campus life: Did he or she run an organization? Stage an event or fund-raiser that was wildly successful? Pull off some difficult project? And Ruderfer pays careful attention to how applicants present and comport themselves in an interview. That's a harbinger of what they'll be like to work with, both for colleagues and clients.

"If you're looking only at the elite schools, you're going to miss some very talented people," Ruderfer said. "There are a lot of reasons why people go and don't go to the elite schools. There's money, geography. In some cases, people were perhaps not as focused in high school, so they don't have the grades or such, but then they get to college and they turn it on with a level of intensity that, for whatever reason, they hadn't turned up earlier in their lives. But they've got it now. And that's what you want. That intensity is going to be a much bigger factor in their success."

The longer a person has been out of college, the less relevant a college is to an employer. By the time someone is forty years old, it probably doesn't matter at all, but even by thirty-five or thirty, there's a whole new body of information to judge him or her by, and it's what most employers will choose to judge.

"Demonstrated success and a track record relevant to the need we're trying to fill is far more important to me than where someone went to school eons ago," said Kevin Reddy, the chief executive officer and chairman of Noodles & Company, a Colorado-based chain of restaurants that's one of the biggest success stories of the last few decades in what's called the "fast casual" space. Kevin has the ultimate say in hiring the chain's senior management.

His own rise didn't involve elite schools. It did involve an entrepreneurial spirit and work ethic that predated college and can't be taught. When he was eleven years old, he struck up a conversation one day with the man who delivered milk and eggs to the houses in his suburban Pittsburgh neighborhood. The man complained that the eggs were his fragile enemies, because they could break so easily and thus prevented him from moving too quickly as he made his rounds. Kevin told the man that for a modest fee, he'd take the eggs off his hands and deliver them himself to all of the houses near his family's. He'd just put them in his wagon and be sure to pull gently on it. "I wanted to earn a little money," Kevin said, "so I could buy a baseball glove."

His parents weren't particularly well-off, so Kevin always worked. He took a job at McDonald's when he was fifteen. "It was growing and advertising a lot, and there were several that were reasonably close to my house and I could get there quick enough. I told them, 'Here's my school schedule, here's my sports schedule, other than those times, I'll work whenever you want.' When I was that young, I wasn't allowed to cook on the grill, so I cleaned the dining room, cleaned the bathrooms. I worked the shake machine. Gradually I made it to the point where I could get to the grill." During his last years of high school he spent up to twenty hours a week at McDonald's, and he continued to devote the same amount to McDonald's during college, although by that point he had managerial responsibilities and, in his junior and senior years, worked in the corporate offices. It helped pay his college expenses.

He went to Duquesne University, a Catholic school near Pittsburgh. "I lived at home, because I couldn't afford to live in the dorms," he said. He majored in business and accounting, but when I asked him to recall a class that had held particular meaning for him, he mentioned one outside of those areas. It was called Marriage and Family Relationships and taught by a priest.

"He had this constant theme about not overreacting and not underreacting in times of stress," Kevin recalled. "And he said that you can't really argue with, debate or change somebody's mind if you don't understand their belief system, and so you really need to listen. For all walks of life, that was very sound advice. Let's face it: The business world is about relationships. You've got to have intelligent people. But once you understand the intellectual plan and you've analyzed it, you still have to bring it to life. And you bring it to life through relationships, through being able to work with people." Kevin said that while he honed those skills in college, he didn't need a college of any particular altitude to do that, and he'd honed those skills at McDonald's as well.

"There's so much more than raw intellect if you're going to influence people and accomplish things, and I don't think you can map it all out as some of the Tiger Moms are trying to," he said. "In the short run, college opens doors. But I think real success, enduring success, in life, in any arena, requires substance, and that substance is much more about what people do every day than where they went to school or where they grew up. It's a function of choice and persistence and being a student of *life*. Once you get out of college, so much of life is being able to relate to people, to influence people, to take risks, how well you listen. I don't think people's real character and real skills shine until they've been doing something for a long time, had their asses kicked and had to get up off the ground a few times."

When he's hiring, he's asking not only whether a candidate has precisely what the position needs but also, he said, "What kind of person are they? Are they genuine? Do they respect other people? Are they passionate?" He can sometimes sense that from interviews. He can sometimes glean it from references, or from noting the sequence of jobs that the candidate has held over time, the frequency and manner in which he or she has been promoted. But from the college a person attended? Not really. Not usually.

Shortly after I spoke with Kevin, I had a conversation with Bradley Tusk, someone I first met nearly fifteen years ago, when he was the communications director for U.S. senator Chuck Schumer of New York. Since then he's been a deputy governor for the state of Illinois, a senior vice president with Lehman Brothers, a special assistant to Mike Bloomberg when Bloomberg was mayor of New York City, and the manager of Bloomberg's 2009 reelection campaign. He currently runs Tusk Strategies, a political and strategic consulting firm based in New York City.

"Over the last twenty years," Tusk said, "I've hired hundreds and hundreds of people." And while he himself went to UPenn for college and the University of Chicago for law school, he said that he has not found that elite schools are any guarantor or predictor that someone will turn out to be a great employee and excel. "In most jobs, there's a base level of intelligence that's needed, and after that, success is typically determined by other factors: work ethic, hustle, instincts, communication skills, street smarts, character, creativity, persistence. I haven't seen any evidence that going to an elite school inherently means you have any of these skills (other than work ethic). And I've found that people who've had to struggle a little will often develop more of these skills—especially persistence—and they also don't have the same kind of entitlement and expectations you sometimes see from employees from top schools.

"So at least based on my experience in government, politics and business, I haven't seen any particular reason to focus our hiring on students from elite schools," he summed up. Then he laughed, because it occurred to him that he had recently made three offers for senior jobs to people in their thirties and, he said, "I don't know where any of them went to college. I *think* I know where one of them went, but I'm not sure. The two others? I have no idea."

Toward the end of 2013, in mid-December, Gallup and Purdue University announced a partnership, supported by funding from the Lumina Foundation, "to conduct the largest representative study of college graduates in U.S. history." The study was christened the Gallup-Purdue Index, and its goal, according to the initial press release, was to "measure the most important outcomes of higher education—great careers and lives that matter—and provide higher education leaders with productive insights." The index is a telling indication of just how consumed Americans have become with the question of college: why it costs so much; whether its returns warrant the investment; how it can best be used to students', and the country's, advantage.

"As it finally did in K–12, an accountability era has begun for higher education," said Mitch Daniels, the president of Purdue and the former two-term governor of Indiana, upon the unveiling of the project, which would quiz college graduates about what was described as "five key dimensions of well-being: purpose, social, physical, financial and community."

In May 2014, the first annual report, based on a survey of more than thirty thousand graduates, came out. The headline on the summary distributed to the news media: "It's Not 'Where' You Go to College, But 'How' You Go to College."

"There is no difference in workplace engagement or a college graduate's well-being if they attended a public or private not-for-profit institution, a highly selective institution, or a top 100-ranked school in *U.S. News & World Report*," the first paragraph of that summary proclaimed. Right out of the gate, Gallup and Purdue confronted the obsession with elite colleges, and right out of the gate, they confronted the unwarranted obeisance to *U.S. News*. They understood the era, and it was as if they were taking aim at a mass psychosis.

The report didn't measure graduates' salaries: a poor stand-in for achievement and a flawed, irrelevant predictor of happiness. Instead it measured their own professed satisfaction with their jobs. Its separate (though related) verdict on their well-being was cobbled together from those key dimensions, meaning how much the respondents said that they liked what they were doing (purpose); how supportive they found the relationships in their lives (social); whether they felt healthy and energetic (physical); whether they felt that they were managing their economic lives in a way that made them less stressed and more secure (financial); and whether they felt connected to, and proud of, the places where they lived and spent most of their time (community). Depending on their own assessments of these criteria, they were characterized as thriving, struggling or suffering.

According to the report, which will be revisited annually over a five-year period, student debt had a significant impact on well-being and workplace engagement. Graduates with between $20,000 and $40,000 in loans, which the report defined as the average student loan debt, were much less likely to be thriving than graduates without any loans to repay.

People's lives were improved if, in college, they'd found some sort of academic mentor. "For example," the report said, "if graduates had a professor who cared about them as a person, made them excited about learning, and encouraged them to pursue their dreams, their odds of being engaged at work more than doubled, as did their odds of thriving in their well-being.

"And if graduates had an internship or job where they were able to apply what they were learning in the classroom, were actively involved in extracurricular activities and organizations, and worked on projects that took a semester or more to complete, their odds of being engaged at work doubled also," the report said.

In other words, the nature and quality of the time spent in college—including, as it turned out, the major someone chose and the efficiency with which he or she zipped toward a diploma—were paramount. Employed graduates who'd majored in the arts and humanities or the social sciences were slightly more engaged at work than those who'd majored in science or business. And graduates who'd finished school in four years or less were much more likely to be engaged at work than those who'd taken longer.

But the clout or selectiveness of the college, so long as it was not-for-profit, had little bearing on graduates' contentment, with tiny exceptions. One of them, interestingly, was that graduates of smaller schools were less likely to be engaged at work than those of schools with full-time undergraduate populations of ten thousand or more. Was this a matter of causation or correlation? That's impossible to say, and it's a question smartly asked about all of the findings of this report and many others.

How you use college. What you demand of it. These dynamics get lost in the admissions mania, which overshadows them, to a point where it makes them seem close to irrelevant. But their importance is vividly underscored by the histories of just about every successful person interviewed for this book. I think back to Peter Hart and his involvement at Indiana University in both its business fraternity and a modest real estate enterprise of his own; to Jenna Leahy and her short trips to Mexico and long ones across the Atlantic to study abroad; to Condoleezza Rice and her lust for extracurricular involvements, along with her habit of arriving to office hours early, with flattering comments at the ready; to Bobbi Brown and her creation of a nonexistent major that she could get truly excited about; to David

Rusenko and his strategy for plucking precisely what he needed from Penn State.

I also think of Jillian Vogel, twenty-four, who did a thorough job of maximizing her four years in college precisely because she didn't end up where she'd hoped to and was determined to turn the consolation prize into something more, into the trophy itself.

Brown University had been her dream, and it hadn't seemed to her like such an impossible one, given that she was in the top 5 of roughly 100 seniors at a selective, well-regarded public school in New York City. She applied to Brown for early admission, was deferred and had a good guess why, because her guidance counselor and others around her had warned her about the problem. She'd scored only 24 out of 36 on the ACT.

After Brown deferred her, she resolved to charm the gatekeepers there into accepting her during the general-admission period in the spring. She drew and sent them a comic strip of all the stuff she'd been up to since she'd first applied. She wrote and mailed them a letter, which she addressed to that cursed 24 on the ACT.

"Dear Composite Score," it read. "It has come to my attention that you are unimpressive. While you represent the hours in a day, the title of a television drama and the product of 3 times 8, you are not an ideal ACT score. I have only a hazy memory of the Saturday morning of your conception, as it was so long ago." It said that back then, "I could not foresee what you would represent and the amount of power you would come to hold over me," and it took issue with that power, arguing that her mind and her potential couldn't be distilled into two measly digits. At the bottom of the letter,

Jillian had a dozen of her teachers sign their names in support. "That's 12 signatures," she wrote, "to compensate for the 12 points" between her 24 and a perfect 36.

Brown did not admit her. Nor did Middlebury, Tufts or Emory. "I felt so rejected," she told me. "I've never felt that kind of rejection before." She ended up with a choice between the University of Vermont and UNC. She headed to the South, feeling lucky to have Chapel Hill but still feeling the sting of not being wanted by all of those other places.

She turned that sting into resolve. She sprang into action. She sought the most interesting classes that she could find, some of them intensive, some of them offbeat, and she wheedled or stormed her way into them. One of the most beloved seminars in the English department, with just twelve to fifteen students per session, was a fanciful exploration of style and usage called Gram-o-Rama. Students in it composed songs, dances, skits and pieces of performance art that were devoted to, or showcases for, the fine points of grammar and wordplay. It was reserved, supposedly, for kids on a creative-writing track; Jillian was a communications major. But she'd met the professor. She pleaded with her. And it worked.

With a ruminative essay about growing up kosher, she also managed to get into a word-of-mouth class about food science and food culture for students in the honors program, which she wasn't even a part of. Limited to fifteen kids, it had an extraordinarily ambitious, encyclopedic syllabus of books and magazine and newspaper articles about everything from overfishing to obesity. It welcomed a who's who of guest speakers. It included a long weekly dinner at the professor's house offcampus, and it culminated in a five-day trip to the Bay Area replete with visits to several of San Francisco's most famous restaurants and to a vineyard in the Napa Valley.

Jillian said that if she wanted an exhilarating experience or an academic challenge at UNC, "I could find it. It just took a little more effort. I was extremely satisfied there, but it took everything I had to make it happen. I couldn't be passive. I had to be proactive." And she carried that gumption back to New York with her, pressing it into the service of a job hunt that led, ultimately, to a position recruiting and developing talent for CollegeHumor Media, an online entertainment company that produces and curates comedic skits, pictures and articles aimed at a young audience.

Then again, she had that gumption all along. It was abundant in her entreaties to Brown, and while it didn't get her an invitation there, I suspect that it will have more to do with what happens to her through the years than will anything else, including which college she went to. The best that college, any college, could do was to draw on it and to draw it out—to give it even more muscle. UNC accomplished that, and UNC taught her, or reaffirmed for her, that you have more options than you initially think you do, if you hunt for and insist on them.

In fact at UNC she discovered and took advantage of something most students there are oblivious to: If there's a course at nearby Duke University that fits into what you're studying and isn't replicated at UNC, you can make arrangements, space permitting, to take it. She did that for a lecture class on contemporary documentary filmmaking. It was terrific, she said, largely because renowned documentarians would drop in to address the roughly 150 students.

But many of those students wouldn't even pay much attention, she said. "Everybody in the classroom had their computers on and Facebook up," she recalled. "And it was like: What are you guys doing? This person is talking to you!" She got the feeling that Duke students had become accustomed, even numb, to the kinds of special opportunities that UNC students appreciated more.

"Maybe I'm just seeing what I wanted to see," she told me. "But I'd sit there and I'd think: Don't take this for granted, guys."

EIGHT

STRANGLED WITH IVY

"Presidents, deans and professors rarely tell students simple truths, for example that the strategizing and diligence that got them into the college of their choice may not, if followed thoughtlessly, lead to an adult life they will find worth living."

—*Harry Lewis, a former dean of Harvard College,
the undergraduate wing of Harvard University, in his
2006 book,* Excellence Without a Soul

While the advantages of going to an elite college aren't questioned as often as they should be, the disadvantages are even less frequently broached, perhaps because a great many people can't imagine that there'd be any. William Deresiewicz can. He's devoted no small part of the last decade to grappling with and articulating them. He does this provocatively, but with some standing and credibility: From 1998 to 2008, he taught English at Yale, and for six years before that, he was a graduate instructor at Columbia University, which is where he got his undergraduate degree, his master's and his PhD (in English). In other words he's frolicked in the Ivies. Only he doesn't make it sound so frolicsome.

In 2008, as he left Yale, he published an essay in the *American Scholar* titled "The Disadvantages of an Elite Education." "Our best universities," said an introductory summary of the essay, "have forgotten that the reason they exist is to make minds, not careers." This was the seed of a book, *Excellent Sheep*, which was in turn previewed, just before its publication in August 2014, in the *New Republic*. The magazine found even sexier language for Deresiewicz's perspective, because that's what magazines do. "Don't Send Your Kid to the Ivy League," read the headline that it slapped on the preview. No equivocation. No qualifications. And the subhead cannily appropriated a booming pop culture trend, warning: "The nation's top colleges are turning our kids into zombies." Bolt your doors and say your prayers. They're on the loose—the flesh-eating hordes from Haverford, the walking dead from Williams.

What Deresiewicz dwells on, and what's so important to keep in mind, are some themes I mentioned earlier in this book, for instance when exploring Rebecca Fabbro's dissatisfactions with Yale, Howard Schultz's satisfactions with Northern Michigan University and the philosophy behind *Washington Monthly*'s evaluation of schools: There's ideally a whole lot more to higher education than a springboard to high-paying careers, and an elite school composed almost entirely of young men and women who have aced the SATs or ACTs isn't likely to be the most exciting, eclectic stew of people and perspectives. It doesn't promise to challenge extant prejudices and topple old expectations. And that's largely because there's a surfeit of students who traveled to their elite destinations on an on-ramp of familiar perks and prods.

"When I speak of elite education, I mean prestigious institutions like Harvard or Stanford or Williams as well as the larger universe of second-tier selective schools, but I also mean everything that leads up to and away from them—the private and affluent public high schools; the ever-growing industry of tutors and consultants and test-prep courses; the admissions process itself, squatting like a dragon at the entrance to adulthood; the brand-name graduate schools and employment opportunities that come after the BA; and the parents and communities, largely upper-middle class, who push their children into the maw of this machine," Deresiewicz wrote in the *New Republic*.

And in the *American Scholar*, this: "Elite schools pride themselves on their diversity, but that diversity is almost entirely a matter of ethnicity and race. With respect to class, these schools are largely—indeed increasingly—homogeneous." He added that because the schools also "cultivate liberal attitudes, they leave their students in the paradoxical position of wanting to advocate on behalf of the working class while being unable to hold a simple conversation with anyone in it." He cited Al Gore and John Kerry, the Democratic presidential nominees in 2000 and 2004 respectively, "one each from Harvard and Yale, both earnest, decent, intelligent men, both utterly incapable of communicating with the larger electorate." Their successor, Barack Obama, was capable, sort of, but even his route to the Ivy League wasn't consistently hardscrabble, and it didn't give him an automatic rapport with working-class Americans. He attended a private secondary school in

Honolulu, called Punahou. It's arguably the best known and most exalted in Hawaii.

Deresiewicz observed that the students at an elite school are prone to vanity, because they are constantly told that they are the chosen, their presence there a testament to how special they are. "There is something wrong with the smugness and self-congratulation that elite schools connive at from the moment the fat envelopes come in the mail," he wrote. "From orientation to graduation, the message is implicit in every tone of voice and tilt of the head, every old-school tradition, every article in the student paper, every speech from the dean. The message is: You have arrived. Welcome to the club. And the corollary is equally clear: You deserve everything your presence here is going to enable you to get. When people say that students at elite schools have a strong sense of entitlement, they mean that those students think they deserve more than other people because their SAT scores are higher."

If you think that sounds like an exaggeration, I'd point you to an acceptance letter from Lawrenceville, a New Jersey prep school that feeds the Ivy League and presages the affirmations that flow so freely there. It came to my attention after its recipient posted it on Facebook. Dated March 10, 2014, it read: "This is the moment a door opened to reveal an educational journey that can shape the rest of your life. Welcome to Lawrenceville. Welcome to the next chapter in your life as a Lawrentian." It proceeded to praise "the remarkable sense of balance our students possess" and to ask its recipient, "Are you ready? We think so, and so do your future classmates." The heart flutters. Goose bumps rise.

Deresiewicz expressed additional concerns. He said that

at elite schools you find "the self-protectiveness of the old-boy network, even if it now includes girls," which means that no one is ever challenged all that mightily or held to stern account, and many students settle into a complacent mediocrity. This, he said, is embodied in the man who kept both Gore and Kerry from the presidency, George W. Bush, who attended both Yale (undergrad) *and* Harvard (business school).

And Deresiewicz's plaint didn't end there. He fretted about a lack of imagination and a dreary careerism in the students at elite schools, which don't challenge those leanings but, rather, instill or amplify them. And he contended that the homogeneous group of overachievers who make it to Princeton or Yale have, to that point, known only one triumph after another, largely because they've been given extensive preparation to master precisely those tasks that the elite educational track values. They can be strangely weak, not strong, as a result.

It's one hell of a laundry list, and I heard some of the same worries expressed by other educators who'd worked at highly selective schools. I saw bits and pieces of his lament all over the place.

"I think we're really screwing them up badly in the long run," said Bruce Poch, the former admissions dean at Pomona, referring to the way in which kids who wind up at elite schools are pointed in that direction from an early age, monitored ceaselessly by their jittery parents and made to believe that a great job and a contented life are a matter of faithful adherence to a program. "These kids are not equipped to get knocked on their tail. At Pomona, one of the things I got really nervous about was looking at these kids who'd had nothing but success. There was a stunning fragility to some of them. The parental bubble wrap and the boot camps got them to their one and only goal in lives," a top-ranked school. Once there, they're sort of frozen, adrift.

And they respond by taking cues from the herd and following what they believe to be the script, because script-following is precisely what they learned to do, and script-following is what got them this far. Act I was admission. Act II is heading in a professional direction deemed worthy of the elite school whose name will be stamped on their diplomas. This means a direction that's reliably lucrative. They avoid risk, because they can't brook the possibility of failure. They conform.

In *Excellent Sheep* Deresiewicz charts the grim ascendance of economics as a major—and finance or management consulting as careers—for a shocking percentage of young people who attend the most highly selective colleges. He writes that while economics was the most popular major at only three of the top 10 national universities in *U.S. News* and three of the top 10 colleges in the mid-1990s, it has tended to reign supreme at 26 of the top 40 schools—the top 20 universities combined with the top 20 colleges—over recent years. There have also been recent years, he writes, when nearly half of students graduating from Harvard and more than half of the students graduating from the University of Pennsylvania have gone into consulting or finance, while more than a third of students graduating from Cornell, Stanford and MIT did so. In 2011, more than a third of Princeton's graduates went into finance alone, he reports. And the focus on just a few professions means the neglect of so many others. "Whole fields have disappeared from view: the clergy, the military, electoral politics, even academia itself, for the most part, including basic science," he writes in *Excellent Sheep.* A lack of imagination and a fear of experimentation constrict, rather than expand, their opportunities.

That same viewpoint is expressed in a small study published in May 2014 by three researchers with an initiative called the Good Project, which is housed within the graduate school of education at Harvard. The authors conducted interviews with forty members of Harvard's undergraduate class of 2013 during their final, senior year. And they concluded that a Harvard education had "a funnel effect."

"Though students enter college with a diverse set of interests, by senior year, most of them seem to focus on a narrow set of jobs," the authors wrote. "The culture at Harvard seems to be dominated by the pursuit of high earning, prestigious jobs, especially in the consulting industries." In students' minds, only some jobs "live up to the degree."

The authors noted that one of the seniors had done some teaching and had loved it, but she eschewed the classroom for "a job at an education-consulting firm," because it felt "more aligned with the kind of work that many of her peers choose to do." Another senior was a fanatic for rare books and rare objects and wrote a thesis on World War II treasures. She then went to work for a medical software company.

This isn't a pattern peculiar to Harvard. Anushka Shenoy, who graduated from Columbia in 2008, told me: "It didn't occur to me to study anything other than economics and go into a banking or consulting career." That's what the people around her at Columbia aspired to and worked toward. That was the vogue. "I didn't know anything about management consulting except that it was really hard to get into," she said. "And I thought, 'Okay! I'll try that!' "

She landed an enviable job at Bain & Company, and moved to San Francisco to work for that management consulting firm there. But after a few years, she realized that she had no passion for what she was doing and that, in retrospect, she'd never really paused at Columbia to take adequate survey of what her heartfelt interests were. Everything there moved too fast for that to happen. It was as if there was no space to wander, no license for it. Once she took a breath and thought more deeply about it all, she changed tacks—and how. Now twenty-eight, she's in medical school in Portland at Oregon Health & Science University. And she's much happier.

What Shenoy felt at Columbia and what the authors of the funnel-effect paper noticed at Harvard are part of what the writer Junot Díaz refers to as "the commodification of the university as a trade guild, a very expensive trade guild." I contacted Díaz, who won the Pulitzer Prize in 2008 for his novel, *The Brief Wondrous Life of Oscar Wao*, and received a MacArthur Foundation "genius grant" four years later, primarily because he'd gone to a state school, Rutgers, and has spoken of how well it served him and how much he loved it. But he has an additional vantage point on higher education and on today's admissions mania, because he's on the faculty of one of the most selective institutions in the country, MIT. He's been teaching creative writing there for twelve years.

"The idea that a university directly feeds into a job: This is sacred law now," said Díaz, forty-six. "When I went to school, yeah, the university was going to help get you a job, but there was an entire experience around the university that was about your life and being educated in ways that weren't about markets. Nowadays, most of my students have a very, very painful or excruciating or overbearing market prerogative on them. The idea that you would go to a university for an education at the level of your soul is considered absurd, and to me that's heartbreaking."

He was speaking of higher education in general—he has taught at Syracuse University and New York University, too—and his observations dovetailed precisely with the results of an annual survey of incoming freshmen at hundreds of colleges nationwide. Administered by the Higher Education Research Institute at UCLA, it shows a striking change in the stated priorities of students over the last half century. For example, in the mid-1960s, only 42 percent of freshmen said that being able to "make more money" was a "very important" goal in their decision to go to college. That number rose to just over 73 percent in the survey results published in March 2014. Between the mid-1970s and 2014, the percentage who said that getting a better job was a "very important" motivation to attend college rose from 67.8 percent to 86.3 percent. Over that same stretch of time, the percentage of students who attached considerable importance to developing a meaningful life philosophy fell sharply.

But the particular culture that Díaz can best vouch for, the one in his mind when he mentions "most of my students," is MIT's. "I've literally had a front-row seat on this crap," he said. "It's just crazy."

An immigrant from the Dominican Republic, Díaz grew up among poor and working-class people who struggled and generally didn't have college educations. "I was a kid stranded in a neighborhood next to the largest active landfill in New Jersey," he said. "Rutgers gave me a passport to the world." It introduced itself to him as the name and logo on a sweatshirt worn by a friend's sister, who went there, and it became a symbol of hope for Díaz, a promise of something larger and better, a focus of his aspirations. "For us working-class kids, it seemed a gold mine," he said.

And it rejected him, at least the first time he applied. In high school he hadn't gotten the grades he'd needed to, and so he spent a year at Kean College (now Kean University) in Union, New Jersey, proving to himself and to Rutgers that he could do better. He transferred to Rutgers for his sophomore year, majored in English and lived in a residence hall favored by students interested in writing. He also worked: pumping gas, washing dishes. And, more than any of that, he opened his eyes to a newly kaleidoscopic community. Communities, really.

"I had never met feminists," he said. "I had never met activists. I'd never met anyone who was openly gay and would organize around that identity. All of this stuff, I'd never had access to. My pre-Rutgers life was like black-and-white television. It was like the first few minutes of *The Wizard of Oz* before the color kicks in."

Is MIT that kind of rainbow? Are any of the elite schools? Not in Díaz's experience.

"If you look at the family backgrounds of my kids, you're not getting a very diverse student body," he said. "They can claim it's diverse. But you're not getting the kind of diversity that I had at Rutgers, where you had kids who were Ivy League–qualified but their parents didn't want to spend that money, and kids like me, immigrants busting their humps. We have in so many ways narrowed it down."

Echoing Poch, he said that what he sees when he looks at many of the students at MIT and at the other revered university in Cambridge, Massachusetts, are what he called "fragile thoroughbreds." They've been trained to peak performance on tests and in term papers, but not to the unpredictability and tumult of adulthood. Many of them come to MIT for specific preparation for a career they've already decided on. They're after a credential they've been told they need. They're executing a plan they brought with them. And the university helps them with that, indulging who they are rather than challenging it, because elite colleges—maybe all colleges—are businesses in the end.

"Customers come in and they want their pickles on their burger," Díaz said. "They don't come in for you to upend everything."

Maybe I got lucky, because my Princeton students didn't seem as intellectually incurious as Deresiewicz found most of the kids at Yale. One was learning Farsi and plotting an ambitious, months-long summer backpacking trip along what used to be the Silk Road, and she wasn't doing this with a big pile of money from her parents, who didn't have it, or to impress the admissions committee, which she'd already done, or with a career in mind, because she hadn't yet decided on one. She was just doing it.

Another, though bound for Wall Street and scarily fluent in the ways of Princeton's status-ratifying eating clubs, had read an array of fiction and nonfiction that only someone who's following his heart and brain rather than any syllabus reads: cult mysteries, bestselling thrillers, books about food, Jonathan Franzen, David Foster Wallace. And another wrote a final paper of such detail, depth and polish that I almost got choked up as I graded it, or rather showered it with compliments. She'd already sewn up an A in the class and was pretty much on track for employment following her imminent graduation, but she had grown fascinated by the topic, was determined to become an expert on it, and seemed interested in doing excellent work for excellent work's sake.

The sixteen kids in my class didn't seem all that fragile, either, though they were less accustomed to criticism than I expected students to be. Isn't digesting negative feedback and turning it into positive fuel the very metabolism of education? Isn't school supposed to humble you?

That's not how it played out at Princeton, which seemed more expressly designed to pump up and prop up its students. I hadn't yet interviewed Díaz, and didn't do so until the semester was long over, but the word *customer* frequently entered my own thoughts while I was teaching there. From the moment I arrived on campus to the moment I left, I got the message that the students were my clients, and I was told more often about what I owed them, in terms of unambiguous explanations, in terms of support, than about what they owed me, their professor.

While I was instructed not to be lavish with A's, I was also informed that virtually nobody got C's. If a student seemed to be descending to a C-plus or even a B-minus, I should check in. I should intervene. Something might be wrong, and it was incumbent on me to look into what that was, whether it could be fixed, and if there was an aspect of the course or of my instruction that wasn't quite working. I caught one student cheating, and when I raised the matter with other faculty, looking for advice, I was asked whether I'd spelled out the rules of the class and the specifics of the assignment with sufficient clarity. And I was encouraged to give the student a do-over.

I liked most of the kids in my class immensely. They were warm and polite. Several had charm to burn. But more than a few of them operated with a literalism that I found dispiriting. They wanted to know *exactly* the minimum number of interviews necessary for a given assignment. They wanted to know *exactly*, point by point and step by step, what they could do to lift the B-plus they'd just received for one paper to an A-minus for the next. They seemed to be calibrating their efforts and meting out their exertions with pinpoint precision, focused on discrete markers instead of anything larger. I kept wishing for less cunning and more heart.

In many ways I was in awe of Princeton. It's a magnificent haven, gorgeous to look at, brimming with talent, rich with world-renowned faculty. But I was sometimes unsettled by many students' tone-deafness to the good fortune embedded in all of that, to the stereotype of Ivy League kids as the cosseted denizens of an aloof caste.

I learned that one of the eating clubs hosted an especially raucous, beer-soaked party known as "State Night," the idea being that on this sloppy occasion, everyone would party as if at a state school. They were encouraged to wear T-shirts or sweatshirts with the names of such institutions—I'm sure that Díaz's alma mater, Rutgers, made the occasional cameo— though some kids would come in garb from other, supposedly lesser rivals in the Ivy League, which, they would reportedly joke, might as well be public universities. Another eating club had "Titanic Night," when partygoers were assigned to different classes of the ship—steerage, et cetera—and told to dress as they imagined those status-sorted seafarers would.

But I was most struck by something I noticed in my own seminar, which was devoted to food writing. Before it began, more than 45 students signed up for the 16 slots. In situations like that, the university has them write letters of application to introduce themselves and describe their interest in the course; the professor then makes the cut. I read the letters, with a smile and with welling excitement. These kids were so mature, articulate, enthusiastic.

Then, deep into the semester, I realized that more than half of my sixteen students hadn't written anything *for* the class that showed the verve and care of their letters. I mentioned this to several full-time professors at Princeton. All nodded, unsurprised. They explained that what many Princeton students excelled at, as demonstrated by the fact that they were there, at a school with an acceptance rate that's now about 7 percent, was *getting into* things, and that the message these kids had received from the college admissions mania was that gaining access, besting the competition, was the principal goal and primary accomplishment. You rallied your best self, or struck your comeliest pose, for that. You didn't worry as much about what came after.

Those same full-time professors theorized that Wall Street was such a common destination for Princeton's graduating seniors precisely because the process of getting the most desirable jobs there was a competition among peers that was familiar from the college admissions sweepstakes. It gave their college years a rhythm, shape and purpose that they recognized, pointing them toward another culling, and promising, if all went well, the satisfaction of having acquired something that many classmates didn't.

One Princeton student, not in my seminar, and not willing to be identified, told me that his lack of interest in any future as a financier left him feeling lost, because he'd never stopped, on his path to Princeton, to figure out what he expected to get out of the university. He just knew that he was supposed to fight for admission to it. After he arrived on campus, he said, he experienced a palpable letdown, a loss of velocity. "A lot of my friends have experienced similar things," he said. "In high school, getting to college was what everyone's doing. That's what everyone is focused on. And then once you get to college, it becomes ambiguous. I kind of felt like I put so much energy getting in in the first place that once I got in, I didn't know what to do."

"What's that last line in *The Candidate*?" asked Bruce Poch, referring to the political classic, starring Robert Redford, about the triumph of process over substance, image over truth. At the very end of the movie, Redford's character wins his election but seems lost, and asks his equally victory-focused team what happens next. "The whole thing was getting it, getting it, whoring himself in ways that are just stunning, and then they find that they don't know what to do," Poch remembered. He said that there's an element of that in the kids who wind up at elite colleges.

I put this observation to Anthony Marx, the former Amherst president, who fell silent for about fifteen seconds. I couldn't tell if he was mulling whether he agreed with it or just trying to choose his words with diplomatic care. Finally he spoke: "It's interesting to think about how this is shaping

America. If our elite is to some extent being formed by this powerful experience of frenzied admissions, does it suggest that we're creating a culture in which the sale is more important than the product?"

That's just one of the frenzy's many troubling implications. The kids who strap themselves into it get the signal, or convince themselves, that they must assemble their high school records in a particular way—this many AP courses, that many extracurricular activities, a memorable summer job, an area of study to which they show profound attachment—whether it tracks with their real interests or not, whether it's who they are or some contrived mannequin. A contrived mannequin is okay.

"We've spent so much time talking about packaging that it suggests that the real trick of the collegiate endeavor *is* to be packaged," said Andre Phillips, the senior associate director of recruitment and outreach at the main campus of the University of Wisconsin. There's too little emphasis on authenticity, which has too unreliable a reward.

And there's so much talk of the trickery that applicants employ, of the connections they exploit and of favoritism and gullibility in admissions offices that too many kids feel licensed, even compelled, to do whatever it takes: hired guns, massaged credentials, outright lies. "The message a kid hears is: I can't do it on my own, I'm not worth enough," said Lloyd Thacker, the executive director of the Education Conservancy, a nonprofit devoted to changing and restoring calm to the admissions process.

"There's real evidence of the deleterious effect—the cumulative impact—of this process," he said, alluding to scattered cheating scandals around the country, both among kids taking the SATs to get into college and kids already there. He recalled that a few years ago, "I'm giving a talk at a school in Bellevue, Washington: Bill Gates territory. I talk about bad behavior in gaming the system, and the audience is really quiet. Then the counselor tells me that two weeks earlier, kids were caught breaking into the principal's office to change their AP scores. And a mother then asked a counselor at the school, 'You're not going to change the recommendation you wrote for Johnny because of this, are you?'"

From him and others I kept hearing the same apprehension: If you hold up certain metrics as the very determinants of children's futures, if you invest those metrics with too much importance and allow too blinding a focus on them, don't you essentially instruct kids to define and see themselves in terms of those very measurements? Isn't it unconstructively clinical, and doesn't it turn them inward on themselves rather than outward toward the world?

"The kids in my grade—the 'smart' ones—grade their success purely on a points system," Jess Silverman, a seventeen-year-old senior at a New Jersey high school, marveled to me. "They measure everything down to the decimal, charting their happiness based on a test curve. It's given me an ideal to strive against. It scares me to become so dependent on a number, because that's not what I am." But, she added, it's what the culture around her seems to want her to be.

I worry just as much about the pecking order that the admissions process creates, or at least affirms. That order is so entrenched and pervasive that even Deresiewicz, who is clearly and rightly disapproving of it, falls prey to its vocabulary in a passage that I quoted above, referring to "prestigious institutions like Harvard or Stanford or Williams as well as the larger universe of *second-tier* selective schools." The italics are mine, used to point out that even within the stratum of selectivity, there are yet more tiers, yet finer gradations. From these microcategories kids develop lists of "reach schools" and "safety schools," of fantasies and fallbacks. They stretch hopefully for some. They settle dejectedly for others.

And they are acutely aware of where they end up. This came through in a letter published in response to a column in the *Times* in 2012 by Andrew Delbanco, a professor of American studies at Columbia University and the author of the book *College: What It Was, Is, and Should Be*. Delbanco had written that there was "a germ of truth" to the charge that elite colleges bred self-satisfaction, and he expressed the wish that they "encouraged more humility and less hubris."

"A germ?" asked the author of the letter. "Has he ever been to a sports event where one team is an Ivy League school and its entire student section engages in the chant 'Safety school! Saaaaa-fety school!' at the opponents?"

Caste consciousness also popped up in a conversation I had with Harry Segal, a senior lecturer in psychology at Cornell. Segal was reflecting on the way that people in general and today's kids in particular can lose sight of how fortunate they really are, always glancing around them and spotting someone with a seemingly better lot. He was also remarking on the unnecessary distinctions made in contemporary America. And he told me that because he's fascinated by those habits and curious about them, he routinely puts a particular question to the two-hundred-odd students in his largest lecture class. He asks how many of them feel bad that they didn't get into Harvard or Yale.

"Lots of hands go up," he told me. "Probably sixty percent

of the class. And the ones that don't? I'm not convinced that they don't want to go up."

This is a lecture with seniors, juniors, sophomores. They're years past the college admissions process. They're *in* the Ivy League. And they're still thinking of what might have been, and still mulling their exact place in the nonsensical college hierarchy that our society has constructed.

NINE

HUMBLED, HUNGRY AND FLOURISHING

"Whenever I do graduation speeches, I always tell students; Yes, yes, often the name of your university can open doors for you. But in the end, it is so up to you. I know that's a cliché. But I think that sometimes the very, very fortunate people who've gone to the Ivy League or Cambridge or Oxford are a little entitled, and I don't think entitlement is good for a career."

— Christiane Amanpour, CNN anchor and 1983 graduate of the University of Rhode Island

Justin de Benedictis-Kessner won't lie. He did not arrive at the College of William and Mary in the fall of 2007 thinking, "This is really for the best." He did not arrive with the belief that everything happens for a reason or with any other, similarly sunny platitude in mind.

He arrived skeptically, even bitterly, still aware, he said, that "this is my safety school," and still smarting over his inability to go elsewhere. Although William and Mary is routinely ranked among the top 50 national universities by *U.S. News*, it wasn't what prep school graduates like him aspired to; only two students from his class at Exeter would be joining him there, many fewer than were heading to any given Ivy League school. "I arrived on campus a naive and preemptively arrogant freshman, ready to excel in classes and to get the whole college thing done with," he said. And he feels embarrassed about that now.

Raised in Berkeley, California, he went to Exeter because his father had gone there many years before and because he was given a scholarship that covered all of his expenses, which his parents weren't in a position to afford. When junior year dawned, the talk about college spiked.

"They've got the process down to a science there," he said, explaining that there were perhaps eight full-time college counselors and that each student was assigned to a specific one, who would provide advice about "how to structure your classes, what classes you might want to take, whether you should focus on grades or leadership activities." And as he and his classmates began to obsess about admissions, people outside the school assured him that he'd fare brilliantly. "They'd say, 'Oh, you go to Exeter? You'll get into Harvard, Yale or Princeton, because it's a feeder school,'" Justin recalled. "And my dad echoed that."

He didn't apply to those three schools, but he did apply to Dartmouth, Middlebury, Tufts, Swarthmore. "I was really, really into Swarthmore," he said. "And then, as a backup, I applied to Kenyon, William and Mary and some California state schools." After he got his acceptances and rejections, he was left to choose among UCLA, UCSD, UC Davis, Tufts, George Washington University, Kenyon and William and

Mary. Of those schools Tufts excited him the most by far. It was in the Northeast, where the lion's share of his friends would be attending college, and it was somewhere Exeter kids routinely went. But neither it nor GWU nor Kenyon was offering him as much financial aid as William and Mary was, and, he said, "My parents were adamant that I not take on a lot of debt for college.

"I took the train down to Tufts, because I was dead set on it," he recalled. "I thought I wanted to study developmental psychology and do this particular program there. I visited the financial aid office. They laid out the books: Here's your family's situation, here's why we can't give you more money. I'm pretty sure I was in a chair crying. I was as close to begging as you can get without being on the floor."

So William and Mary it was. And while regret trailed him there, he was smart and practical enough to try to convert it into a kind of gameness. "That sense of disappointment motivated me," he said, and he set about making William and Mary its own adventure—not the one he'd wanted, not the one he'd planned, but a worthwhile side trip, a diversion that surely had virtues all its own.

Because William and Mary was a relatively small school and he didn't feel intimidated by it, he signed up for stuff. He joined groups—the rowing team, for example. He'd been, in his own estimation, "a mediocre rower" at Exeter, so he hadn't resolved to continue the sport in college. But William and Mary's team was modest and approachable.

"I had the chance to be in some of the varsity boats as a freshman and to excel in a sport that I loved," he said. "That was awesome, and it couldn't have happened at some of those other schools. I ended up being the president of the rowing team by the time I left. I even raised a bunch of money for the school, helped to build the boathouse."

On William and Mary's stage, he became a star, a leader. "I ran for the student honor council," he said, and he was elected, so he spent several years adjudicating ethics violations like plagiarism cases. It fascinated him. "I learned a lot about how people's minds work," he said.

And in his government and psychology classes—he was a double major—he found that he stood out and that professors noticed and appreciated him, extending opportunities his way. During his freshman year, a psychology professor invited him to help with a research project over the summer, and he eagerly agreed to. Another professor later put him on another research project, actually hired him for it, paid him and then wrote him a glowing recommendation for grad school.

"He's the reason I'm here," Justin said, referring to MIT, where he's pursuing a doctorate in political science and working as a research coordinator in the political experiments lab. His dissertation examines how public services and government accountability at the local level influence and interact with people's political opinions, and he said that it could logically lead to a job in academia or in the private sector, doing data analysis. He hasn't decided which he wants.

But he's sure that he's on the right page. And he's grateful for his years at William and Mary, where he had not only a great time but also a meaningful one that pointed him as sharply as he could be pointed in an academic and professional direction that feels exactly right. Justin doesn't wonder what Swarthmore might have meant to him or what Tufts might have done for him. He doesn't feel so much as a twinge of regret.

"There was a lot more that I could do in a new environment than I could have done if I'd gone to a college with a huge bunch of people I'd been to high school with," he explained. William and Mary, he said, was nothing less than "a chance to reinvent myself."

It's impossible, and therefore foolish, to say definitively that some students are better served by going to colleges that aren't their first or third or fifth choices; that aren't quite as prestigious as the ones that they had hoped for or actually decided to pass up; or that aren't on anyone's list of elite standouts. And the students themselves are perhaps the worst judges of the situation. After all, it's a human tendency, and a merciful one at that, to develop and hold tight to a conviction that the assigned or chosen course turned out to be the optimal one, especially if the alternatives are no longer in play. Regret is corrosive; many people surrender it as quickly as possible. And if they can't be with the one they thought they would love, well, they love the one they're with.

But some of these students, like Justin, really do develop an assurance that might have been suffocated on a campus of kids with a more uniform academic fluency and more obvious self-possession. They sidestep the peril, explored by Malcolm Gladwell in a passage of his book *David and Goliath*, that threw one Brown University student he profiled off her longtime desire to be a scientist. "She was a Little Fish in one of the deepest and most competitive ponds in the country," Gladwell wrote, "and the experience of comparing herself to all the other brilliant fish shattered her confidence. It made her feel stupid, even though she isn't stupid at all." In a less daunting body of water, she might have escaped the currents of self-doubt.

And some students at smaller, more obscure colleges discover that what these schools lack in a bounty of resources they often make up for in the availability of the resources that do exist. This was the experience that Todd Martinez had at Calvin College, in Grand Rapids, Michigan.

I briefly mentioned Martinez, forty-seven, a Stanford chemistry professor and (like Díaz) a MacArthur Foundation "genius grant" winner, earlier in the book, in connection with his belief that there's not likely to be all that much difference between the prowess of students at a school with a 5 percent acceptance rate, like Stanford's, and students at a school with a 20 percent acceptance rate. He went to Calvin College largely because it's run by the Christian Reformed Church, for which his father was a missionary. It has about four thousand students and an acceptance rate now of just under 70 percent. He then did his graduate work at UCLA and taught at the University of Illinois as well as at Stanford, so he has seen the world of higher education through disparate lenses.

And he told me that at many small schools like Calvin, "you have much more access much earlier to both equipment and to professors." He gave the example of a nuclear magnetic resonance, or NMR, machine. "Most schools that have a chemistry program will have an NMR machine. But at UCLA, where I was a grad student, the undergraduates are not going to touch it, whereas we at Calvin were able to take apart the NMR machine if we wanted." It wasn't the fastest, most powerful, most sophisticated kind of NMR machine, he said. But it was theirs. They could have at it. Similarly, he said, professors were approachable in a way that they sometimes aren't at larger schools.

The novelist John Green, who wrote the bestselling phenomenon *The Fault in Our Stars*, certainly found that to be true when he was a student in the late 1990s at Kenyon, in Gambier, Ohio. It has about 1,700 students, and Green told me that he got to know many professors there extremely well. An exchange with one of them stays with him always. It had no small bearing on his ability to forge a career as a writer after he graduated, he said.

At Kenyon, Green took an introductory fiction-writing class, after which he applied to take another, more advanced one. It was open to only twelve students. A total of sixteen, including him, wanted in, and he was one of the four turned away. "I was decimated," he said. "I thought, 'If you can't be one of the best twelve writers in your class at your tiny Midwestern college, how are you ever going to have a career?'"

Fred Kluge, the professor who taught the class that Green had completed but not the follow-up, took note of his reaction. "Without me even saying anything to him, he invited me to his house," Green recalled. "He sat me down. He poured himself a glass of Scotch. He poured me a glass of seltzer water. And he told me I was a good writer, 'a solid B-plus writer,' as he put it, and then he told me that the stories I told before class and on breaks were really, really good, and if I could figure out a way to write the way I told those stories, I could have a life in writing." Green's problem, Kluge suggested, was that he was trying too hard to be lofty and literary; he wasn't writing from emotion, in a true voice.

The advice was precise, and it was pivotal.

"I needed someone to tell me that I had potential, but I also needed someone to tell me why I didn't get into that class," Green said, adding that Kluge's intervention "was *way* above and beyond the call of duty." Green holds on to, and sometimes revisits, a particular photograph from his graduation ceremony at Kenyon, and the reason isn't the way he looks in it but the fact that Kluge can be seen in the background, watching over him and smiling.

Green, who is now thirty-seven, said that before Kenyon, he wasn't an especially good student, and had perhaps a 2.9 GPA at the prestigious boarding school he attended in Birmingham, Alabama. His SAT scores were "reasonable," he said; he did better, oddly, in the math than in the verbal component. Many of his classmates applied to Ivy League schools. He didn't dare. As he remembers it, his applications went to Emory University, Grinnell College, Kenyon, Macalester College and Guilford College, in Greensboro, North Carolina. He was put on the wait list at Emory, rejected at Macalester and got into the rest. Back then, he said, Kenyon took more than 50 percent of its applicants. These days it takes between 35 and 40 percent.

"It isn't any better or worse a college," he laughed. "It's mostly the same teachers as when I went."

And he thought it was terrific. He loved it. He did a double major in English and religion, and he said that most of his classes had between eight and thirty students. One had four. It was called "Reading *Ulysses*," he said, and it was devoted entirely to James Joyce's masterpiece. One of the other three students was Ransom Riggs, who went on to write the bestseller *Miss Peregrine's Home for Peculiar Children*.

"Looking back on it, I got such tremendous value out of the classes," Green said, and he recalled many of them with a detail that made clear just how much they'd meant to him. He talked about a class on Islamic history. He also talked about a class on Jesus in which he learned that "the idea that there were sons of gods wasn't in any way uncommon in the first century," he said. "That wasn't the radical idea. The radical idea was that Jesus of Nazareth was *the* son of God. And that just blew my mind."

He relished his excursions into nineteenth-century British romantic literature. "There's just so much stuff in those classes that I use in my books," he said. "I'm always cheating and stealing from them. I wish that I could go to college again, so that I could have four more years to steal and cheat from.

"There's something magical about that time," he continued, and it's not primarily that you're living among all your friends or going to so many parties. It's not the beauty of a campus or the first taste of something verging on adult independence. It's the permission to sit still, to *think*. It's the lull, the space and the freedom for that. "Spending six hours on a Sunday reading *Jane Eyre* and *Jane Eyre* criticism is by far the best use of your time," he said. He wishes he'd done more of that.

And while he could have done it at any number of schools, he said that he's not sure that many of them would have served him nearly as well as Kenyon did. And that's not because Kenyon is famous as a cradle for writers, the school that gave birth to the *Kenyon Review*, which is still published in Gambier. It's because of Kenyon's personal touch, its intimacy. One of his religion professors, Don Rogan, would invite him over for evenings when various professors recited poetry. And he became a coach and an audience for Green when Green found his way back to fiction writing.

Green said that after the rejection from the advanced class, "I stopped for about a year and felt totally useless, but started up again my senior year and wrote a story that—while still very bad—was a huge leap forward for me. It was about a re-cently ordained Lutheran minister traveling home to perform a wedding who ends up also overseeing a funeral, and it was longer than anything I'd ever written and I remember it as *brilliant*, but then of course I dredged up a copy and it turns out to be pretty awful. These things should live in memory, where they can glister.

"Anyway," Green continued, "Don treated the story with total respect and encouraged me to finish it, and I still re-member his comments about it after I gave it to him upon my graduation. He said, 'This is a very promising story. The fu-neral went on too long, but then, funerals generally do.'"

Reflecting on Rogan, reflecting on Kluge, Green said, "I do think that those relationships were more available to me than if I'd gone to Harvard.

"My closest friend in high school went to Princeton," he said. "A couple of months after he started, he sent me an email: 'There are a lot of stupid people here.' He got 1600 on the SATs and was searingly brilliant. He was really offended that all of these people didn't live up to his expectations." Green wasn't making a dig at Princeton. He was making the point that the experience a person has at any school depends on hopes, prejudices, unforeseeable interactions, attitude. It's subjective.

"I believe that you can get a good education at most Amer-ican universities," Green said. "You can also get a not-good education anywhere. You can scrape by." That's what he sees when he looks at the people and the world around him.

"I might be wrong about this," he said, "but I don't think it matters that much where you go."

*   *   *

I'm inclined to agree, but then I recognize just how right Kenyon was for him and William and Mary for Justin. I consider how many kids seem to find, at schools well outside the Ivy League, a reassurance, an impetus or a spark that they might not have found at schools inside of it. Those schools do seem to matter. They do seem to make a difference. Just as Harvard is the crucial launch for one person, the University of Maryland or the University of Rochester can be essential for another.

I cite Maryland for a reason. I interviewed one young lawyer who went there, but only after rejections from Columbia and UPenn that were such a "personal blow to my identity," he said, that he posted them on the wall above his bed in his boarding school dormitory room, "to remind myself to do better." At Maryland he was a standout in the criminal justice department, because he resolved to be and because he could be. As a result, he got into the highly regarded law school at New York University. Upon his graduation from it last year, he nabbed a coveted associate's position with a major Manhattan firm.

And I cite Rochester because that's Joseph Ross's alma mater.

Ross, now forty, attended high school in the suburbs of Buffalo, and he said that his best friends in his graduating class headed alternately to Harvard, Yale, Amherst, UPenn and Smith. "I was the dumb one among them," he said. "I applied to UPenn and Cornell. Didn't get into either."

So he went to Rochester, where he didn't feel at all like the dumb one. "My high school had been very competitive," he said, "and I did much better in college." He developed an assertiveness, academically speaking, that he hadn't possessed before, and he stretched further than he might otherwise have, attempting and completing not only two majors, in psychology and neuroscience, but also a minor in creative writing.

When he turned his gaze toward becoming a physician, he didn't bother with the top-ranked medical schools. After all, Rochester had wholly satisfied him, and it didn't sit at the summit of rankings. As best he can recall, he applied to just two places, SUNY Buffalo and SUNY Syracuse, both of which made sense in terms of cost. He ended up at SUNY Buffalo, and eventually made his way to where he is now: on the faculty of the Yale University School of Medicine.

He teaches internal medicine there and also writes frequently and extensively for various blogs and publications, a passion that has been helped enormously by classes he took at Rochester. At an unusually young age, he's an associate editor for *JAMA Internal Medicine.* "I can't imagine a better job," he told me. As for the way he got there, he said, "I think that what served me well, and this is part of what I look for when I'm selecting research fellows, was focusing on what I was passionate about rather than focusing on getting into School X." Perhaps partly because of Rochester, Ross concentrated on deeds, not labels.

And perhaps partly because of Northwestern Oklahoma State University, Travis F. Jackson, who is also forty, concentrated on working harder than many of the people around him.

Jackson is a Los Angeles–based lawyer with a nationwide firm that's a major player in the health-care industry. His career has gone about as well as he could have imagined, and it has taken him far from the Oklahoma farmland where he grew up. "My town had a population of about one thousand," he told me, "though I think there may have been some cattle in that count."

He went to college at Northwestern Oklahoma State because it was nearby and affordable. He graduated summa cum laude. He went to law school at the University of Notre Dame because he got a scholarship that paid for enough of his expenses to keep his student loan debt manageable. He graduated summa cum laude there, too.

At Notre Dame he was around many alumni of elite colleges, and he's been around many more of them since. And he said that because his own undergraduate alma mater doesn't have any particular glimmer, "I was intimidated to compete with these people. But that made me not take things for granted.

"With all due respect to some of my friends who have gone to Ivy League schools," he said, "I think they have a tendency to do that." They're not as intent on proving themselves, because in their own minds, their diploma has already made their case for them. And consciously or unconsciously, they count on it to be a safety net. "If I didn't put the effort in," Jackson said, "I didn't have anything to fall back on."

Indeed, students at less lavishly celebrated colleges are sometimes motivated by their institutions' lack of luster. They don't assume that the names of their schools will propel them into the job market and through life, so they take greater care to acquit themselves in a way that might. Nor do they assume that the college atmosphere they inhabit is so rich with positive influences that they'll simply prosper by osmosis. They're prodded to be scrappier, and that can turn into its own advantage.

"You're going to be forced to be more entrepreneurial at a small school," said Martinez, reflecting on his experience at Calvin. He developed an interest in theoretical chemistry early on there, and the college couldn't offer him every last bit of instruction he craved. But it had a library and affiliations and concerned, generous faculty. He discovered that he could improvise and patch together what he needed. Looking back, he sees enormous merit in having been compelled to take that kind of initiative.

"It's not necessary to get into a highly selective school in order to be successful," he said. "What's necessary is to understand what you want to do and how to do it well, and to be a self-starter."

As I listened to Jackson, Ross and others whom I interviewed, I searched for any and all commonalities, themes, ways of thinking and strategies for behaving that departed from a lockstep striving for the school with the "best" name. And I spotted, in the stories of many of the people happiest with the way things had turned out for them, an openness to serendipity that sometimes gets edited out of the equation when you're blindly accepting the marks that your parents and your peers have all agreed on and you're dutifully hitting them, one after the other. I noticed a nimbleness in adapting to change, a willingness to shoot off in a new direction and an attention to the particular virtues of the landscape right around them rather than an obsession with the promised glories of the imagined terrain around the bend.

I saw qualities that Hiram Chodosh, the Claremont McKenna president, told me were in woefully short supply these days. He remarked on, and rued, a "propensity to be very linear" in too many of today's overachievers. He conceded that this wasn't a wholly new phenomenon, remembering his time at Yale Law School and the way many of his peers there drew up and executed their plans to become law professors down the line. Their thinking, he said, went like this: "I need to get a great federal court clerkship, ideally with the Supreme Court. To get that, I need to have a recommendation from a prominent Yale law professor. To get *that*, I need to TA for him my third year. To do *that*, I need to work for the law review under their supervision my second year."

As Chodosh flashed back on that, he shook his head. "You don't become a great academic because you're trying to become a great academic," he said. "You become a great academic when you look out the window and you have something to say about what's wrong with this picture that's unique."

Not enough of the students arriving at elite schools are looking out the window. Instead, he said, "There's this job they want, and they've benchmarked someone's career, and they've created a straight-line path. Frankly, I don't know people who've been successful who've worked in a straight line. Maybe they exist, but I don't know them."

I know some, but their straight lines usually didn't begin all the way back in kindergarten or for that matter middle or high school, and their mile markers weren't SAT scores and enrollment at a college with an acceptance rate below 15 percent. Their focus was the actual work they intended to do: preparing themselves for it, picking up the skills they needed, snatching small chances to show what they were capable of and then using those to grab hold of even bigger chances. That's how success generally happens.

It's how it happened for Christiane Amanpour, the CNN correspondent who occupies an altitude in the news business so lofty that when the writer Sheila Weller chose three TV journalists to profile in her 2014 book, *The News Sorority*, she grouped Amanpour with Katie Couric and Diane Sawyer. I'd met Amanpour a few times and knew her a bit before I thought to inquire about where she'd gone to school. I can be as pitiful a slave to stereotypes as anyone else, and the erudition that she exhibits on air, coupled with her plummy English accent, led me to expect Oxford or Cambridge. The University of Rhode Island surprised me.

Amanpour grew up in privileged circumstances in Iran and indeed attended boarding school in England. "My original desire to be a doctor didn't pan out," she told me. "I didn't get the right grades. I was a bit lost and roaming in the academic wilderness. And I didn't go to school again after high school for a number of years."

The revolution in Iran sharpened her interest in international affairs and gave her the idea of becoming a journalist, but it also wiped out her parents' funds and put many colleges out of financial reach. She knew she wanted to study in America—it was where so many friends had fled—and was steered to the University of Rhode Island because it didn't cost as much as many private colleges and because a family friend knew the school's president. The reasons were that mundane and the process that quick and blunt. Like Dick Parsons, Condoleezza Rice, Howard Schultz and so many others, she pivoted to college in a manner that bore positively no relation to what so many kids and parents today put themselves through.

Partly because Amanpour didn't start college until she was

twenty-one and partly because money was a concern, she did a swift sprint toward her diploma, beginning school in January 1980 and finishing, after six semesters, in December 1982. She worked during that time, at a local television station in Providence, about a forty-minute drive from the school's location in Kingston, Rhode Island. And, she said, "I did not live on campus. I lived with friends in Providence, who, actually, hilariously, were at Brown, so I got the best of both worlds." (For one period, one of those housemates was a Brown student by the name of John F. Kennedy Jr.)

She said that the education that she got in her journalism classes was helpful, but her time off-campus was at least as important, and what mattered most of all was that she had figured out what she wanted—a journalism career—and she summoned a drive to match that direction. Perhaps it had to do with the upset of the Iranian Revolution and with being so far from home. "My life experience made me much more worldly than most of the freshmen, sophomores and juniors I encountered," she said, adding that her subsequent success "was a combination of the education I got and a deep, deep commitment and understanding that I had to work hard in the world. It was my own personal motivation. I climbed the ladder very systematically and dogmatically—internships, ground level at CNN, up the ladder. At no point did the name of my college make any difference in my career."

My friend Scott Pask could—and would—say the same about the name of his college, and with him, as with Amanpour, I didn't know for the longest time which college that was. I was aware that he'd received a master's in fine art at Yale University and that he'd done so when he was around thirty, and not right after his undergraduate education. But where that undergraduate education happened didn't come up in our conversations until several years into our friendship, which goes back about a decade now. Pask went to the University of Arizona.

He's a prodigiously respected Broadway set designer, with three Tony Awards to his credit, along with a slew of additional nominations. And he's exactly the kind of person Hiram Chodosh envisions when he sings the virtues of not working in a straight line.

Scott grew up in Yuma, Arizona, without much money, so cost was a major consideration when he decided on college. He chose the University of Arizona. He wanted to study architecture—"I loved drawing houses," he said, "and I loved looking at houses"—and according to his research, Arizona was a fine place to do that. He enrolled in its College of Architecture, which he said was "a very small and rigorous institution within the greater structure of the university." And he quickly came to know the other students and the professors in the college well. The conversation among them was constant, enlightened, intense.

He reveled in that. Even so, he didn't tamp down interests other than architecture when they flared. Didn't tame or limit his curiosity. Occasionally, Broadway musicals would come to town, and he found himself drawn to them. Watching the spectacle of *Cats*, he wondered who conceived and built the sets and how the whole process worked. "I thought it was some elaborate hobby that people had," he said. "I couldn't imagine that these were jobs: the design and the costumes and lighting. I thought, 'Wow, how do they have the time to do that?'" They were surely doing something else, something real, to pay the bills.

Although the theater program at Arizona was mostly limited to students who had chosen it as a major, Pask was determined to sign up for a set design class that he'd learned about. "It had all these prerequisites, none of which I had," he said. "But I took over some models I'd been building, and they let me in." After that he persuaded someone to let him help with a campus production. "It was like a light going on," he said.

He went ahead and got his architecture degree, but there were new thoughts bubbling in his head, new schemes being entertained. He set out for New York City without any detailed agenda. His first steady job was in a Paul Smith clothing store on Fifth Avenue. He usually manned the counter, though sometimes he folded shirts. "I was an ace folder," he said. "I was also really good at accessories." One year, he was even allowed to decorate the Christmas windows.

He assiduously cultivated friendships with the artists and performers he met, and he seized opportunities for obscure, offbeat collaborations with them. He volunteered to create huge murals for regular parties at a New York nightclub. He contributed the scenery for the modest shows of aspiring dancers. And when he started to get paying jobs in set design, he threw himself into them, not principally out of ambition but because he loved what he was doing. It wasn't until he was nearing thirty that he realized he had the makings of a lifelong career and enrolled at Yale, eager to expand his knowledge and raise his game.

He now runs his business—and it's a serious, successful business—out of a studio in Manhattan, and college students and recent graduates routinely ask to stop by. He says yes as often as he can. And he's frustrated by how many of them are looking not for general advice or inspiration but for step-by-step marching orders. They want it all laid out for them.

"There is no map!" he told me, his voice rising, his words emphatic. And if someone insisted on drawing one, with a destination of his brilliant career, they probably wouldn't put Arizona and a Paul Smith store on it.

TEN

FIRE OVER FORMULA

"If you are extremely smart but you're only partially engaged, you will be outperformed, and you should be, by people who are sufficiently smart but fully engaged."

—Britt Harris, the former chief executive of the
Bridgewater Associates hedge fund and
a 1980 graduate of Texas A&M

College has long been seen as a pivotal gateway—even *the* pivotal gateway—to professional success and overall fulfillment. Parents have long had strong feelings about where their kids should go. Kids have long felt enormous pride about where they were welcomed. And a hierarchy of colleges, with some eliciting more admiration than others, isn't anything new. So what explains the particular fever of the college admissions process over the last decade? Why has the temperature risen so high?

When I sat down with Anthony Marx, the former Amherst president, and asked him what he thought was driving the admissions mania, he first brought up something that was also very much on my mind: the heightened consciousness in America with status and labels and the thoroughness with which higher education has been absorbed into that. "People don't advertise their names, their hometowns or their high schools," he said. "What do people put on the back windshields of their cars? Colleges. Surely that says something about the branding aspect of higher education. Yes, we hope for our kids to get great educations and meet friends who will change their lives. And they do. But there is also the halo effect."

That can't be all or even most of it, though: The stickers have been around for decades. A factor that hasn't is the cult of the expert. Twenty years ago, you never heard about personal trainers; people believed in the possibility of squatting, sweating and slimming on their own. But trainers are now ubiquitous in the upper-middle-class neighborhoods of major metropolitan areas, whose most pampered, indulgent denizens may also have nutritionists and therapists and personal shoppers, in a few cases for their children as well as themselves. Many people of means seem to believe that there's no problem, from a belly's sprawl to a child's sloth, that isn't best fixed by throwing money and a specialist at it. Anything can be delegated. Everything can be outsourced. This mindset is the fertile climate for all of those independent college consultants, whose proliferation has invariably turned up the heat of the admissions process, both for the families who use them and the families who are then forced to worry about a possible penalty for not doing so.

The cost of college aggravates the situation. Parents poised to spend as much as sixty thousand dollars a year on tuition, room and board want whatever's deemed to be the luxury model and push their kids to attain it, while the children of the much greater number of parents who can't swing a bill that enormous vie for scholarships whose acquisition and generosity hinge on board scores and GPAs higher than those of their peers.

Several college placement counselors told me that the oft-rued narcissism of the so-called selfie generation may sometimes come into play, with kids intent on going to a revered institution that validates their self-regard. It's where they belong. It's what they deserve. On top of that, social media has given kids ways to keep track of one another and to issue widely seen bulletins about their lives that didn't exist before, and what kids often want and choose to do with those bulletins, whether the news is related to college or something else, is impress. Check out the Facebook pages of high school seniors around the days that early-admission or general-admission notices are released, and you'll see a blizzard of updates communicating who got in where. The process, like so much of modern life, is public as never before.

But counselors said that mothers and fathers are the principal agents of the frenzy, which is the apotheosis of their efforts to micromanage every last moment of their children's lives and protect them from all injury, especially to their self-esteem. If they've been run-of-the-mill helicopter parents up until they start plotting college, they become Black Hawks at that point.

"Parents have put so much into kids, kids have put so much work in," said Tim Levin, the head of the tutoring service Bespoke Education. "You get to this process that you don't have a lot of control over—maybe for the first time in your life—and it's so quirky that even if you do everything right, you may not get what you want. And that drives parents crazy. They've chosen the right schools, the right tutors, the right museums. They've controlled *all* the variables. And suddenly they get to something that they can't control so well, and they can flip out a bit."

Especially because many of them sense that this passage in American life isn't like others. That's a key part of all of this, maybe *the* key part of all of this. The world is a more competitive place, in which the hegemony and influence of the United States are no longer the givens that they were in the past. The gap between the haves and the have-nots has widened, raising the stakes of which side of the divide you wind up on. "The difference between being in the top one or five or ten percent and not is bigger than ever before, so if people think going to a highly selective school will get you there, they're going to care more," said Alan Krueger, the Princeton economics professor.

Like Krueger, Catharine Bond Hill, the Vassar president, is an economist, and like him she sees "increasing income inequality" behind the college admissions mania. "The reward for getting into the top X percent of the income distribution now is a multiple of what it was thirty or forty years ago, and people perceive the access to that as coming through these elite schools."

There are fewer and fewer well-paying jobs for people without college degrees and, over recent years, there hasn't been any surfeit of great options for people *with* college degrees. The fear and awareness of this among young people were captured in a short graphic and story that ran in the summer of 2014 on Mic.com, a news and commentary website aimed at an audience of those under thirty years old. It showed that from 2000 to 2010, the number of people between 18 and 24 who were enrolled in college climbed by 29 percent; during the same period, the number of college-educated janitors rose by 69 percent. The post framed this, melodramatically, as possibly "the saddest economic statistic ever."

For most of the last decade, the gross domestic product has grown at a snail's pace, and the optimism that once seemed inextricable from the American spirit has flatlined. In this century, there have been only three fleeing points when most Americans signaled satisfaction with the direction in which the country was headed, and all came at tense, fraught junctures when Americans had reasons to will themselves into a sort of defensive confidence: the month when George W. Bush took office, which followed the furious legal contest over vote counting in Florida and the intervention of the Supreme Court; the days following the 9/11 terrorists attacks; and the month when the United States invaded Iraq. All of those came in the first four years of the century.

Over the next ten years, which the Democratic political strategist Doug Sosnik has referred to as "a decade of anger and dissatisfaction," polling by the *Wall Street Journal* and NBC News continuously showed that the number of Americans who believed the country was on the wrong track exceeded those who thought that it was on the right track. "For the first time in our country's history," Sosnik wrote in a political memo that he shared with the newspaper and website *Politico* in late 2013, "there is more social mobility in Europe than in the United States."

Americans had been so humbled, and become so pessimistic, that when a Gallup poll asked them in mid-2014 which country was the world's "leading economic power," 52 percent said China, while only 31 percent gave the correct response: the United States. It was the sixth consecutive year in which more Americans had mistakenly answered China instead of our own country. And that downbeat, doubting frame of mind came through in a *Wall Street Journal*/NBC News poll in August 2014, when 76 percent of Americans ages eighteen and older said they weren't confident that their children's generation would fare better than their own. That same survey showed that the percentage of Americans who felt that the United States was on the wrong track had shot up to 71.

"It's been a long time since Americans felt that way or at least had that aggregate fear," said Anthony Marx. "So, understandably, you look for every angle that you can that will give your kid an advantage." And a selective college that commands pronounced respect is perceived as one of those angles. In the eyes of apprehensive parents, it's a possible guarantor, or at least an extra arrow in the quiver.

So they meddle and wheedle and marshal whatever resources they have toward the goal of a college that gleams in the public eye, convinced that this is the responsible, caring thing to do. Or at least too many of them do this, setting their children up for what is very likely to be disappointment, infusing the effort with an emotionalism that can turn that disappointment into heartbreak and planting the notion that there's a clear winner's circle and, outside of it, a tundra of uncertainty.

"It's ironic because what, in the end, do parents really want?" said Andrew Delbanco, the American studies professor at Columbia. "They want their children to be happy. And

I don't see how buying into the college admissions process is accomplishing that."

I don't, either. And I have two particular complaints about the mania that I'd perhaps put above others, two primary reasons that I wish kids and their parents wouldn't be drawn into it. The first is this, and it's an echo of Scott Pask's lament and of one of William Deresiewicz's concerns: The mania's focus on such a limited number of acceptable outcomes, coupled with its attention to minutely detailed instructions for achieving them, suggests that life yields to meticulous recipes. That's a comforting thought but a fraudulent one. The second reason is that the admissions mania perverts the true meaning and value of hard work, encouraging such effort in the designated service of a specifically defined goal, as a pragmatic bridge from point A to point B, not as an act of passion, not as a lifetime habit, not as a renewable resource, which is what it should be and how it bears the ripest, sweetest fruit.

Speaking of recipes, Steve Schmidt, the McCain campaign strategist, told me that his interactions with students at elite colleges over recent years had given him a set of impressions about them much like Hiram Chodosh's. "I'll talk to a group at Stanford and I've spoken at the Kennedy School at Harvard on any number of occasions," he said. "You have a bunch of hyperambitious kids, and they're nice kids, they're earnest, they're engaged. But they have their notepads out. 'How did you get where you are?' They're almost looking for you to give them a formula: 'On Day 246 of your career, you should do this.' I said to one kid, 'I'm going to give you a piece of advice. You should go and get a job working on a sailboat in the Caribbean for six months. Or maybe work behind a bar.' He was shocked. And I said, 'I'm serious as a heart attack. Life isn't reduced to a formula. Luck enters into it. It's a chance event.'"

As for hard work, that's what nearly all of the most accomplished people I've interviewed attribute their achievements to. They sometimes call it different things, dress it up in different semantic finery. But it's always there in the gist of what they're saying, the cream of their advice, and the work they're talking about isn't the narrowly targeted kind that goes into anything as prosaic as an SAT score, a science project or an essay. They're talking about something that overarches all of these and is sustained well beyond them.

It's what Sam Altman of Y Combinator identified when I asked him what distinguished the entrepreneurs behind the startups that took off from the ones behind the startups that went nowhere. He said that what mattered most in the end was a true, deep attachment to whatever you're making, whatever you're selling, whatever you're doing. He praised intensity and stamina. "Sheer determination" was how he put it. It sounded to me like a synonym for hard work, which is at the very least a component or by-product of it.

It was about a week after my phone conversation with him that I happened to meet and have drinks with Britt Harris, the rich financier who teaches the "Titans of Investing" course at Texas A&M, his alma mater. He told me that largely because of the Titans class, he had given extensive thought to the real secret of the most successful people. Ambition? Sure, they all had that, but many unsuccessful people did as well, and sometimes in greater measure. Competence? Yes, but that doesn't take a person all the way to the top. Mentors? Those helped, and anyone who finds a shrewd and generous one should by all means make the most of him or her. But mentors weren't the decisive edge.

Harris shared his conclusion with me by recounting a guest lecture that he'd given to a hundred or so students at Princeton about five years ago. He told the students that he was humbled to be appearing before them and conceded as much, saying to them: "Your level of intelligence is literally off the charts. I want to admit to you—and this is not false humility—there was never a day in my life when I could reasonably be considered to be accepted into Princeton. I would have rejected myself!

"I'm in my fifties," he recalls telling them. "I've run seven relatively important organizations, and I've been fortunate enough to have people from Princeton work for me. But I've never worked for somebody from Princeton. How do you explain that?"

He then gave them *his* explanation for it: "I'm fully engaged. If I decide to get involved, I'm all in. Every day is one hundred percent." That's his greatest asset, he told them and, later, me, explaining that a robust and lasting energy for hard work is always going to be more consequential than any college.

Few of the parents I know would dispute that. Most feel it in their bones. It's common sense. And that's exactly what the college admissions mania squeezes out of us. It makes us forget what we inherently know.

We know, for instance, that many people hit their strides late in life—later than college, sometimes by decades—and that who they are when an admissions office evaluates them and even who they are when they finish their higher education isn't who they'll be years later. We know that extrapolating too far from the present into the future is a fool's game: At different times, we're different versions of ourselves. One version exists on the cusp of college. There will be other versions down the road. And they'll be dealing with circumstances, professionally and personally, that we can't begin to imagine.

We know that many of the attributes that best position someone for professional success—and for contentment, which isn't the same thing—aren't fully reflected in a high school transcript or easily distilled in a college admissions application. Many people flourish in their careers and their relationships because of the buoyancy of their spirits, their talents for establishing a positive rapport with everyone around them and the emotional wisdom with which they separate what's vitally important from what's not. Their gift isn't their measurable intellect but their personality, and while it may come through in better grades and flattering references from teachers who take a shine to them, or in leadership positions attained by dint of their popularity, it's probably not going to show up as readily in the material that an admissions officer evaluates as other, more quantifiable gifts do.

We know that people are often defined as sharply by setbacks, and by their responses to them, as by getting what they want when they want it, including a "yes" from Yale or a welcome from the University of Chicago. One of the most potentially meaningful aspects of the college admissions process is, in fact, rejection. And that's partly because college is, or should be, disruptive. It's about becoming a new person, not letting the ink dry on who, at seventeen or eighteen, you already are. In that sense defeat can be a springboard. And figuring out how to rebound from disappointment is infinitely more beneficial than any diploma.

We also know, or should know, that by infusing the choice of a college with so much anxiety, we're taking an exhilarating crossroads and turning it into something sour and sinister and gratuitously injurious. *Going to college*: That phrase—that adventure—has lost some of the thrill it once had, and not just because so many Americans now pursue higher education, making it a more routine occurrence. No, we've sucked some of the magic from college by letting college get sucked into our tedious, soulless preoccupation with status.

But not entirely, at least not yet. And that's what keeps Tara Dowling, the Choate college counselor, moving forward, despite all of the parents who ask her why their kids didn't get into an Ivy, despite the cynical games that some students play, despite their insistence on looking past and down on so many terrific but underexposed schools, despite every other facet of the frenzy.

"Every year I ask myself: 'Do I want to do this again?'" Dowling said. "'Do I want to do this one more year?' But in the end, as a first-generation college student who got no help from a counselor and whose life was changed by college one hundred percent, I believe in the transformational power of higher education and the self-awareness and self-actualization that comes from the process of applying to college."

If students are steered through it correctly, if at least some measure of calm can be made to prevail, "kids become aware of who they are," she said. "Kids become aware of what they want. I love being part of that process: watching the light bulb go on, watching them work their buns off. And in the end they all go to college, and their lives *are* changed."

There's something else we know, and it's the forgetting of this that's perhaps most curious, and saddest. We know that where we go to college will have infinitely less bearing on our fulfillment in life than so much else: the wisdom with which we choose our romantic partners; our interactions with the communities that we inhabit; our generosity toward the families that we inherit and the families that we make. We know that no college can compete with getting any one of those things right, let alone getting several or all of them right. Then the admissions process comes along, and it shoves all that knowledge to the side.

That's what baffled and horrified Susan Bodnar.

EPILOGUE

You met Bodnar in an earlier chapter. She was the one whose son, Ronen, was rejected from an elite preschool. It was his frog that was only hopping. When I corresponded with her in the spring and summer of 2014, as Ronen finished his junior year and began his summer break before senior year, she told me, "It feels a bit like that right now. His frog is only hopping."

We were on the phone, and it was one of Ronen's last days of school, and he was awaiting word on a final paper in an English class for which he desperately wanted an A-minus. He feared that he'd get only a B or B-plus. Because English was supposed to be one of his strengths, a B or B-plus wouldn't look good to an Ivy League school.

"My son is texting me his final grades right now," Bodnar said at the start of our conversation. Her voice was tense. She knew that. She apologized for it. She hated herself for being so wound up but she wasn't sure how not to be. She vowed to stop mentioning the imminent English grade. She repeatedly broke that vow. "He's going to get a B in English," she predicted. "His first B. End of his college dreams."

Ronen goes to Manhattan's Trinity School, which I mentioned earlier in terms of its low kindergarten acceptance rate. His sister, who is younger than he is, goes to Horace Mann, another private school in New York City's "Ivy Preparatory School League." But Bodnar, a psychologist, and her husband, a technology researcher, don't have the kind of money that Trinity and Horace Mann cost; both kids are on half scholarships. And up until Ronen's junior year, she took pride in not leading a life as posh and pampered as so many of the other families with children at those schools, at not participating in all of their expensive rituals, at having to find ways at home to economize, like most Americans do.

For their vacations, the family doesn't go to fancy resorts. They hike and camp. Dinners out in restaurants are rare. "I cook all of our meals," Bodnar said. And while other families turned to caterers and decorators for their kids' birthday parties, Bodnar felt that she could do as well with her own efforts and ingenuity. "There was a way that we felt we were on some sort of equal footing, and everything was hunky dory," she said.

Then, she said, "It was like someone skied into me and I was knocked on my face."

What happened was all the junior year talk at Trinity about college admissions. Belatedly, she realized that the families and kids around her and Ronen had been doing all of this concerted prepping, all of this vigorous strategizing. She also had her eyes opened to just how unforgiving the odds for getting into the most selective schools had become. Ronen was an exemplary student; she'd always assumed he'd go to the school of his choice. But exemplary wasn't good enough anymore.

She said that as summer approached, "one friend said to me very casually, 'My son is going to Yale for pre-law for a week and then studying (acting) with Stella Adler for four weeks and then going to Harvard for a pre-med program.' He's between his *sophomore* and junior years. You hear that and you shrink. You just shrink. My son's going to music camp, again, for the fourth year, because he really loves music."

Trinity provides dedicated SAT tutoring for small groups of its students, and Ronen had of course participated in that. But he didn't do an additional private tutor: That was outside the family's budget and their sense of how much privilege and entitlement anyone should exploit. Ronen was already going to what was considered one of the finest secondary schools in New York City. All these add-ons seemed sort of obscene. Still, Bodnar wondered: Had it been a mistake not to sign her son up for them, to figure out a way?

For instance, she said, "It never occurred to us to put him in a Saturday pre-college program. It turns out that's a big deal. And there are people in the summertime who aren't hiking or camping but going on world community-service trips that cost a lot of money." But not Ronen.

"We just don't stack up," she said. "We're just not going to stack up."

She'd never thought that way before, she said, and she didn't want to think that way now, but she also wanted her son to have every option in life and, yes, every advantage, including a school with a name that snapped people to attention, at least if that was the school he preferred. And she didn't want him doubting himself or feeling hurt. But they were hurtling toward a junction that seemed designed to diminish him.

"Suddenly we have been transported to an alternate universe known as the potential applicant," she wrote to me in an email. "We speak a new language with words like *legacy* and *diversity* and *institutional priorities* and *Ivy League.* Suddenly our son is being looked at through rubrics, assessments and cutoffs." She didn't want Ronen to buy into all of that but wasn't sure how to responsibly pull out of it. "We don't know how to get off this train," she continued. "I haven't slept since we went on our college tours during spring break. I wake up crying and hurting. I'm considering medication. Yes, me. Ms. Natural, who never even takes cold medicine."

What Bodnar found especially odd about her susceptibility to all of this was that she saw, in her very own psychotherapy practice, how damaging it could be when a kid was allowed or encouraged to become too invested in the admissions game and its results. She treated young people in their teens and twenties who'd been pulled into "the vortex," as she called it. "It's like we are mass-producing perfect robots posing as kids," she wrote to me in one email.

And on the phone she said, "They have no space to be kids. They're not feeling that the work they're doing is their own. They're succeeding, but it's not coming from within. And they're having a lot of psychological problems because of it: obsessive-compulsive disorder; freaking out because they're not perfect." She wondered aloud about some of the blackout drug-taking and binge drinking that's happening on college campuses. Were the roots of it in the high-pressure, overprogrammed secondary school experience that a kid doggedly pursuing the most elite colleges has?

The possibility spooked her, so she was working on some kind of balance. She was trying to celebrate Ronen for who he was, whether it turned out to be admissions bait or not. She was reminding herself that a place like Harvard or Princeton or Yale probably wasn't even right for him. "He's not an alpha male," she said. "He loves the woods. He loves poetry. That kind of school could be a disaster, not a boost. So who knows? Where's he going to feel happy? Where are they going to like him? We're telling him: Be honest. Be yourself. His Common Application essay is going to be about his joy of being in the wilderness. Is that going to be a winning essay? Probably not. But it's who he is."

The verdict on his English paper did arrive before the end of the phone call during which she'd been waiting for it. He got a B-plus, which would also, then, be his grade for the course. The next day, Bodnar emailed me and told me that Ronen had come home "angry with himself for failing" to do better. "He believed he failed his passion," she wrote. "He is 16!

"This is what we told our son," she continued, and in her message I heard echoes of the reassurance that Diana Levin had given her son, Matt, the boy who'd fantasized about Yale, Princeton and Brown but was heading off to Lehigh instead. Bodnar said to Ronen: "This is not the end of your journey. This is a learning experience. You will be better at whatever college you attend because you have had this experience. You still have time to develop the competence to match your passion. It will happen. Trust your inner voice and one day it will match up with what you can demonstrate on the outside. Do not give up."

Here is what I would like to say to her: Those very words prove that your son has something so much more essential and nourishing and lasting than whatever he's going to get on whichever campus becomes his home, because that's only his temporary home. You've given him his real home, the one he had before college and the one he'll have after, and just look at all that it brims with, and consider all that it will bequeath him.

You once told me that when he and his sister and you and your husband go camping, you not only "talk a lot" but "sing together." Ronen will always have that music. You once told me that for you and your husband, your family "has been the center of our existence, and our love for our children our heartbeat." That rhythm will forever be his. So will the wilderness and so will poetry, so long as he isn't permitted to lose sight of them.

You told me that "enthusiasm inhabits his every gesture." If that stays true through this crazy college crossroads and remains the case beyond it, he'll be a graced man. Probably a happy one, too.

Acknowledgments

If I named all of the people who helped me in some way—with interviews, with suggestions, with encouragement, with friendship—I'd need pages and pages. I hope that all of you know who you are and that you have my gratitude. I'll confine this very short list to those people without whom this book simply wouldn't exist. Thank you, thank you, thank you to Tom Nickolas, Elinor Burkett, Jennifer Steinhauer, Alessandra Stanley, Gail Collins, Trish Hall, Andy Rosenthal, Barbara Laing, Anne Kornblut, Campbell Brown, Ben Greenberg, Maddie Caldwell, Jamie Raab, Lisa Bankoff, Robert Niles, Alex Halpern Levy, Susan Bodnar, Diana Levin and my uncle James Bruni, the educator in the Bruni clan.

Index

LISA GREENWALD

Welcome to Dog Beach

Library of Congress Cataloging-in-Publication Data
Greenwald, Lisa.
Dog Beach / Lisa Greenwald.
pages cm
Summary: Eleven-year-old Remy loves the traditions of Seagate, the island where her family spends every summer vacation, but after her grandmother and a special dog dies, and her relationships with best friends Bennett and Micayla change, Remy takes comfort in the company of Dog Beach—where she hatches a plan to bring her friends closer and recapture the Seagate magic.
ISBN 978-1-4197-1018-6 (alk. paper)
[1. Summer—Fiction. 2. Vacations—Fiction. 3. Beaches—Fiction. 4. Friendship—Fiction. 5. Dogs—Fiction. 6. Dog walking—Fiction.] I. Title.
PZ7.G85199Do 2014
[Fic]—dc23
2013023282

THE ART OF BOOKS SINCE 1949
115 West 18th Street
New York, NY 10011
www.abramsbooks.com

For Aunt Emily, dog lover extraordinaire

And in memory of my beloved apricot poodle
Yoffi, the best dog in the history of dogs,
who I still believe may have been part human

On Seagate Island, there are three kinds of people: the lucky ones, the luckier ones, and the luckiest ones.

The lucky ones are the people who come for a weekend or maybe even a week. They stay at the Seagate Inn or they find a last-minute rental.

The luckier ones are the people who rent a house for the whole summer, Memorial Day to Labor Day. They usually come back summer after summer and stay in the same house.

And the luckiest ones are the people like me. I don't want to sound conceited—I'm grateful for how lucky I am. Because when it comes to Seagate Island, there's no doubt that I am the luckiest. I've spent every summer of my life on Seagate Island in my grandmother's house.

I was born at the end of May, so I spent my first three

months here. And I'll spend every summer here for the rest of my life. It's probably weird for me to think that far ahead, since I'm only eleven. But trust me—I will.

"Remy," I hear my mom calling from inside the house. I give her a few minutes to come outside and find me. It's kind of an unofficial house rule that if one of us is outside, the other one has to come out if they want to talk. No one should have to go inside to talk unless it's raining. On Seagate Island, our time outside by the sea is sacred. We've only been here for a week, and we have the whole summer stretched out in front of us, but we still don't take our outside time for granted.

I hear the quiet creak of the screen door, and then my mom pulls over the other wicker chair to sit next to me.

"Don't be mad, okay?" she asks, but it sounds more like a command than a question.

This can't be good.

"I just ran into Amber Seasons, and she's in a pickle," my mom starts. I wonder why people use the word *pickle* to mean a problem. In my mind, pickles are one of the most delicious foods. But I also get why people hate them. Bennett hates pickles. In fact, if he orders a hamburger and someone puts a pickle on his plate, he has to send the whole meal back. He feels bad about it, but he does it anyway. That's how much he hates pickles.

But Amber Seasons's being in a pickle isn't surprising. I've known her since I was born, pretty much, and she's always been in a pickle. She's fifteen years older than I am, and no matter what's going on, she always seems frazzled.

"What kind of pickle?" I ask.

"She offered to teach an art class for Seagate Seniors on Monday and Wednesday mornings at ten. But then her babysitter ended up staying in New Jersey for the summer, and now she needs someone to watch her son. She told me that's when he naps, so you'd just be sitting in her house every morning for a few hours."

I can't believe this is happening. This was going to be the first real summer that Micayla, Bennett, and I were allowed to roam free, all day, and do whatever we wanted.

In previous summers we were allowed to go off on our own, but only for a few hours at a time, and we needed to check in and always tell our parents where we were. But this summer was going to be different.

We're eleven now, going into sixth grade. That's middle school for Bennett and Micayla; it'll be the last year of elementary school for me.

And now I have to cut into that completely free time to watch Amber Seasons's son.

On the other hand, babysitting is kind of cool and something real teenagers do. I guess I'm older now and my mom thinks I'm more mature. I'm flattered that she thinks I can handle it.

"Please, Remy," my mom says. She's sitting on the wicker armchair with her head resting on her hands, and she looks pretty desperate. It's not even a favor for her, it's a favor for Amber Seasons, but I bet my mom already said that I'd do it. My mom has this weird thing about helping people solve their problems. She gets all jazzed up and has this intense, burning desire to help them, like she can't stop until she makes whatever situation they're in a little better. Helping other people makes her happier than anything else.

"Fine." I sigh, all defeated, but knowing I would never get out of it. "Maybe Micayla and Bennett can come with me some mornings?"

My mom considers that for a moment. "Well, you can certainly talk to Amber and ask her if it's okay."

She goes inside to finish getting ready for her afternoon swimming session, and I sit back in my chair and think. How bad will it really be? It's only a few hours two mornings a week.

My mom always says how good it makes her feel when she helps other people. So maybe I'll be like that too. I'll help Amber, and then I'll feel better. About everything.

Being sad on Seagate is kind of an oxymoron. The two things don't go together at all. But this year is different. I'm sad on Seagate, and I can't seem to help it.

"I got you two scoops," Micayla tells me when she walks through the house and finds me on the back porch. That's another thing about Seagate—no one locks their doors, and we all just barge into each other's homes. It can be awkward sometimes, like when I saw Bennett's mom getting out of the shower, but she had a towel on, and we just laughed about it. But the rest of the time it feels like the whole island's our home.

The turquoise ice cream cups from Sundae Best, Seagate Island's oldest and best ice cream shop, somehow make the ice cream taste even more delicious. I always get espresso cookie, and Micayla always gets cherry chip. When it comes to ice cream, we are as different as can be. But when it comes to almost everything else, we're pretty much the same.

Well, except that I'm white and she's black. And then there's also the difference of our hair—she wears it in braids year-round, and I have thin, straight, boring, not-quite-blonde and not-quite-brown hair that barely stays in an elastic band. Hers always looks good, even after she's just woken up.

Her parents are both from St. Lucia, in the Caribbean. They moved to the United States when they were kids but didn't meet until college. They have amazing accents, and when we're a little bit older, they're going to take me with them when they go back to visit Micayla's grandma in St. Lucia.

We take our ice cream cups and walk down the wooden stairs of my deck to the beach. Even though I do this at least ten times a day, I feel lucky every single time. On Seagate, the beach is my backyard, and I'm pretty sure there is nothing better than that in the whole world.

Sometimes we don't even bother with towels or chairs—we just sit down on the sand. We dig our feet in as far as they will go and we eat our ice cream. Our plan is to meet up with Bennett when he's done playing Ping-Pong with his dad, and then we'll decide what to do for the rest of the day.

"I hope this will cheer you up," Micayla says, burrowing through her ice cream cup for a chunk of chocolate. "I've never seen you sad on Seagate before."

She's right about that. But she's also never really seen me anywhere else, except for the time her dad brought her to New York City for a last-minute meeting. Her mom had flown to St. Lucia to visit Micayla's grandma, and Micayla couldn't stay home alone. So Micayla came to New York and we spent the day together. I don't think I was sad that day, so she's never really seen me sad anywhere, not just on Seagate. But I know what she means.

"I'm happy to be here. I just keep picturing Danish running on the beach . . . And his dog bed is still upstairs. I wish my parents would just throw it out, but I think they're too sad to do it. And the Pooch Parade during Seagate Halloween will be so horrible without him."

"I know," she says, not looking at me. "Well, maybe we can figure out something else to do during the Pooch Parade."

It's probably weird that it's not even July yet and I'm already thinking about Seagate Halloween, which takes place over Labor Day weekend. But it's one of the biggest traditions of the summer—everyone participates. Seagate Halloween is exactly the same every year, and that's the way I like it.

Bennett dresses up as Harvey from Sundae Best. He wears his shorts really high and a Seagate baseball cap. Micayla dresses up as a mermaid, like the statue you see when you first get off the ferry. I dress up as a beach pail. My mom makes me a new costume every year out of painted cardboard, and it comes out awesome every time. And the best part was that Danish would dress up as the shovel! We'd get the biggest sand shovel we could find and strap it to his back, and I'd carry him, so we looked like a perfect pair—beach pail and sand shovel. So happy together.

We've been on Seagate Island for a week, and I've been partially sad the whole time. Happy to be here, but sad without Danish. I don't want to be sad here. It's my most favorite place in the universe. But I can't seem to help it.

Danish was my grandma's dog, so for many years I only ever saw him on Seagate. Our house here was Grandma's house. When she died three years ago, we got Danish and the house, although it always seemed like they were partially ours to begin with.

During the summer, Danish slept in my bed. He spent all day with Micayla, Bennett, and me. Everyone thought he was my dog. And the house—well, the house felt like ours too. The yellow room with the canopy bed was mine. No one else slept there. Mom and Dad had the room around the corner with the blue-and-ivory-striped wallpaper. And Grandma's room was at the end of the hallway. She had her own bathroom, but she'd let us use it.

All year she'd be busy on Seagate, volunteering at the elementary school to help the kids with math, setting up the concert schedule for the summer, taking Danish to Dog Beach even when it was a little bit cold outside. Even though I knew all that, I always imagined her waiting patiently for us to come back for the summer. We'd come for weekends sometimes, but that didn't really count. Summer was summer.

Summer was when we were all together. Grandma would make her famous corn chowder. Mom would set up her easel on the back deck and paint landscapes of the ocean, and Dad would try to play Ping-Pong with everyone on the island at least once.

After Grandma died, we were all really sad. We couldn't imagine being on Seagate without her. But when we came back that next summer, being there was more comforting than we expected it to be. Everyone wanted to tell us stories about Grandma. Dad did some work on the house to spruce it up a little bit, and Mom organized a special concert in Grandma's memory. Now the annual concert series is known as the Sally Bell Seagate Concert Calendar.

Danish died this past December. It was sudden, and I don't really like to even think about it. All winter and spring, I kept hoping that being back on Seagate would be comforting, the way it was after Grandma died. But so far, it's not. So far, I just miss him. It was always Micayla, Bennett, and me—with Danish running along with us.

A key member of our crew is missing.

"I have to tell you something," Micayla and I say at the exact same time, and then we both burst into laughter.

"You first," I say. She probably has more exciting news than my babysitting job.

"Avery Sanders has a boyfriend," Micayla tells me.

"Yeah?" I ask. "She didn't mention it to me when I saw her at Pastrami on Rye the other night."

"Just saw her at Sundae Best. She was going on and on about it. She said this new kid moved to Seagate in the middle of the year. And he's, like, a real-life boyfriend."

I look at Micayla, surprised. "I wonder why she didn't tell me before."

Avery Sanders is a friend of ours, but not a best friend. She moved to Seagate four years ago, and she lives here year-round. She's the type of friend that we never really call to make plans, but if we run into each other, we'll hang out.

She's nice, but she's one of those girls who seemed like a teenager when we were, like, nine, and she'd always say that Bennett was my boyfriend, even when I didn't really know what a boyfriend was.

The past few times I talked to her, she told me that she was bored with Seagate and that it has really changed since she moved here.

I always listened to what she said, even though none of it made sense. How could Seagate be boring? And how could it change? Seagate will always be perfect, and summer after summer, it always stays the same. That's the beauty of it.

"I think her grandparents live here year-round now too," Micayla tells me. "That's what my mom said."

Actually, that's another group of lucky people on Seagate—the year-rounders. I always wonder if that makes them luckier than the luckiest or somewhere in between. On the one hand, they never have to leave Seagate. But on the other hand, they have to see almost everyone else leave. And they don't get that amazing anticipation—the excited, heart-bursting feeling of coming back.

"What did you have to tell me?" Micayla asks.

I explain the whole pickle situation with Amber Seasons.

"That's cool," Micayla says. "It's, like, your first real job."

"You think?"

"Yeah, for sure." She digs deep in her cup for the last little bit of ice cream. "And it's only a few hours. You won't miss anything."

"I guess."

Micayla gives me her please-cheer-up smile again and taps my leg. "Come on. Let's go meet Bennett at Ping-Pong. Bennett always makes you laugh after five minutes."

She's right about that.

"Who's he playing?" I ask Micayla as we get closer to the stadium. It's not really a stadium, but since Ping-Pong is such a huge deal on Seagate Island, that's what we call it. It's really just a big overhang in the middle of the island with fifteen Ping-Pong tables underneath it. This way people can play rain or shine.

"He said he was meeting his dad here. You know they take their Sunday games really seriously."

Bennett's dad only comes to Seagate on the weekends. He's a big lawyer in Boston. He flies in every Friday and flies back every Sunday on these teeny-tiny planes. Bennett and his dad always have a heated Ping-Pong match right before he leaves on Sunday afternoon. Bennett usually wins.

"Remy! Mic!" Bennett shouts to us. "Where have you guys been?"

We walk closer to his table and see that he's playing against a kid with spiky hair and a shirt with a picture of a video game controller on it.

"Yo, Calvin." Bennett turns to the spiky-haired kid. He's really not the type of person to use the word *yo*, so hearing him say it is strange. "This is Remy." Bennett points to me. "And this is Micayla." He points to her.

"Hey," Calvin says, looking down at his untied sneakers like he doesn't really care to talk to us. We say "hey" back, and then Bennett and Calvin return to their game.

There's a girl sitting on one of the wooden benches along the side of the stadium. "Calvin, come on," she says. "Grandpa said we needed to be back by three."

"Claire." He keeps playing and doesn't look at her. "Shut up."

"Calvin!" The girl yells this time. "Fine. Whatever. I'm leaving you here. I hope you get lost."

I guess she doesn't realize that it's pretty much impossible to be lost on Seagate.

She huffs, annoyed, as she stands up and walks away. She doesn't introduce herself to us, and she doesn't say good-bye to Bennett. She's wearing white cutoffs, and they're really, really short, so she adjusts them as she walks away.

"My sister is such a bore," Calvin says.

"Most girls are," Bennett replies.

What did he just say? I look at Micayla to see if she heard it, but she's more involved in their game than I realized. Bennett Newhouse, one of my best friends since birth, just said that most girls are bores. At least he said "most" and not "all," but *still*.

Finally Calvin leaves and Bennett walks over to Micayla and me. "Surfing?" he asks. As much as I want to go surf, I'm still kind of shaken up. If he thinks most girls are bores, does he think I'm a bore? Or does he not think of me as a girl?

"There will be time for surfing after we discuss what just happened," I tell Bennett. Micayla cracks up. She says that I speak in a really formal way because both of my parents are on-air journalists. She tells me I should talk more like a kid. I think I talk like a kid most of the time, but my more formal speech comes out when I'm angry. Like I am right now. "Why did you say that girls are bores?"

"Uh-oh, Investigator Remy is here again!" Bennett laughs and raises a hand to slap Micayla five, but she denies him. "Rem, relax. I just met the kid. I was trying to make him feel comfortable."

I give him a casual eye roll. That's a lame excuse if I ever heard one. "Well, who is he anyway? A weekender?"

Bennett shuffles some stray sand around with the toe of his flip-flop. "No. He's my next-door neighbor."

"What?" Micayla exclaims. "What happened to Mr. Brookfield?"

"That's his grandson! The one he was always telling us about." Bennett widens his eyes at us, and I can't tell if he wants us to be excited or not. "Remember?"

"Kind of." I shrug. I do remember, but I don't want to admit it; I'm still mad at Bennett. Mr. Brookfield always went on and on about his grandchildren and how we'd love them if we only knew them. But they always went to camp in the summer and had no interest in Seagate.

That was okay with me. I already had friends, and while people say you can never have too many, I was happy with the way things had always been.

"That girl was his twin, then," I say, putting it all together. "Didn't Mr. Brookfield always say he had twin grandchildren?"

"Yup. Calvin and Claire."

Calvin and Claire—sounds like a matched pair. I decide that I'll think of them as the C Twins.

"Please tell me they're just here for the week," Micayla says, and I'm glad she does, because that means I don't have to. "July Fourth week and then they're going home?"

"Nope. They'll be here all summer." Bennett raises his eyebrows, like he's not sure why this is such a big deal. "So? Surfing?"

"Why are they here?" I ask.

Micayla chimes in, "Yeah. I thought they loooved camp."

It's not that we don't believe camp can be great. I go to school with a girl named Rachel Kleiger who claims camp is the best place on earth. She feels about camp the way I feel about Seagate. But we just never understood how these twins could choose a camp over Seagate. Seagate is perfect.

And anyone who has an option to be here should be here.

"I don't know, guys," Bennett says. "I just met them today." He backs up a little bit. "You're both acting weird. I'm going to surf."

Micayla and I hang back a minute and tell Bennett that we'll meet him at the beach. After he leaves, I say, *"We're* acting weird? *He's* acting weird." I look at Micayla and wait for her to say something. "Right?"

She shrugs. I wish she'd agree with me more. "I'm still thinking about that kid Calvin's hair. It was unusual, right?"

"I forgot what it looked like already," I lie. I don't know why I lie, but I do.

"Brown and spiky?" I can't believe Micayla just believed me.

"Oh yeah. That's not really so unusual."

On the way back to the beach we pick up our surfboards and change into our bathing suits. They're still wet from our morning swim, but we don't mind. They're just going to get wet again anyway. On Seagate, it's okay to walk around in a damp bathing suit. No one judges you. There's no pressure to show off. I feel kind of guilty that I'm so judgy about Calvin and his sister. Maybe they're not that bad.

Maybe it's just that I'm still feeling off. Things are different. Without Danish, I can't seem to get into the summer groove. Add to that Bennett's weird comment, and Micayla being so focused on their game and Calvin's hair. Everything seems a little strange.

I decide to put it all out of my head and try to stop thinking for just a minute. Micayla and I run into the sea holding hands like we always do. We like to swim for a few minutes before we attempt to surf. It's kind of like how the Olympic divers go into that hot tub before they dive, or runners stretch before a race.

We need to warm up.

Maybe that's kind of how it is with summer too. You have to get back into the swing of things. I decide that this past week has been my warm-up week, my few minutes in the ocean before surfing.

Everyone needs time to adjust. Even on Seagate. Even me.

Danish was a miniature poodle. He had apricot fur
and weighed thirteen pounds, and he acted more like a
human than a dog. He also had expensive taste. One time,
for my cousin's bar mitzvah, we had to stay at a motel in
Toronto. It was an okay place, but Danish hated it there. He
barked the whole time. We had to take him to the bar mitzvah party because the other hotel guests were so sick of his
barking! At the party, he sat at the table with us and even
won the limbo competition.

Then, a few months later, we traveled to Washington, DC,
for my mom's friend's wedding, and we stayed at a real hotel
with a pool and a ballroom and everything. It was way fancier, and Danish loved it. They gave him special dog treats
and had a dog sitter come and walk him while we were at
the wedding. He didn't even care that we left and didn't bark

once. We were treated like celebrities there, and Danish knew it.

Danish liked going for walks, but he preferred to sit with us on the couch while we watched TV. He ate his meals when we ate our meals. His food bowl and water bowl sat on a mat beside our kitchen table. When he was done eating, he'd hop up onto his bench near the kitchen window and wait for us to finish.

After Grandma died, my mom bought that bench just for Danish. It's antique, with a gold velvet cushion and brass finishes, and it was the perfect width for Danish. Most people don't buy human furniture specifically for their dogs. But Danish had human tastes, and we did what made him happy.

Danish adjusted to life in Manhattan, but he was happiest on Seagate, just like all of us. He could roam free there, like I could, and he didn't really need a leash anyway—he always stayed right by my side.

This is going to sound crazy and it doesn't make any sense, but I always believed Danish would live forever. We read that book *Tuck Everlasting* last year in school, and so I'd tell myself that Danish drank the magic potion, just like Jesse. And that Danish and I would always be together.

I guess most of me knew that was totally made up and that no one lives forever—but a tiny part of me believed it anyway.

I wait a moment, wipe my tears, and take a deep breath before I go into Amber Seasons's house. It's my first day of work, and I don't want to look like a complete basket case. Her son'll be napping, but I still need to seem professional. At least that's what my mom said.

I'll be okay eventually. I know that. I asked the vet, Dr. Laterno, how long people usually feel sad after their dog dies, and she said it depends. That everyone is different. I just wanted a set answer. Like, six weeks and you'll feel much better. Or even six months. Just so I knew what I'd be dealing with. But I guess it doesn't work that way.

"Remy, I can't thank you enough," Amber says as she opens the door to let me in. "You're a lifesaver. Hudson is upstairs sleeping, and he'll probably nap the whole time I'm out. I was lucky to get a good sleeper." She says the last part under her breath.

I nod. Don't people say that "they slept like a baby" when they've had a good night's sleep? I thought that meant that all babies slept well.

"My girl is the difficult one," she continues.

"You have two kids?" I ask. "My mom only mentioned one."

"Oh, no." She laughs. "I have one kid and one dog. I refer to her as my girl." Right then a little Yorkie comes running in. "This is my darling, Marilyn Monroe. But ever since Hudson was born, she's become ultra-feisty and jealous and, let's face it, pretty demanding."

I nod, slowly, trying to see what she's talking about. But all I observe is an adorable little Yorkie with a hot pink bow on her head. She jumps up as high as my knee and wags her tail, and when I pet her, I swear she smiles. A smiling dog! Danish was a smiler too, though I think I was the only one who could really see it.

"So Hudson will be asleep, but if you can give Mari a little attention, that would be amazing." She smiles and gives me a hug. "You're the best, Remy."

A few minutes later, Amber is out the door carrying an easel and a coffee can of paintbrushes. I quickly tiptoe upstairs and put my ear to the door of Hudson's room. Nothing. Good.

I tiptoe back downstairs and make myself comfortable on Amber's gray burlap couch. I take a copy of *Ocean Living* magazine off the coffee table, but before I even pull back the front cover, I hear the jingling of Marilyn Monroe's tags and she jumps up onto the couch and starts licking my face like I'm her new favorite person in the world.

"I'm happy to see you too, Marilyn Monroe."

She licks me even more and then settles down, sitting so close to me that one of her paws rests on my leg.

I try to go back to reading, but it's difficult because Marilyn Monroe is just sitting there, staring at me, as if she's asking me, "What's next?" or "What are we going to do now?" So I put down the magazine and look back at her.

"I used to have a dog," I start. And I tell her all about Danish. She barks at just the right spots, like she understands me and gets what I'm saying. And when I tell her that Danish died this past winter, she lets out a little whimper.

"You're sweet, Marilyn Monroe," I say. "Thanks for listening." She licks my hand, as if to say she's always here to listen. For some reason, she's the easiest person to talk to. Okay, I know she's not a person. Easiest creature to talk to?

I wonder why that is. I never had trouble talking to Micayla before, but I haven't told her all this stuff about Danish and how I'm feeling. Maybe it's gotten harder for some reason.

"If I had known you'd be here, I wouldn't have been so grumbly about taking this job." She looks at me, head tilted. "Don't tell Amber I said that. Or Hudson."

She lets out a little yelp, and I'm pretty sure my secret is safe with her.

I'm surprised when Amber shows up just a little bit later. It feels like she's only been gone ten minutes, but I look at the clock, and it's noon. Hudson's still asleep, and Marilyn Monroe is sipping some water out of her bowl, dainty and delicate, not getting any on the floor and very little on her face.

Amber thanks me again and again, and I tell her it was no trouble, but in my head, I'm wondering if I'm the one who should be thanking her.

Micayla has a theory that avoiding Dog Beach is making me sadder about Danish.

"Let's just go there. It's your favorite place, and turning away every time we walk by isn't helping," she says one morning.

Dog Beach is pretty crowded for only eleven in the morning. It's at the farthest end of Seagate, but since Seagate is a pretty small island, nothing is really that far from anything else. With unobstructed views of the ocean and the signature Seagate white fencing, Dog Beach is one of the prettiest places on the island. Even non-dog-owners think so.

I look around at all the dogs, and I'm not sure Micayla's theory is right. I'm sad all over again. Danish's friend Cookie the beagle is here, and Palm the Pomeranian. Palm's owners live on Seagate half the year, and West Palm Beach, Florida, the other half, so that's why they named him Palm. Most of Danish's friends were little dogs, but his best friend was a Dalmatian named Hampton. They were an odd pair, one so big and one so little, but they'd play together and look out for each other. And now Hampton's here on his own, off to the side playing with a yellow Lab. Must be a newcomer. I get a scraped-knee stinging feeling that maybe Danish has been replaced.

In a way, Hampton and Danish kind of reminded me of Bennett and me. Hampton was outgoing and boisterous while Danish was quiet, taking everything in. But they got along so well.

The dogs on Seagate are like the people—you can tell which ones are here for a week for the first time and which ones will be here until August, like they are every summer.

"Aren't you glad to be here?" Micayla asks, tying her braids into a low ponytail. "Let's go sit on one of the benches and people- and dog-watch. I'm too hot to stand up."

I nod. "Are you sure you're okay? You're not going to have some crazy allergic attack?"

Micayla is seriously allergic to dogs that shed, but she loves them anyway. She can't resist petting them, and then she gets all sneezy and her eyes turn red and watery and she complains a lot. But she still loves them.

"Of course, I'm fine." She smiles.

Bennett goes to play with the dogs. He picks up one of the extra Frisbees and starts playing fetch with a golden retriever. Bennett's a dog person even though his family has never had one.

The golden retriever's owner (who must be a newcomer, since I don't recognize her) comes over to play too. She looks like she's around forty, but I can see Bennett saying something that's making her laugh.

Bennett can talk to anyone. It doesn't matter how old they are, if they're a girl or a boy, even if they're human, really. I just saw him talking to that golden retriever. He called out, "Mickey, here boy!" just like he'd been friends with that dog for years.

While we're watching the dogs and Bennett play, I tell Micayla about Marilyn Monroe and how we had a pretty awesome time together.

"Is she here now?" Micayla asks.

"No, I don't see her." I admit—I'm a little disappointed. I was sort of hoping she'd be here.

"Well, she can be, like, your almost-dog this summer," Micayla says. "Do you think your parents will want to get another dog one day?"

"I doubt it. A dog isn't like a new pair of flip-flops that you can just replace," I tell her. "It takes time."

"I know," she says. "I mean, I don't know, because I've never had a dog, but I know you can't just trade one for another."

Micayla links arms with me even though we're still sitting on the bench. "Come on, let's walk and look at the dogs."

We spend the next hour playing with a pair of Malteses named Snowball and Marshmallow. They're puppies, and the Howells just got them. The Howells are an older couple who live on the other side of the island. We always see them at the deli, Pastrami on Rye. My mom always jokes that they don't even need a kitchen since it seems that they eat every meal there.

"How are you, Remy?" Mrs. Howell asks.

"Good," I reply. "Happy to be back on Seagate." I usually answer this way. I wish I had more to say, but nothing seems to come to mind. I used to be so good at talking to adults, but now I get nervous. I'm not sure why.

"Us too," Mrs. Howell says. "And these guys are so happy to be here. They were running in circles in our Brooklyn apartment. That hasn't been fun for any of us."

Snowball keeps jumping up on my legs and licking my knees, and it makes me laugh.

"She likes you, Rem," Micayla tells me.

The two white fluff balls keep jumping on us, and I love watching them. But they're not my dogs, and eventually we have to leave them behind. Micayla and I wave good-bye to Bennett, who says he'll catch up with us at my house, and we start walking home.

"It's settled," Micayla says. "You're amazing with dogs, and you're going to be a vet when you grow up."

"I don't know, Mic," I say. "But I'm glad I have you as my cheerleader."

"Speaking of cheerleaders," she says, kicking a rock along the path, "did you hear that Seagate is getting a basketball team this year? Avery Sanders told me, of course. Her boyfriend can't wait to try out."

"I didn't hear that." To be honest, I never think about the school here. I don't like to think about kids being here when I'm not. Maybe that's really selfish of me. But Seagate feels like a summer-only place sometimes.

"Yeah, for seventh and eighth graders."

"But who would they play? They'd have to take the bridge or the ferry for any matches." There's only one school on Seagate. It goes from kindergarten to eighth grade, and after that the kids have to go off the island for high school. It's only about a twenty-minute ferry ride or a quick drive over the bridge. It's not a big deal, but it's very different from what I'm used to. Back home in New York, I can walk to my school, and when I'm in high school, I'll probably take the subway. You're always connected when you've got a subway.

"Yeah, they play the other schools in Ferry Port and Seaside, I guess."

Micayla doesn't say much after that, and when we get to my house, my parents are sitting on the back porch reading the newspaper and drinking pink lemonade. They're both here for all of July, and then when August comes they take turns going back and forth to the city. When Grandma was here, they would go to the city more often, but even though I'm allowed to be alone a lot of the time, I can't stay alone overnight.

"Hi, girls," my mom says in her cheerful Seagate voice. I call it her Seagate voice because I rarely hear it in New York City. Back in New York, she's stressed and frazzled. She complains about people who honk too much, people who push on the subway, her boss, and how much everything costs. But on Seagate, that fades away. It's all painting and reading the newspaper and walks on the beach.

"Hi," I say. "Micayla's mom invited me to go for fish sandwiches with them tonight. Can I go?"

"No interest in my famous salmon casserole?" my dad asks. "Micayla?"

He always asks this, even though he knows the answer. I think that's why he asks, because he likes to see how we'll respond. Micayla always tries to be super polite and give a reasonable answer for why she can't eat it. He's been asking this same question for years, but she's still polite. That says something about her, I think.

"Well, I would, but my parents have been talking about fish sandwiches for days, and now I'm really craving one," she says. "But thanks anyway."

Super polite. Always. That's my best friend Micayla.

"Okay, okay. I'll try not to cry," my dad says. "Good thing Abby likes it."

My mom rolls her eyes. "Oh, I love it."

My dad's salmon casserole is one of the only things he can make, and it's his favorite. He tries really hard and adds new touches to it all the time, like green peppers and bread crumbs. But it's really just a mishmash of canned salmon, mayonnaise, spiral pasta, and random stuff he finds around the house. It kind of gives me a stomachache when I think about it. But my dad really wants us to like it, so we try to pretend that we do.

"So, Mr. and Mrs. Boltuck, how's the summer going?" Micayla starts, sitting next to my mom on the wicker love seat.

"Micayla, please." My mom smiles. "Call us Abby and Reed."

"Okay. Do-over." Micayla laughs. "Abby and Reed, how's the summer going?"

We sit around chatting, waiting for Bennett to show up, and then we'll walk over to Frederick's Fish together.

Micayla's telling us this story about how her dad's computer crashed and he lost the whole draft of the biography he's working on when I hear the creak of the screen door. I turn around and see Bennett running through the house. He bursts out onto the back deck. "Am I late? I'm so sorry. Little Jakey Steinman lured me in for a game of Ping-Pong. You know those six-year-olds. You can't say no. And he plays a mean game."

"Hi, Bennett," my dad says. "Have a seat."

Bennett sits way back in the chair, and it almost falls over. He makes this weird face, and Micayla and I crack up.

"You guys seem like you're up to no good," my dad says.

"Huh?" I ask.

"We were just at Dog Beach," Bennett says. "It's kind of like Remy's therapy. We think it will help her feel better about Danish."

My dad nods, then grins like he's going to say something funny—but I know from experience it won't be funny. At all. "Got it. For a second, I thought you and Remy were eloping!"

"Dad!" I yell. And even though he's made this joke a million times, it feels different this summer. I want to sink into the indentation in the middle of my lounge chair and bury myself in the sand. I can't look at my dad and I can't look at Bennett. All I can see is the wicker ottoman in the corner, the one that Danish liked to use for sunbathing. And then my sadness wipes away my embarrassment.

I'm not sure which feeling is worse.

People have been making jokes about Bennett and me getting married since we were tiny babies. His birthday is the day after mine. Apparently we were both terrible newborns, and we both spent our first summers on Seagate. His mom met my mom at a Seagate new mothers group, and they became best friends immediately.

They say we were the worst babies on the whole island, and they were so glad they found each other so that they could commiserate.

There are pictures of us as babies in sun tents on the beach, sleeping in our strollers side by side as our dads played Ping-Pong. Summer after summer, as we got older, the pictures evolved. They morphed into us trying to eat soft-serve in cones, the ice cream melting all over our faces, and of us burying each other in the sand or wearing different homemade costumes at the annual Seagate Halloween Parade.

We never really paid much attention to these jokes when Avery Sanders said them, or my dad or Bennett's dad or anyone else. But it feels different now. I just wish people would stop saying it.

My dad puts his feet up on the ottoman and looks at his watch. "Well, if you three are going for fish sandwiches, you'd better skedaddle."

He's right. It's a little after five and Frederick's Fish always gets lines for dinner. Micayla's brother and sister are here this week, so we'll be a big group.

Micayla, Bennett, and I walk over to Frederick's Fish, dragging our feet a little, not talking much.

"You seem better today," Micayla says, as we walk past SGI Sweets, Seagate's famous candy store. "I mean, not your usual Seagate happy, but better than you've been."

"I guess." When I hear myself say it, I can tell I'm acting like a downer. I should be more appreciative to Micayla for being so supportive. "Let's go into SGI," I tell her. "I want to buy you some of those gummy apples."

She doesn't argue with me. I knew she wouldn't. They're her absolute favorite candy, and they're impossible to find anywhere but Seagate. We buy a big bag and share them as we walk.

At the fish place, Micayla's family is already waiting in line. Her mom is sitting on one of the benches, and her dad, brother, and sister are standing a few feet away. They're smiling, but as we get closer, it seems that they're talking about something important—they're leaning in and speaking quietly. Micayla's mom is not a part of the conversation, and she seems to be daydreaming a little bit. We have to tap her a few times before she realizes that we're there.

"Are Zane and Ivy staying the whole week?" Micayla asks her mom.

When her mom replies, "I'm not sure yet," I start to get the feeling that something weird is going on. Micayla's mom is a super planner and she always knows what's going on— today, three weeks away, even a year from now.

I start to wonder why Bennett and I were invited to this family dinner. Even though we always do everything together, we usually have some separate family time. It's expected that there will be some nights when we're each with our own family; no one gets mad about it.

But as the meal goes on, no one says anything to explain the weird feeling in the air. I wonder if Bennett notices it too. Ivy and Zane make jokes about the new Seagate basketball team, and Micayla's dad talks about the biography he's working on about Franklin D. Roosevelt. Micayla's mom asks us questions about the other kids on Seagate and if the new salted caramel flavor at Sundae Best is as good as everyone says it is.

I keep sensing that something unusual is going on, but I have no idea what it is.

Good thing the fish sandwiches at Frederick's are as delicious as always, because when the food comes, eating it up is all I can think about.

A few mornings later, I wake up to a text from Bennett saying that he and Micayla are going to get egg-and-cheese sandwiches at Breakfast by the Boardwalk and that I should meet them there.

They get up much earlier than I do, so they usually don't text me until at least nine in the morning. When I look at the seashell clock above my doorway, I see that it's already close to ten. The text message came in at exactly nine, and I doubt they're still there. I sleep later on the mornings I'm not babysitting Hudson and hanging out with Marilyn Monroe.

When I text him back, he says that they already finished eating and that they're over at Mr. Brookfield's house and that I should come over.

I haven't seen the C Twins since the other day at Ping-Pong, and I'd nearly forgotten about them.

My parents are down by the community pool when I tell them I'm heading out. They look up from their books and tell me to have fun.

I'm wearing my yellow halter one-piece under my rainbow cover-up, and I realize it's the first time I've walked alone on Seagate since we got here. Normally I'm with Bennett or Micayla or both. And in the past, I never walked alone. I always had Danish with me.

I ring the doorbell to Mr. Brookfield's. I hardly ever ring doorbells on Seagate, but I don't know Mr. Brookfield well enough to just barge right in. He greets me at the door with a "howdy" and tells me how much taller I've gotten since last summer. I never know what to say to this, so I just smile.

"The gang's in the back," he tells me.

I'm on my way there when I hear the screaming. It startles me so much that I jump back a few feet and knock over one of Mr. Brookfield's porcelain director's chairs. He has them all over the house—miniature ones, wooden ones, metal ones, even a few large enough to sit on. Bennett told us that he was a movie fanatic, and when we'd visit before, we were always super careful not to break any of them.

I hear the screaming again, and I try to figure out who it is. Bennett never screams like that. It's definitely not Micayla. Claire is super girly and dainty—at least that's how she seemed the other day. Calvin? I can't figure out why he'd be screaming so loud.

It's not like any old scream, like during a fight or when

someone's scared, or even when they drop a mug accidentally. It's a high-powered scream, almost like in a cartoon,
but realistic, like it's coming from a regular person.

On Seagate, nothing all that scary happens, so no one
really screams. There aren't any mice or rats—at least, I
haven't seen any, thank God. There's no armed robbery or
mugging. There's the occasional ocean rescue, when a little
kid goes out too far, but they're always rescued right away.
The lifeguards on Seagate are the best in the world. That's
what my mom says.

I look around, wondering why Mr. Brookfield hasn't come
running out. When I finally spot him, he's just sitting in his
sunroom reading a magazine. I guess he's not worried that
someone is screaming really loudly in his backyard, so I try
not to worry about it either and head back.

Bennett, Micayla, and the C Twins sit crouched around
a little tape player. My grandma used to have one of them,
but we got rid of it after she died. We didn't even own any
cassette tapes, so there was no reason to own a player.

"Rem, come listen to this," Bennett yells to me. "You're
never going to believe it."

I walk down the few steps from the deck to the backyard
but stop when I hear Rae and Rudy Spitz bickering. They've
been married for more than sixty years, but we never see
them talking nicely to each other, only fighting. We figure
that's just how they communicate.

"I told you thirty times to water those flowers!" Rae yells.

"All right, all right. Enough."

"Don't *enough* me, Rudy!"

"Rae! You're making me crazy!"

"Those Spitzes!" Calvin says under his breath, cracking up. "We've heard my grandfather say that a million times already, and we've only been here a few days."

"I don't know how he's lived next door to them all these years," Claire says, looking unimpressed and sort of bored with the conversation. "Oh. Hi, Remy."

"Hi," I say back to be nice. Claire's one of those girls who always seems to be bothered. It could be the weather or the way her sneakers fit or that she's not allowed to have dessert, but it's always something. I've only known her for a few days, but that type of thing is really obvious.

"Rem, come here," Bennett says again, and I finally make my way to the tape player. "You gotta hear this."

He presses Play and I hear that scream, the one I heard just a few minutes ago. It sounded so clear and lifelike that I had no idea it was a recording. Bennett then proceeds to play it ten more times. He seems so interested in it that I can't help but be interested in it too.

When Bennett gets enthusiastic about something, I automatically want to know more about it. He just has this way of making even everyday things seem more interesting.

"Okay, whoa," I say, laughing. "That's a lot of screaming. Explain?"

I don't know how it's possible for a scream to sound so

incredible, but this one does. There's something almost magical about it.

Bennett turns to Calvin and Claire, who are eating a sleeve of Chips Ahoy like they haven't seen food in years. "You guys want to tell the story?" he asks them.

Micayla reaches in for a cookie and shrugs. "I don't really know what's going on either," she whispers to me.

Calvin sighs and plops down on the grass. He puts his baseball cap across his face like he needs a second to regain his concentration, and then he says, "Our grandfather is that scream."

I've known Mr. Brookfield forever, and he's always been the nice older man who lives next door to Bennett's family. He was friends with my grandma. He likes to walk around Seagate and pick up any trash, even though that's not a huge job because no one really litters here. He also plays cards down by the Ping-Pong stadium and was a judge for the Sandcastle Contest a few times. But that's really all I know about him.

I've never heard him raise his voice. I have no idea what Calvin means when he says that Mr. Brookfield "is that scream."

Claire's pulling up grass to make bracelets, but she chimes in, "His scream has been in a million movies." She rolls her eyes. "But he has no connections. I really wanted to meet someone famous, but he says he can't do anything."

"Mr. Brookfield is famous?" I look at Bennett when I ask

this because I feel uncomfortable talking to Claire, and Calvin doesn't really make much sense.

"Well, no. I mean, um, he's not, right?" Bennett asks Calvin. "I think he should be, though."

"He doesn't even really seem to care," Calvin says, twirling a finger beside his head, the universal sign for cuckoo. I can't believe Calvin and Claire talk about their own grandfather, sweet Mr. Brookfield, this way.

"Wait," Micayla says, crumpling up the empty sleeve of cookies. "Why isn't he famous if his scream was in a million movies? I'm so confused."

Claire looks up at the sky, as if searching for some kind of divine help to get her out of this annoying situation. "Basically they just paid him to record the scream once, but it's been in, like, billions of movies, and no one knows it's him. I swear, if you watch movies like *Star Wars* and *Indiana Jones* and even some Disney cartoons, you'll hear it."

"That's really cool and kind of crazy," I say, making eye contact with Bennett, hoping he realizes that I think it's cool too. I could tell Bennett was all excited about it, but Claire and Calvin act like it's no big deal.

"You guys don't get it. It would be cool if he was actually, like, famous," Claire says. "But he's *not*."

Claire has to be the most negative person on Seagate. She doesn't belong here. She belongs in New York City on the hottest day of the year, on garbage pickup day; that way she'd be able to find a million more negative people.

I keep thinking about the Scream, and as cool as it is, it also kind of freaks me out. How can I have lived near Mr. Brookfield for so long and never known this about him? It makes me feel nervous.

"So why are you on Seagate this summer anyway?" Micayla asks Claire.

"We were forced to come," Claire says. "Grandpa's getting older and our parents want us to spend time with him."

"We love the guy, but no offense, it's kind of slow here." Calvin widens his eyes at us. "And the guy may be getting weirder; he's talking about his scream more, which only makes me think he's going crazy."

He did *not* just say what I thought he did. Newcomers talking badly about our beloved Seagate? I want to get up and walk away and not talk to these two ever again. If it's slow here, it's because *they're* boring. They obviously don't get the magic of this place, and I don't really care to show it to them.

Besides, is revealing a secret really a sign of someone going crazy? I don't think so. Plus, I don't want that to be true. Even though Bennett thinks it's awesome, part of me hopes Mr. Brookfield will stop talking about this weird scream and go back to being the nice old man who picks up any litter he sees—this changes everything about him.

"Well, if you think it's slow here, you'll just have to hang with us," Bennett says. "We'll show you how awesome it is."

I literally feel my mouth dropping open like an exaggerated cartoon character. I look at Micayla to commiserate, but she seems distracted, ripping the strands of her cutoffs. She doesn't seem to understand what a serious disaster has occurred.

Bennett Newhouse, one of my best friends in the entire world, just invited these two downers to hang with us.

The worst part is, they still don't seem happy. Claire goes on and on about the celebrities she'd like to meet if only her grandfather was famous enough to actually help her meet them, and Calvin just plays with his hat.

It occurs to me that instead of sitting around talking about celebrities we're never going to meet, we could go inside and ask Mr. Brookfield about the Scream and get him to tell us why he kept it a secret all these years. It explains his director's chair collection, for one thing. But I also want to ask him how it happened, and what it was like to be in the movies, and if he ever screams to himself every now and again.

He has this mystery past. Everyone just sees him as nice Mr. Brookfield, but there's actually so much more to him, and hardly anyone even knows about it. Only us.

I start to get the feeling that maybe that's true for everyone. Maybe all grown-ups have mystery pasts, and it takes random old artifacts to discover what they are. Maybe kids have the same thing. Not mystery pasts, but secret feelings. Only a few people know how sad I am about Danish. I just carry it around with me like an oversized backpack, one that's invisible to pretty much everyone.

I think about all of this as the rest of the group goes on and on about what it's like to be famous.

When there's a lull in the conversation, I suggest we go for a swim. It's getting really hot out here. And underwater, I can think all I want about secret lives, and I don't have to listen to the C Twins at all.

Micayla and her mom are going to get their hair rebraided this morning. I've gone with them a few times, and it's cool, but it takes a really long time.

Bennett's mom is taking him and his little brother, Asher, on a fishing expedition. If Danish were here, we'd go for an early-morning stroll along the beach and then stop at Daisy's for pancakes on the way home. Daisy's is a restaurant for humans and canines. That's what the sign says. Daisy McDougal is a dog lover through and through, and so she set up a little doggie eating area on the porch of her restaurant. There are bowls of water and buckets of treats for the dogs.

It's one of my favorite places on Seagate. I've been avoiding it this summer for obvious reasons.

So instead of pancakes, I decide to smear some cream cheese on a bagel and head over to Marilyn Monroe's. I know it's Amber's house and I'm really there to watch her son, but after just a few mornings together, it seems that my main purpose is to spend time with Marilyn Monroe. And I'm okay with that.

"Oh, what a morning!" Amber says as soon as she sees me. "My personal trainer canceled my afternoon appointment, and Marilyn Monroe was craving a trip to Daisy's—I could tell. But we never made it out for our morning walk."

"That sounds . . . stressful," I say. Sometimes it's hard for me to really understand what she's worried about.

"But Hudson is down, finally, and Marilyn Monroe was somewhat satisfied with a few extra treats," she tells me. "Thanks again, Remy."

"No problem," I say. "And . . . um . . . I could take Marilyn Monroe to Daisy's later, I mean, if you want."

"You'd do that?" she asks. "She can be a handful. She never quite got the hang of walking on a leash, heeling, and all that."

"I can handle it," I say. "I mean, if you want. We can talk about it when you get back. I don't want you to be late."

"You're the best, Remy." Amber grabs all her supplies and her iced coffee and heads out for the art class.

"I love Daisy's too," I tell Mari when we're settled and cozy on the couch. "I understand how you feel."

She does her little "I agree" yelp, and we settle back into the couch for our usual morning chatting session.

"I went to Dog Beach finally," I tell her. "I had been avoiding it, but my friends dragged me there. You haven't met them yet—Micayla and Bennett—but they're pretty awesome."

She looks up at me with her big brown eyes, her ears up as high as they can go, as if she wants to hear more about them. So I tell her about how my mom met Bennett's mom when we were babies and how Micayla came to Seagate the summer before second grade. She sits close to me, not making a peep, with her lips curved up slightly in what I like to call her listening smile.

"Micayla's getting her hair braided this morning and I'm super jealous." I show Marilyn Monroe my boring straight hair. "I wonder what color beads she's going to get."

Marilyn Monroe listens to me, but I can tell she's getting bored. She probably doesn't think much about human hair problems.

"You still want Daisy's," I say. "I can tell. We'll go later."

She jumps onto my lap and licks my face and then settles down.

"Oh, and this other thing happened since I saw you last," I tell her. "So there's this guy, you've probably seen him around, his name is Mr. Brookfield. Anyway, he can do this crazy scream, and it's been in movies."

I try to imitate the Scream, and it sounds really bad. And then Marilyn Monroe starts barking like crazy, like she's trying to imitate it too. And then I get worried we're going to wake Hudson up.

"Shh," I say, and she immediately gets what I'm saying and stops barking. "We make a good team, Marilyn Monroe."

Her lips go from her listening smile to her smiling smile, and I know she agrees.

It takes me a few days to come up with my best new idea, but I'm glad it didn't take all summer. I'm sitting on the bench outside Sundae Best eating espresso cookie ice cream in a sugar cone, and that's when I realize that you can feel so happy about something (espresso cookie ice cream) and so sad about something (Danish) at the exact same time. But you can also wipe away a sad thing with a happy thing. Temporarily, at least.

So I decide to make a pact with myself that whenever I start to get sad missing Danish, I immediately give myself something happy to think about. It's not hard to find happy things on Seagate, so my pact is pretty easy to keep.

Walking to Micayla's yesterday, I got sad because I saw a teenager walking an apricot poodle pretty much exactly Danish's size. My throat started to get a sunburny feeling, and I immediately wanted to turn around and go home. But then I passed a pretty white house with a million beach pails lined up on the ledge of the front porch.

I stopped for a second and wondered why I'd never noticed it before. Maybe because Micayla usually picks me up and we walk the other way to the beach? Or maybe because I've been looking down as I walk this summer since I'm feeling so sad?

But it didn't matter why I'd never seen it before—I was seeing it now. And it was the picture of happiness. You can never have too many beach pails, and these were all different colors—turquoise, hot pink, yellow, Kelly green. Some handles were up; some were down. It didn't look arranged in any artful way, but that made it even more beautiful.

So basically, whenever I get sad about Danish, I will think about those beach pails. I'll try to remember all the different colors and the order they were in, and then sometimes I'll stop just to visit them and see if they've changed.

It's such a simple thing, but seeing it made me so happy.

I even snapped a picture with my phone before anyone inside caught me doing it. If they did catch me, I figured I'd just tell them how much I loved it.

I pick Micayla up and show her the house, and then we walk together to meet Bennett. After we pick him up by the Ping-Pong stadium, the three of us are going to the free concert by the gazebo in the middle of the island. They have concerts every Wednesday, and we try to be the first ones there. It doesn't really matter if we like the band or not, we just like sitting right up front and then dancing like maniacs.

We started doing this the summer we were eight, and we've been doing it ever since. Only, back then, our moms would have to take us, and they'd tell us to calm down, asking us if we could just sit and relax and enjoy the music. We were enjoying it, though—just in our own way.

Micayla's been doing this thing lately: No matter where we're going, she takes me past Dog Beach. It started that she just wanted to take me there to help me stop feeling so sad about Danish. But now it seems like something else is going on.

Mason Redmond, who we've known forever, is helping out at Dog Beach this summer. He doesn't really do much except encourage people to pick up after the dogs and occasionally throw a ball around, but he says it's helpful for him because he wants to be a veterinarian one day. He's only eleven, like us, but my mom says he's a forward thinker. I guess she means that he plans ahead.

I'm pretty sure Micayla has a crush on Mason, but she hasn't admitted it yet. Micayla started having crushes last summer, when we were only going into fifth grade. I didn't have any crushes, but it was kind of fun to talk to Micayla about hers. Micayla's older sister, Ivy, always has crushes, so maybe that's why Micayla got them earlier than me.

The crushes only lasted like three days, anyway. I feel like when I get a crush, it will last a long time.

This summer, though, she's been acting all funny when she sees Mason. She doesn't want to get too close, but he has to be within sight. She wants to wait a few minutes, and then when she thinks that Mason sees us, she wants to leave.

I don't really get it.

Plus, we've known Mason as long as we've known each other—since the summer before second grade. That's when Micayla's family bought the house here, and that's when Mason started spending summers on Seagate with his aunt and uncle.

He's just an average kid, except for his whole "forward thinking" thing.

"Okay, let's go," Micayla says five minutes after we've gotten to Dog Beach. I timed it, because I was wondering if we were actually staying for such a short amount of time or if I was just imagining it. You know how they say time flies when you're having fun? I thought it could have been that kind of thing. But it isn't—it's just Micayla's secret crush.

"Already?" I ask. "I wanted to play with the pair of Malteses again."

"Sorry, Rem, we'll be late for the concert," Micayla tells me, grabbing my hand and gently pulling me away. At the same time, I notice Mason hopping off the lifeguard's chair and walking closer to us. "And you spent all morning hanging out with Marilyn Monroe, so you're not too dog-deprived."

Sooner or later Mason's going to start thinking that we really hate him, but I don't want to tell Micayla that. Since she hasn't yet told me about her crush, we haven't been mentioning Mason at all.

When we get to the concert, Bennett's in front, in our usual spot, and he's saving us seats. But as we get closer, I notice that he's with those twins again. They're everywhere.

They're sitting on the grass, texting or playing games on their phones, and they barely say hi to us. I want to ask Bennett why they're here, but I know that would be rude.

Finally the music starts. It's one of the local Seagate bands. I don't think the band members play together during the year, but once summer comes, they play all over the island—at the free concerts, at the coffee shops, at baby music classes in the mornings, even at some of the beach bonfires.

The band is called Saturday We Tennis, which doesn't really make any sense, and none of us know what it means. When you first hear it, you probably think it means that they play tennis on Saturdays, but Micayla guessed that Saturday is actually the name of a person they play tennis with. We don't even know if they play tennis.

Anyway, the band is three guys named Everett, Aiden, and George, and they're in college, but they all grew up spending summers on Seagate.

They're pretty much our local celebrities.

Their most popular song is called "Photo Booth Jam," and it's kind of silly, describing all the kinds of pictures people take in photo booths. Micayla, Bennett, and I know all the words, of course, so we stand up and start singing along with them. Aiden always encourages audience participation.

After a few minutes, Avery Sanders joins us in our section. She high-fives me when she sees me and then starts dancing with us.

"Silly face with glasses," I sing. "Oh yeah."

"Kissy face with Amy," Micayla sings. "Oh yeaaaahhh." The end of that verse drags on, and she does it perfectly.

"Thumbs-up! High five! Fish face, smooch, eyebrow twist." This is the part of the song that starts to go really fast, and Bennett can totally keep up with them. They usually find Bennett in the crowd after and tell him that he can fill in if one of them gets sick.

Bennett gets all excited when they tell him this, and I think he secretly hopes one of them does get sick so he can be in the band. So far it hasn't happened. But it would be so cool to see Bennett up there. I'd cheer for him as loud as I possibly could.

"That song was really crazy," Claire says, as we're applauding. "I mean, photo booths are fun and everything, but who sings about them?" She looks at us to agree with her, but obviously we're not going to.

"Shh," I say. "They could hear you. And their feelings would get hurt."

"What?" She makes a face at me. "They're grown-ups in a band. You don't need to worry about them, Remy."

She didn't say much, but the few words she did say made

me feel like the stupidest, most immature person in the world. I don't know how she was able to accomplish that so quickly.

And I don't know why she even came down here if all she was going to do was insult the songs of one of our favorite bands.

I remember how my mom always tells me to ignore the kids at school when they say dumb things, so I try to do that now. But it seems harder than usual, like I'm out of practice.

I never had to worry about stuff like this on Seagate before, and I shouldn't have to worry about it now. This Claire girl doesn't even belong here, especially because she doesn't want to be here in the first place.

The band starts playing their next song, "Friend Me," and this one is really fast-paced, and Micayla and I always hold hands and dance around to it while Bennett sings as loud as he can.

I'm about to hop up and start dancing when I notice that Micayla and Bennett are staying seated. It doesn't take me long to figure out why—they're embarrassed in front of Claire.

Don't they know that she doesn't really matter?

Ever since Claire and Calvin got to Seagate, I've noticed that I have been thinking really mean thoughts. I never thought these things about people before. Sure, I really don't like wheelie-backpack girls in my school, but I pretty much just stay away from them.

But with Calvin and Claire here, I'm turning into a mean person.

After a few weeks on Seagate, they started complaining to their mom that they were really bored, so she signed them up for two weeks of tennis camp in Westchester, near where they live. And when I found that out, I was ecstatically happy. Too happy. I felt bad about how happy I was. But they were just such a drag to have around. They were always complaining, and Bennett was always trying to include them in things, and then they would still complain.

So now they're gone and it's just Bennett, Micayla, and me again. I still miss Danish, but things are starting to feel close to right.

The annual Seagate Fourth of July Celebration is great, the way it always is: fireworks on the beach, the staff from Shazamburger grilling hot dogs and hamburgers on the boardwalk, enough for everyone on the island to have two of each.

There's a pickle-eating contest, but Bennett is grossed out by pickles, so we never stick around for that. There's a line at Sundae Best that wraps around the whole island, practically, but no one seems to mind. No one worries about their kids staying up late, because everyone can just sleep in the next day. That's the beauty of Seagate: No one is in a rush. Time doesn't really matter, because everyone has so much of it.

"Y'know that kid Mason Redmond?" Bennett asks us as we're on the way to the beach. I'm starting to get a sense that he knows about Micayla's crush, but I'm not sure. Bennett was never involved in our crush talk last summer, even though he was around us all the time. I'm not sure how that worked out, but it did.

We nod.

"He knows what he wants to do when he grows up," Bennett says. "Do you think that's weird or cool?"

"Weird," I jump right in. "Kids should be kids, I think."

Micayla laughs. "You always talk like a grown-up, though, Remy!"

"You know what I mean, Mic." I nudge her with my shoulder.

Bennett ignores our little back-and-forth. "But he's our age, so how does he know he wants to be a veterinarian? And why is he working on it over the summer?" He seems really concerned, but there's no reason to be.

"Don't worry," I tell Bennett. "We're kids. We can just focus on being kids. That's what my mom always tells me."

"My mom tells me that sixth grade at my school is going to be really serious and I'm going to need to buckle down," Bennett says. "I don't even know what that means, and isn't that a weird expression?"

"Yeah," Micayla says. "I don't think of buckles as being down; I think of them as, like, being through something."

They go back and forth about the expression, and then I start laughing, because the whole thing just sounds so silly.

I say, "Guys, we really only get two months of summer, so let's just enjoy it and not think about school, okay?"

They nod.

I'm not sure they agree with me, but at least they go along for the moment. We never used to talk about what we want to do when we grow up. Talking about it now gives me a funny feeling, like I'm lost in a crowd and can't find Bennett or Micayla anywhere.

We're almost at the beach when a poster catches my eye. It's haphazardly stuck to one of the streetlights with masking tape, and it has a picture of a dog on it.

"Guys, hang on one second," I say. "I have to look at this."

Micayla and Bennett hang back, and I hear them talking about the whole "knowing what you want to do when you grow up" thing, and I try to tune it out. I'm not sure when my friends became so serious, but I think I liked them better before.

The poster says:

OUR BELOVED OSCAR IS MISSING!

Help us find our amazing boxer Oscar. He has brown fur everywhere except his stomach and his paws, where he has white fur. He answers to the names Oscar, Oscie, or Cuddle Cookies (don't ask). Email DawnRam200@gmail.com if you find him. Reward if found and returned. Thank you!

I stand there for a second after reading the sign. Then I rip it down. For the first time in forever, I have this feeling like I really need to do something. I have to find Oscar. I know how hard it is to be without a pet, but these people don't have to. And especially since I've become so attached to Marilyn Monroe, the sting of missing a pet feels even more brutal.

"You guys." I run over to them. "We have to find this dog." I show them the poster, then feel a little bit guilty for ripping it down. Other people need to see it too, if we're going to be able to find Oscar. But I also need to take it with us—I need to keep looking at his picture to remember what Oscar looks like, and I need to keep the email address handy for when we find him.

"I've definitely seen this dog around," Micayla says. "Should we go ask Mason at Dog Beach?"

I cover my mouth and try not to laugh. This crush is becoming totally obvious.

"No, let's not talk to Mason," Bennett says. "He stresses me out. I thought summer reading was enough to be worried about, but now I have to think about my career?" Bennett shakes his head. "I can't handle that kid this summer."

I walk them over to one of the wooden benches on the path to the beach, and we sit down for a second to talk. "Plus, don't you think Dog Beach would be the first place that his owners would look for Oscar?" I ask.

"You're probably right," Micayla says, slightly defeated.

"Do you know Oscar's family?" I ask them. "I think he looks familiar, but I'm not sure. Danish usually stayed away from the bigger dogs."

"Danish was a little wimpy," Bennett says, and then moves back a little bit because he knows I'm about to hit him.

I hit his arm anyway. "Hey! Bennett Newhouse, take that back!"

"Come on, Rem, we loved him, but he tried to drink coffee out of your dad's mug that one time. He didn't even like doggie treats; he always wanted his own croissant from Mornings."

Bennett's right about that. We said it again and again that Danish was more human than canine, and he did sometimes prefer a croissant from Mornings to a treat from Daisy's. The owners of Mornings (Seagate's fanciest breakfast place) are a couple named Beverly and Sidney, and they're really *not* dog people. I guess Danish knew that, and he was constantly trying to get them to change their mind.

Danish was never allowed inside, but I'd usually get him his own croissant. They made him so happy. How could I refuse him?

We all agree that we've seen Oscar around but we're not sure where, and we're not sure who he was with. So we take the poster and we walk around Seagate and go up to as many people as we can, asking, "Have you seen this dog?"

Most people shake their heads.

One old lady says, "I think I saw him at Daisy's. He was stealing treats from the other dogs! No one did anything to stop him!" She shakes her head like it was a complete travesty, and then she walks away.

Micayla suggests that we ask Avery Sanders. "She's such a gossip, and she knows everybody, so she'd probably be able to help."

She has a point, and I haven't seen Avery in a few days, come to think of it. The last time I saw her was at the Wednesday concert when Claire made us feel bad about dancing.

After a few more minutes of searching, I can tell that Micayla and Bennett really want to go to the beach. It's not hard to figure it out, since Micayla keeps saying, "Can we take a break, Rem? I really want to swim. They said it might rain later."

And Bennett says, "Let's go looking again tonight. Everyone's out now, and Oscar's probably scared and hiding."

I don't know if boxers even get scared. I think they're often used as watchdogs and sometimes help the police catch criminals. I was reading a book on dog breeds at the school library so I could help my parents choose our next dog, and I seem to remember that.

"You guys can go," I tell them. "I'm going to keep looking."

They tell me to stop being crazy and that of course they're coming, but a few minutes later they go to the beach for real, and I'm left walking around alone.

I don't know why it's so important to me that I find Oscar, but it really is. I guess it's because my dog-free life is pretty permanent right now, but Oscar's family's life doesn't have to be.

After a few hours of looking, I still haven't been able to find Oscar the boxer, and I have to go home. I even stopped to ask Amber and to quickly say hi to Marilyn Monroe, but neither of them had any information.

On the way home, I see Avery sitting on the bench outside Novel Ideas, Seagate's bookstore.

"Hi, Remy," she says. "You look lost, but I know that's impossible."

"Oh." I laugh. "Yeah, I'd never be lost on Seagate. But maybe you can help me?" I tell her the whole story about Oscar the boxer, but unfortunately she doesn't have any clues.

"Where's Micayla?" she asks, folding down the corner of a page of the novel she's reading.

I shrug. "Home, I guess?"

"Oh, okay. I'll call her later."

It seems weird that Avery's calling Micayla, since we're pretty much "see you around" friends, but I guess things can change.

The whole way home, I keep my eyes peeled for Oscar the boxer. I know his name is just Oscar, but I think *Oscar the boxer* sounds so cute. I'm starting to get worried that he jumped into the ocean and swam away when no one was looking. Dogs are good swimmers, and he could probably make it to the mainland somewhere, but I'm not sure how anyone would ever find him then.

"You really think he has tags and identification?" I ask my dad while he's making dinner. It's stir-fried-chicken night. Aside from his famous salmon casserole, it's the only thing my dad makes, but his stir-fry is actually edible.

"I do, Remy." He turns around from the stove and smiles at me. "Can you grab some plates? Do you want to eat inside or out?"

"Out," I tell him. I grab our wooden tray with the blue-and-white tile, the one I use when I serve my parents breakfast in bed. I only do that once a year, on their anniversary, which is August 14, so we leave the tray on Seagate. I stack the tray with plates and silverware, fill up two tall glasses with pink lemonade, and bring everything out to the back porch.

My dad brings out the sizzling frying pan and the bowl from the rice cooker and puts everything out on the picnic table. When my mom serves dinner, she puts everything onto serving platters and into fancy bowls, but my dad serves the food in whatever he cooked it in. To me, that just makes sense. Fewer dishes to wash.

"Do you think Mom's going to get in trouble?" Dad asks, putting some stir-fry on my plate.

"She didn't read the book again?"

"Nope!"

My mom loves reading, but she hates the books that her book club picks. They're usually dark and depressing, about a war or a missing child or a woman leaving her husband. I don't read them—my mom just tells me about them, usually explaining why she wasn't able to get through the book.

She keeps going to the book club meetings anyway, because she loves seeing her friends there—Bennett's mom, Micayla's mom, her other friends Barbara, Faye, and Gina. To be honest, they may never actually discuss books; they might spend the whole time talking about their families and stuff. I don't really know.

But when Mom goes out, it's just Dad and me for dinner, and sometimes that's really nice too. I used to wish I had a sibling, but I've gotten pretty used to being an only child. Maybe I'm kind of like Danish that way—I enjoy spending time with adults, even a little bit more than I like spending time with kids, the same way he preferred people to dogs.

I ask my dad a million more questions about where he thinks Oscar might be, and then he tells me that maybe we can go out searching for him after dinner, after the dishes are done. We can search for Oscar and meet Mom at the book club and maybe get ice cream for the walk home.

But as we're doing the dishes, which really only involves loading the dishwasher and hoping Mom doesn't notice that we didn't rinse everything first, we hear a knock on the door.

I immediately assume it's Mom coming home early. Which is disappointing because it means we probably won't go out for ice cream. But when I get to the door, I see that it's Bennett. And he's holding a leash.

My heart starts pounding. Did Bennett buy me a dog? I immediately get excited and scared all at once. Maybe my parents will be upset at first but then they'll say we can keep him, of course. Or maybe it's a girl dog. I don't know. I'll pretend that I'm mad at Bennett for doing that, but of course I'll be thrilled.

But then I get some sense. Bennett didn't buy me a dog. Where would he find one, first of all? And he'd never go behind my parents' back for something like that—or anything, really.

I look closer. Attached to the leash that Bennett is holding is Oscar!

"You found him?" I scream, and then I hear a dish break, and my dad comes running in. Oops. It's a good thing we don't use Mom's fancy platters.

"What's going on?" my dad asks.

"I don't know!" I yell. I'm so pumped up that I can't stop shouting.

"I was walking back from the pool after Asher's swimming lesson, and I saw a dog wandering around outside that store that sells all the beachy decorations."

"Beach House is the name of the store. Yeah?" I don't know why we're stopping this story for such insignificant details, even though I really do love that store.

"Maybe he was hungry and wandered over from Shazamburger? I don't know," Bennett says. "But I looked closer. I told Asher to sit down on the bench because I wanted to see if it was really Oscar, but I was nervous that maybe it wasn't and maybe the dog would bite Asher. Y'know?"

"Yeah!" I yell again. Sometimes it takes Bennett forever to tell a story.

"So I looked closer! And it was Oscar. He had tags and everything!" Bennett is yelling now too, and my dad backs away a little bit. "His fur is all wet. Maybe he was swimming in the ocean, like you said?"

"Yeah!"

I realize I am saying the same thing over and over again, but I can't stop because I am totally freaking out. Bennett found Oscar! Sure, I wish I was the one to find him, but at least he's been found. Then it occurs to me—if he's found, why did Bennett bring him here?

"Wait. Bennett." I pause to catch my breath, and my dad goes back into the kitchen, probably to pick up the broken pieces from the plate he dropped a few minutes ago. "Did you contact the owners?"

He sits down on the little bench outside our front door, the one Grandma always used to take off her muddy shoes after gardening. "I was about to," he says. "But then I had to come here first. You were really the one searching for him, and I just happened to see him. So I think you should contact the owners. You should get the reward and the credit."

"Bennett," I say, and all of a sudden I want to sit down next to him and give him a kiss on the cheek, even though I haven't done that for at least five years. "You found him. And they're probably worried sick. So we should tell them soon—or tell them right now, actually!"

"Let's go," he says. "But first, do you have any of those treats that Danish used to love?"

I'm sure we have them. I saw them at the back of the pantry a few days ago, and I wanted to tell my parents to throw them out, but I couldn't get up the courage to say anything.

At first it feels weird to give Oscar one of Danish's treats, but then it feels like the absolute right thing to do.

I go back inside and grab the box and then tell Dad we're going to bring Oscar back to his owners. His address, 87 Sand Lane (two streets away from me), is written right there on the little dog-bone charm hanging from his collar.

We give Oscar a few treats and take the box with us. His owners will probably be happy to have them. It's not always easy to find good dog treats on Seagate, and we always got Danish the best.

For a dog who has been missing from his family, Oscar

doesn't seem that upset. He's happy with his treats, and he's playing with me like he's known me his whole life.

Either I'm really good with dogs (and I know that I am, but I don't like to brag about it) or Oscar is really good with people.

It could be both, actually.

We almost ring the doorbell at Oscar's owners' house before we realize that someone's already sitting out on the front porch. Then I hear a small cry, and I turn and see a tired woman pushing a stroller with three seats in it.

"Triplets," she whispers. I wonder why she's not screaming with joy that we have Oscar with us, but it's because she hasn't seen him yet. He's hiding behind me—until he hears the woman's voice. When he sees her, he jumps up on her, and then jumps up a little bit more so that he can see inside the stroller. He starts panting and wagging his tail furiously and licking the lady's face. And she's so excited to see him, but I think she's trying to stay quiet too, since the babies are sleeping.

Bennett starts telling the story of how he found Oscar but stops himself when he notices the stroller.

Then all three of us are just standing there in silence, but our smiles are speaking louder than our voices ever could. It's like that whole "a picture is worth a thousand words" thing, except it's not a picture, it's the real thing.

The lady puts a finger to her lips in the universal *shh* sign and motions for us to follow her inside. She leaves the jumbo stroller out on the porch. If that's not a sign that Seagate is the safest place in the whole world, I don't know what is.

Oscar runs inside like it's the happiest day of his life, and we follow behind. Inside on the couch we find a sleeping man. I'm guessing he's the father of the babies. The TV is still on, and he's holding the remote as if he's about to change the channel, but he's totally asleep.

It's the kind of funny picture you'd see posted online for everyone to email to their friends, only I don't think I should be the one to take it.

The lady exhales and fills Oscar's water bowl, and he runs over.

"We gave him water," I say. "Don't worry."

"I'm not worried." She grins at us. "I'm just so grateful that you found him. Please sit down. Can I get you a drink? Please tell me how you found him."

Bennett starts the story again. "I was waiting for my brother at his swim lesson, and then I saw Oscar roaming around. I recognized him from the picture and also because there aren't many dogs on Seagate with brown fur every-where except their stomachs and their paws." Oscar walks over to us, and Bennett starts petting him. Then Oscar sits on the floor between us and we're both petting him. He has soft fur—wiry and silky—and it seems to fall out all over the place. His owner must spend all day vacuuming.

"So I checked his collar," Bennett continues, "and it was definitely him. I had to stop at Remy's first, though, because Remy was the one who really started everyone on this mission to find your dog."

The lady raises her eyebrows. "You're Remy?" she asks.

I nod.

"Wow. You are one special girl," the lady says. "And let me just say that Oscar doesn't respond this way to just everyone. He seems to really like you guys."

"Thanks. He's an awesome dog." I smile. "This is Bennett. Did we already say that?"

I crack up and realize that I'm feeling kind of nervous all of a sudden, though I don't know why.

"I'm Dawn Ramirez," she says. "The exhausted, sleeping man on the couch is my husband, Mateo. And Oscar is my first baby. I don't even know how he got out. Maybe he's feeling neglected. We have triplets—you probably noticed." She laughs and then takes a deep breath. "And it's pretty crazy. All I can say is, thank you guys so, so much for finding him."

"You're welcome," I say. "It was all Bennett."

"It was pretty much all Remy," he says, hitting me gently on the arm. "If you didn't mention it, I wouldn't have paid attention."

"Well, I'm giving you both the reward," she says. She leaves the room for a minute and then comes back with two envelopes. One for Bennett and one for me.

She sits down at the table and asks us if we want ice cream. While she's dishing it out into bowls from the to-go containers from Sundae Best, we hear screaming. Really loud baby screaming. It's coming in surprisingly clear, since they're out on the front porch.

Then Bennett points to a flashing gray walkie-talkie-like device. I'm guessing it's some kind of baby monitor, and I understand why Dawn was so comfortable leaving the triplets sleeping outside.

"They sleep best out there," she explains. "I'm going to give it a second and see if she falls asleep."

"You can tell which one is crying just by listening?" I ask.

She nods. "That was Mia. The other two are boys, Felipe and Alexander. Mia's cry is distinct, and she cries the most." Dawn puts her head down on the table and stares at the monitor. Bennett and I eat our ice cream quietly and quickly. I think we're both getting the feeling that it's almost time to go.

"Listen, I'm going to ask you something," Dawn says. "You can totally say no. I'm sure you're busy and everything. But Oscar really responded well to you. And as you can probably tell, I'm in over my head with these babies. Would you be interested in watching him? Like a dog sitter? Walks, trips to Dog Beach, stuff like that? We'd pay you and everything, of course."

Bennett and I look at each other. I think he's talking with his eyes, the way we used to do when we were little, but I can't be sure. The summer we were seven, Bennett and I made up this intricate blinking code, so that we would always be able to communicate, even when other people were around. Micayla tried to learn it too, but it was really just a thing between Bennett and me.

I can't wait any longer to figure out if Bennett wants to do this or not. If Calvin and Claire were here, he might say no. But they're away, and so Bennett's my friend again, the way he used to be.

"I'd love to," I say. "Dogs are my favorite animal, and we spend a lot of time at Dog Beach, anyway."

"Oh, you have a dog?" Dawn asks.

Now Bennett is blinking a little too much, and I know he's speaking with his eyes; that was our code for danger, which ultimately became our code for when people asked us awkward questions, like if we were going to get married someday, or when we'd eat dinner over at Mrs. Shanley's house and she'd try to serve us mushy cauliflower.

"I used to," I tell Dawn. "He died this past year."

She nods. "Are you guys brother and sister?"

Bennett and I widen our eyes—the signal for shock, which is probably not a very good secret code, but we never came up with anything better.

"No," Bennett says, laughing a little. "We're just friends."

Brother and sister? We look nothing alike. Bennett has

floppy brown hair that usually falls into his eyes until his mom bribes him to get a haircut. My hair is somewhere between blonde and brown. Plus, Bennett's, like, three inches taller than I am.

I don't know why that question bothers me.

I hate it when people ask us if we're in love or if we're going to get married. We're only eleven and it's a dumb question. But now I'm annoyed that Dawn asked us if we're brother and sister.

Something in the way Bennett says "We're just friends" makes me upset. It's true. We are just friends. But not like any pair of friends you'd find in a school or on a soccer team or something. We're different. We're lifelong Seagate friends. Best friends, even.

All our lives Bennett told everyone that I was his best friend. I have two best friends—Bennett and Micayla—but as far as I knew, I was Bennett's only best friend. And I liked it that way.

I wonder why he didn't say it just now.

I wonder if things changed and I didn't even notice.

"I'm sorry about your dog," Dawn says, and I remember that's what we were talking about before I got distracted about me and Bennett. "It's really hard to lose a dog. I've been through it a few times, and it never gets easier."

"Yeah, that's what people say," I mumble. I want to finalize the arrangements for watching Oscar and then I want to go home. It suddenly feels awkward being in this kitchen, and even though there's still a spoonful of ice cream left, I don't really feel like eating it.

"Well, why don't you take a day to think it over? And if you're interested in dog-sitting for Oscar, come by tomorrow. I usually take the babies out for a morning walk, but we're never too far." She smiles. "That's the beauty of Seagate, right?"

"Yup!" I stand up and put my bowl in the sink, and Bennett follows me. "I'm a mother's helper right now for Amber Seasons on Monday and Wednesday mornings, but I'm free the other days."

"Okay. Well, we'd work around your schedule, of course. Thank you guys so much again," Dawn says as she's walking us to the door. "If I wasn't so tired, I'd sound more excited, but please know how absolutely, completely grateful I am."

We leave Dawn's house, and the triplets are now sleeping peacefully in their gigantic stroller. I wonder how long they sleep outside, or if they ever move into their cribs. They can't possibly sleep out here all night; it gets chilly.

Bennett's house is closer to Dawn's than to mine, but he walks me home anyway. He says his dad always tells him that it's safer for boys to walk alone than it is for girls. On Seagate, though, it's safe for anyone to walk alone. But I don't argue, because I like his company. Even right now, when we're not really talking, it's just nice to walk together. And the nicest thing about being best friends is that you can walk in complete silence and not feel weird about it.

Sometimes you just don't have anything to say, and that's okay.

It's quiet for so long that I'm startled when Bennett asks, "Wasn't it weird that she thought we were brother and sister?"

I'm surprised he's thinking about it too, but in a way I'm glad I'm not the only one who still is.

"Yeah," I say. "Are they new here? I don't think I've seen them before. Or maybe I just don't recognize her now that she has the babies."

"Huh?"

"I mean, maybe Dawn and her husband were the kind of couple who were always going out to eat late at night and staying in their cabana by the beach and weren't really out and about. And they're completely different people now with the triplets."

"Oh. Yeah. That could be."

After I say it, I realize that every change in life—big or small—can change you as a person. The way having babies changed Dawn and Amber. I wonder how I've changed since Danish died. I know I've changed, but I wonder how exactly, and if everyone can tell.

All this change can be frustrating if things are good and all you want is for them to stay the same. That's part of the beauty of hanging out with dogs: They're pretty predictable. They like to eat and go out for walks and have belly rubs. And they'll always be there to greet you and welcome you home.

When we get to my house, Bennett tells me he'll see me in the morning. He'll come by and then we'll walk to Micayla's, and we'll all bring Asher over to day camp. We used to go to Seagate day camp, and it was fun, but now we're old enough to entertain ourselves. And that's even better.

At home, it's probably annoying for Bennett to help out with Asher so much. But here he doesn't seem to mind it. Everyone wants to be walking around on Seagate anyway, because there are so many people out and about, and you don't have to worry about cars, and no one is in a hurry. Plus, Bennett doesn't have to take Asher everywhere by himself; he has Micayla and me to go with him.

It doesn't really matter what we do together—we always have fun.

One time we spent a whole afternoon throwing pebbles across the walkway to the beach. It was a rainy day, so no one was really walking there, and we made up this whole game, seeing how far the pebbles could go. Most people would have probably thought it was really dumb, but we loved it.

That's just the kind of friends we are.

I don't really need a day to think about Dawn's job offer. Of course I am going to watch Oscar. We bonded immediately. I have Marilyn Monroe, and she's great, but it's kind of like the saying that you can never have too many friends. You can never have too many dog friends either!

Plus, I feel a little bit bad for Oscar. He was Dawn's first baby (she even said it herself), and now she doesn't really have time for him. I wonder how often dogs are replaced by babies. It makes sense, I guess, but it must be really hard for the dog.

There should be some kind of doggie support group where they could go and bark as loud and as often as they need to and get out their frustrations. Maybe Oscar ran away because he needed attention and wasn't getting it.

Poor guy. I want to help him.

My Oscar-watching time might cut into my Micayla and Bennett time, but I'm sure we can work it out. We've navigated the two mornings I'm with Marilyn Monroe, and we can navigate this too.

I daydream a perfect schedule while I eat my Froot Loops on the front porch and wait for Bennett and Micayla to get here.

My parents are at the Seagate Art Festival today. It starts at ten, but they got special passes for the early exhibit that started at eight. I don't think anything is worth getting up at eight in the morning, but they do. I'm just glad they didn't make me go with them.

They are making me meet them there later, to see the special exhibit on Minnie Lions, an artist who spent her whole life on Seagate, photographing everyday objects. My parents are obsessed with her work, and I'm a fan too.

I'm excited to see it, just not so early in the morning.

In my perfect schedule, I would watch Oscar in the mornings, bring him back to his home, and then maybe watch him again in the afternoons. That way I can spend the middle chunk of the day with my friends. That's when we go swimming or surfing or just relax on the beach.

I finish my Froot Loops and then run upstairs to put on a bathing suit. It's so easy to get dressed on Seagate. Breakfast in pajamas, never worrying about what to wear for the day—always just a bathing suit with shorts and a T-shirt over it. When I was little, I would walk around Seagate in only a bathing suit and no one minded, but now it just feels awkward to do that.

When you think about bathing suits too much, you realize how weird they are. You're pretty much just wearing underwear, but underwear that everyone can see.

I'm upstairs changing into my turquoise-and-white two-piece when I hear Bennett and Micayla downstairs. I quickly make sure my door is closed. The safety of Seagate is also a little bit nerve-racking—friends can walk into your house anytime, including when you're changing!

When I'm dressed, I find them downstairs looking through one of my mom's furniture catalogs and eating Cheerios out of the box.

"This chair is way awesome," Bennett says. "It's like a chair bed. Right? Doesn't it look big enough to sleep on?"

"Sure." Micayla turns the page.

I wonder how long I can stand here without them noticing me. It's strange how engrossed they are in this catalog. My mom is obsessed with furniture, so she subscribes to tons of magazines, and pretty much every furniture designer in the world sends her a catalog. The same way I like to imagine perfect schedules, she likes to daydream about redecorating.

If it were up to her, she'd redecorate every year. She loves changing things up. And I'm exactly the opposite. If it were up to me, my room on Seagate would still look the way it did when Grandma owned the house. And my room in Manhattan would look the same way it did when I was a little girl.

I just like things to stay the same.

"Oh, hey, Rem," Bennett says. Is it possible that he's gotten taller in just one day? Looking at him sitting in one of our wooden kitchen chairs, it seems like his head is a whole foot above Micayla's. I wonder if it was always like this and I just didn't notice. "People are setting up the Sandcastle Contest and I said I'd help. Micayla's in too. You're gonna come, right?"

We always help set up the Sandcastle Contest. We help get all the supplies organized and hang the banners and walk around Seagate getting people to sign up. But I'd totally forgotten about it. I need to go to Dawn's and tell her that I will help with Oscar.

Then I realize that Bennett and I never officially said we were going to watch Oscar together, but Dawn asked him too—not just me. In my head, I made the decision that I'd do it, but I don't know if he did. And he's actually the one who found Oscar in the first place.

I reach into the box for a handful of Cheerios. I never get sick of cereal. I could eat cereal all day, every day, and be fine with it.

"Oh, what'd you decide to do about watching Oscar?" Bennett asks as if he read my mind. "I really want to, but it's going to be hard on the days I have to walk Asher to and from camp. My mom ended up taking him today because I forgot about the Sandcastle Contest."

"I want to do it," I tell them with my mouth full of Cheerios. It sounds gross, but sometimes it's okay to be gross with your best friends.

"What are you guys talking about?" Micayla asks. "Anything I should know about?"

Micayla was out to dinner at Picnic last night for her parents' anniversary. Picnic is Seagate's fanciest restaurant, and it's a really ironic name. When people think about picnics, they think casual and sitting on the grass and stuff, but this place is super fancy—white tablecloths, tall crystal glasses just for water, and even the salads cost a lot of money. The food is good, but it's the kind of place where you have to whisper during the meal, and eating there always takes forever. It's not really my kind of restaurant.

So we tell Micayla the whole story, and she says, "Well, I want to watch Oscar too!"

I look at Bennett and he looks at me and again I wonder if we're talking with our eyes or not. We're going to have to have a real conversation with words about whether we can still talk with our eyes.

"Remember how I was the one who was really able to communicate with Danish?" Micayla reminds us. "I mean, I have a gift. I'm practically Mary Poppins."

We were obsessed with that movie when we were little, especially the parts when Mary was able to communicate with Andrew, the dog. So over the years, Micayla convinced us that she was able to have conversations with dogs too.

Danish would bark, and Micayla would talk, and then

Danish would bark back. But his pitch would always change, and it really seemed like Micayla understood what his barks meant, and that Danish understood Micayla's words.

I had totally forgotten about that, even though I have conversations with Marilyn Monroe all the time. But I didn't think I had magical powers—the conversations just seemed normal to me.

"I don't think Dawn would mind," Bennett says. "And it would really help to have more people, especially when I have to watch Asher and you guys have to do, um, more lying on the beach."

We both hit Bennett at the same time, and he says, "Ouch. I'm getting beaten up by girls!"

We all agree that we'd love to watch Oscar, so we decide to head over to Dawn's right away so that we can get to the Sandcastle Contest prep on time.

Dawn answers the door with one baby in one of those carrier things, one baby over her shoulder, and the third one crying in a swing behind her. Oscar is running around in circles barking and pushing his metal bowl with his nose.

"Oh, I am so glad to see you guys!" I'm not even sure if she notices that Micayla, who she's never met, is with us. "Oscar is hungry and needs to go out. The food is in the cabinet next to the stove. Thanks, guys!"

She leaves us standing in the foyer, puts one baby down on a pillow on the couch, and picks up the crying one in the swing. It feels like she's immediately forgotten we're there. I guess that means we're just supposed to get started.

Bennett grabs the food. I pour some water into Oscar's other bowl. Micayla talks to him and pets him, and he calms down within seconds.

We really are a good team.

I go back to the living room to tell Dawn that we're leaving, but we find her on the couch, asleep, with three sleeping babies around her. Waking any of them up would probably be the worst thing we could do, so we tiptoe out with Oscar on his leash.

We walk him over to Dog Beach, which is luckily right near where the Sandcastle Contest prep is going on.

As soon as we get there, he runs onto the beach as if he's been waiting his whole life to get there. He starts playing with a French bulldog that we always see around. I think her name is Latte. Micayla walks off to start up a Mary Poppins–like conversation with that pair of Malteses we met the other day, and I keep an eye on Oscar, just to make sure he's playing nicely with others.

Bennett tells us he's going to check in with the Sandcastle Contest people.

I watch as he walks away, thinking back to that whole exchange with Dawn last night, the brother and sister thing, and the "We're just friends" thing. I don't know why I'm still thinking about it. It just seems to be stuck in my head, the way a burrito sits in your stomach hours after you eat it.

Bennett is Bennett. No one really spends much time

thinking about him. That sounds kind of mean, but it's just that I know him too well to have to wonder what's going on with him all the time.

Oscar goes over to get a drink of water out of this special doggie water fountain that Daisy Dog Lover Extraordinaire (that's what Daisy McDougal calls herself) had installed a few summers ago. I follow behind him and rub his belly for a minute. And then when I look up, I see Bennett walking toward me, but he's not alone.

He's with two other people.

The C Twins are back.

Bennett and Calvin take off to meet the Sandcastle Contest organizers, leaving me alone with Claire.

"I got kicked out of tennis camp," Claire tells me, digging her toes into the sand.

"Why? How?"

"If you let me talk, I'll tell you," she snaps.

I stay quiet.

"I got kicked out because I didn't want to play," she says, groaning. "I mean, seriously. My parents were paying for me to be there, so why did the counselors care if I played or not?"

I try not to look too confused. "Um? I guess because if you're not playing tennis, what are you really doing there?"

"Yeah, Remy. Thanks." Claire huffs and walks away, leaving me standing alone with Oscar. He seems tired and ready to go home, but I want to wait for Micayla and Bennett to get back before I head out.

Oscar goes back to playing and I sit down on a bench for a few minutes, feeling unsettled. I realize how good it felt when Calvin and Claire weren't here, but now they're back and Claire is being rude and surly and Bennett is busy with Calvin. I'm not sure where Micayla is, but I get this lonely feeling where I just want to go home and crawl under my covers.

I wish Danish were here. Oscar's nice and all, but he's not my dog.

So far, day one of the three of us watching Oscar is turning into me watching him. By myself.

"Remy, right?" I look up and see Mr. Brookfield, Claire and Calvin's grandpa, standing over me.

I nod.

"You running a doggie day care or something?" he asks. For a second I'm confused, and then I look down at my feet and see Oscar and two other dogs just sitting around me. I'm not even sure how or when the other two dogs got there.

"No, just watching one dog." I smile. But then I think about my time with Marilyn Monroe, and I wonder if Mr. Brookfield is on to something. Maybe I *am* on my path to running a doggie day care. "You guys don't have a dog, right?"

I don't ever remember seeing a dog running around inside or outside Mr. Brookfield's house, so I'm not sure what he's doing at Dog Beach.

"No, I just like coming to sit here," he says. "I like the benches. If you get up and stand on that one over there"—he points to the green bench a few feet away from us—"you can see the whole island. Try it sometime."

I want to try it right now, but I'm nervous that someone will see me doing it and tell Dawn that I'm not acting like a professional dog watcher.

"So you come here, just to sit, even though you don't have a dog?" I ask Mr. Brookfield.

"I do," he says. "The main section of beach doesn't have benches. And I don't want to carry a chair. Plus, I like to watch the pooches."

"There are chairs on the south end," I tell him. "When the Seagate Inn remodeled, they donated all their old lounges so that anyone who wanted a lounge chair could have one."

He nods. "That's true. But I'm good here."

I thought I was the only one who liked going to Dog Beach even without a dog.

I want to ask him something, but I don't know if I should. In all the years I have known Mr. Brookfield, I've never really talked to him before. I wonder if he was at Dog Beach all the times I was here with Danish and I never even noticed.

It's strange how you can see something all the time and not even realize it's there. It's like how when Mom rearranges the furniture and I promise myself that I'll remember how it used to look. But then after only a few days, I forget. Even though I saw it the old way for so long, I still can't remember.

In the distance, I see Bennett with a stack of posters that he'll have to hang up, reminding everyone about the Sandcastle Contest, and then I see Micayla talking to someone. It takes me a few seconds to figure out who it is, but when I squint my eyes, it's clear that it's Mason Redmond.

She's actually talking to her crush!

I'm excited and sad at the same time. They've probably forgotten about Oscar.

"So tell me more about that whole scream thing," I say finally, trying to think of something other than myself.

"I'm so glad you asked. What exactly would you like to know?" Mr. Brookfield asks. He stretches his legs out in front of him, and I notice he's wearing bright white sneakers and tall tube socks. It occurs to me that older people don't like to wear sandals as much as young people do. I wonder if there will come a time when I won't want to wear flip-flops every day. It's too sad to think about.

"How come nobody knows it's your scream that's in all those movies?" If Claire were here, she'd probably tell me to be quiet and that nobody really cares about it. But I do care. It's so mysterious.

I'm suddenly grateful that it's just Oscar, Mr. Brookfield, and me right now.

"I had a very small role in a movie, and I was grateful to get it," Mr. Brookfield tells me. "I'd been on a million auditions. In this one, I was cast as the person who was going to get attacked by an alligator. We shot the scene, and then the director told me they'd want to get the screaming sound just right, so we'd record it later. We did record it later, but the scene got cut considerably, so you could really only see the back of my head. And then eventually, even my head got cut. But the scream. Oh, that scream! They kept it. And for years and years, and still today, people are using that scream!"

Mr. Brookfield goes on, telling me details about some of the movies it's in, and it's clear he really does love to talk about this. I wish I'd known before, because I like hearing these kinds of stories. It took Claire to bring all this out of him.

The more Mr. Brookfield talks, the more I realize that he seems so much happier when he's talking about his work and when he's talking about the past and his wife and life on Seagate. He never seems that happy otherwise, just talking about day-to-day life.

"Remy!" Bennett runs over to me, all out of breath, and Calvin follows behind him. "They asked us to put up all these signs for the Sandcastle Contest right away. Are you okay bringing Oscar back by yourself?"

It's nice that he asked, but I wish he'd just come with me.

"Dude, she's fine," Calvin says. "It's Seagate."

Bennett looks at me again, and when I don't say anything right away, he says, "Yeah, you're right. We'll be around, Rem. See you soon."

They walk away with the signs flapping in their hands. Oscar is resting on the sand, and I think I've probably kept him out too long.

"Nice boy, that Bennett," Mr. Brookfield says. "He was always a nice boy."

"Yeah," I grumble. "I guess."

I take Oscar back home, where Dawn seems to be in better shape. Only one of the triplets is up, but he's not crying. The other two are sleeping in their swings.

"He looks exhausted! That's great!" Dawn gives me a hug. "Remy, I really want to thank you so much for taking care of Oscar."

"You're welcome." I laugh a little bit because I don't know what else to do. "Same time tomorrow morning?"

"Unless I need you before." She looks back at Oscar. "I'll text you?"

"Yeah, that would be great. See you later."

I walk back over to the beach, hoping that Calvin and Claire got bored with helping and decided to go back to Mr. Brookfield's to watch TV.

"Where did you go?" Micayla asks as soon as she sees me. She's sitting at the Sandcastle Contest registration table. "I texted you, like, seven times."

Uh-oh. I never even looked at my phone. I was so pre-occupied with thinking about Bennett and talking to Mr. Brookfield, I kind of forgot about Micayla. It's such a terrible thing to do, I feel guilty immediately.

"I didn't look at my phone. I don't know why. I'm so sorry!" I squish up my face in embarrassment and give Micayla a hug. "I had to take Oscar home. He was really tired."

"Yeah, I figured." She gives me a look that says *I'm con-fused* and *You're crazy* at the same time.

"Let's go help set up," I tell her. "I love looking at all the little tools some people use to build sandcastles."

"Me too," she says. "But I have to talk to you."

As we're walking over to get the supplies, I'm dying for Micayla to start talking, but we keep getting interrupted.

"Girls, all the supplies are on one of the picnic tables," Mrs. Pursuit tells us. "So far we have ten teams competing, so I'll need you to organize everything into ten bags and make sure every bag has one of each item."

"On it," I reply.

Mrs. Pursuit was a gym teacher in Connecticut before she retired. Now she lives on Seagate year-round, and the Sandcastle Contest was her idea. She gets really crazy when the day of the contest rolls around every summer. I'm pretty sure she thinks of it as the Olympics of sandcastle building.

Micayla, Bennett, and I were always a team, until last summer. The volunteers who usually help set up canceled at the last minute, and so Mrs. Pursuit asked us to step in.

We were so flattered, we didn't even mind stepping out of the contest.

We finally make it over to the picnic table and begin putting supplies into the royal blue tote bags, donated by Blueberry Crumble, Seagate's bakery.

I'm putting a sand sifter and a shovel into my fifth bag when I can't take the suspense anymore. "What did you have to talk to me about?" I ask.

"Oh, um, it was nothing," Micayla says.

"How could it be nothing?" I give her a crooked look. "Nothing is ever nothing, y'know. Between best friends, I mean."

I continue putting supplies into the bag and wait for her to talk.

She opens her mouth again but hesitates. "Well, I talked to Mason Redmond," she says.

It seems like there was something else she wanted to say, but maybe I'm expecting too much. Maybe she was just nervous about telling me she talked to Mason Redmond.

Mason Redmond is one of those names that can't be separated. I never just say "Mason" aloud. It's always "Mason Redmond." I'm not sure why certain names are like that and other names aren't. People just call me Remy. Only teachers and people reading names off a list call me Remy Boltuck.

Out of the corner of my eye, I see Mrs. Pursuit coming, and so we continue to work as we talk quietly. People come over to us and ask us questions about the contest. A frazzled mom of three little kids comes over, stressed that they hadn't signed up and worried if it's too late to enter.

Micayla finishes the last bag, and we start setting them up in a neat row. "So, let me tell you this story about Mason Redmond."

"Only if you admit that you actually like him," I insist.

"I don't know if I like him like that," Micayla says. "I'm still thinking about it."

"Whatever you say," I grumble.

We organize the bags and tidy up and then go sit on one of the benches by Dog Beach. We still have a few hours before the contest starts, and Bennett hasn't come back from putting up the signs.

"When you were watching Oscar, I just walked over to the volunteer table, and Mrs. Pursuit was panicking, and Mason was trying to calm her down, and he was reminding her that it always ends up being awesome." Micayla takes a deep breath. "Anyway, he just said, 'Hey, Micayla,' and I said, 'Hey, Mason,' and then we talked about how our names were kind of similar, and then he said you are really good with dogs."

"Me?" I gasp a little bit. Mason Redmond was talking about me? It's not like I really care, because I'm not the one with the crush on him. It's just surprising. I never think that anyone is talking about me.

"Yeah," Micayla says, in her no-big-deal tone. "Well, you are, Remy."

"Thanks." I smile, realizing we're off topic. "But what

about Mason Redmond? Do you like him or not?"

"I don't know," she says. "Okay, maybe I do. Today, I think I like him."

I have no idea what she means by *today*. But maybe it goes along with the saying to take things one day at a time. Maybe the person who first said it was dealing with a crush and unsure what to do.

We all go home to change, and I tell Bennett and Micayla that I'll meet them outside my house at five thirty so we can walk over to the beach together.

When Micayla and Bennett come to pick me up, they're laughing about something. When I ask them what it is, Bennett tells me it's some joke that Calvin heard, and they couldn't stop cracking up about it. I didn't ask what the joke was, because I don't really like Calvin, and I figured I wouldn't like the joke.

We get to the beach and Mrs. Pursuit tells us to stand behind the supply table. She hands us the sea-green SEA-GATE SANDCASTLE CONTEST 2014 shirts. Micayla and I had put on ribbed tank tops, because we knew we'd have to put the contest T-shirts on over them. Bennett did not, so he has to take his shirt off. Obviously this isn't a big deal, since he's a guy and guys go shirtless all the time at the beach, but I laugh anyway, and his face turns bright red.

I see him shirtless at the beach all the time, but it looks so funny to me when we're not standing on the sand about to jump into the ocean.

There are ten teams participating and lots of space for anyone who wants to sit and watch. People have been waiting all day for this, staying on the beach since early this morning just so they'd get a good seat.

One of the teams is made up of all the band members from Saturday We Tennis, and I have a feeling they're going to win. They won last year and a few years before that too.

A few of the teams are families with little kids, the way that Mom, Dad, Grandma, and I used to participate. We'd even let Danish help. He'd make cool imprints with his paws, and we always said that was the finishing touch. Memories of him are all over Seagate Island, and even when I'm not feeling entirely sad, something reminds me of him and I get filled with a flash of sadness again, like when the waves wash over your feet really quickly and then disappear moments later.

With a few minutes to go before the contest starts, I see Mr. Brookfield coming over to us, with Calvin and Claire tagging along behind.

I'm happy to see Mr. Brookfield but not the other two. Something about them makes me nervous and defensive. They're always criticizing Seagate, and it hurts. When you love a place so much, you can't stand to hear even one negative word about it. It was already different enough here without Danish by my side, and now these two come out of nowhere, complain about everything, and make the summer feel shaky.

Calvin and Claire don't even stay for the contest. They tell Bennett they're going over to the pool to swim and lie in the sun. But Mr. Brookfield stays.

I watch him in the distance a little bit, sitting on a bench, reading some kind of science fiction novel. He doesn't look happy, but he doesn't look sad either. I think about what it must have been like to finally get that part in the movie, only for it to kind of disappear, and there wasn't much he could do about it.

Mrs. Pursuit runs up to us, a whistle hanging around her neck and her frizzy brown hair in a high ponytail. She looks like an elderly middle school student, if that even makes any sense. "You all ready?" she asks us.

"I have an idea," I tell her. Micayla looks at me, confused, but I continue anyway. "Mr. Brookfield is totally famous—his voice is the scream in so many movies I'm sure you've seen. What if he does his scream into your megaphone to start the contest?"

I turn around to see if Mr. Brookfield hears what I'm saying, but he's too far away. Then it occurs to me that I probably should have asked him if he even wanted to do this.

"Do screams and sandcastles really go together?" Mrs. Pursuit asks us. "Let's think about it for next year."

I turn back again to check on Mr. Brookfield, and I notice that he's dozed off on the bench.

Well, Mrs. Pursuit did say we could think about it, so that's something. I'll have to find the right time to suggest it to Mr. Brookfield, and then we'll have a whole year to make it happen next summer. Maybe there are other ways to get his scream involved in Seagate life.

But it's such a peaceful place. No one screams here usually.

The teams have an hour to build their sandcastles, and they can have as many supplies as they want. Micayla and I are in charge of manning the supply table, in case anyone needs extra shovels or pails or cool sculpting devices.

At the last minute, the person who does all the photography for Seagate events had to cancel. Mrs. Pursuit bought disposable cameras at the general store and asked Bennett if he'd be willing to take some pictures. Of course, Bennett was thrilled to do it, and even from up here, I can see him running along the sand trying to get some great action shots of teams building their sandcastles.

So Micayla and I sit at the table, not really talking. I try to think of things to say, but everything seems wrong. I don't know why I'm having to think about things to say to her. This has never happened before.

"Bennett seems different this summer," I say, finally. It's been on my mind for weeks, but I haven't really had the courage to bring it up.

"Really?" Micayla asks, and I immediately want to take it back. I feel silly for even mentioning it.

"I guess he just seems to want to hang out with Calvin more than I thought he would," I say. "Know what I mean?"

She puts her feet up on the support beam in the folding table. "I guess so. Maybe. He's just Bennett." She hands a white shovel to a little kid who's all out of breath from running over the sand. "I haven't thought about it."

I ponder this for a few seconds. Is it new for me to think about Bennett this much? Maybe I didn't used to think about him at all. I wonder when this really started, and when it will stop. I wonder if there's anything I can do about it.

I drop the subject. Then Micayla spends forever telling me this story about her brother and how his bus broke down on the way back from Washington, DC, and he ended up spending the night at the house of someone he met on the bus. It's not really that interesting a story, but the way Micayla tells it, it sounds like a plot to some crazy movie.

Things start to feel more normal between us.

The Saturday We Tennis team wins the contest, and everyone runs down to see their sandcastle. They built it to look like a town house—tall, with square windows and a steep front stoop.

The Seagate Sandcastle Contest has loose rules—it's not limited to only traditional castles. All kinds of homes are acceptable. And that's what makes it different.

When the contest is over, Micayla, Bennett, and I walk

home together. After Micayla and Bennett drop me off, I think more about the fact that I guess I am thinking about Bennett. And I know that sounds totally crazy—thinking about thinking about something.

Over dinner, my parents can tell I'm acting a little strange, because they keep asking me if there's something on my mind.

I don't want to tell them about Bennett, though. It just doesn't feel like the kind of conversation you have with your parents.

The next morning, Micayla, Bennett, and I meet at Oscar's house. It makes me laugh that we think of it as his house instead of Dawn's house or her husband's house or even the babies' house. But the truth is, we know Oscar better than we know any of the others.

We know that Oscar likes to sit with us for a few minutes before we go out. I know we're not exactly having a conversation, but it almost feels like we're catching each other up on what has happened overnight or in some cases over the past few hours. We sit on the couch, Oscar sits in front of us, and we take turns petting him. His breathing slows down when we do this, and he looks so relaxed. It could be the way the white part of his fur curves, but I swear he even has a smile on his furry face.

After a few minutes of that, Oscar sips his water, we pack

up some treats in a little Tupperware container, and we head out. We leave Dawn either asleep on the couch or dealing with at least one crying baby.

We may leave with a calm Oscar, but we never leave a calm Dawn behind (unless she's asleep). And she always thanks us a million times.

Even though Micayla didn't start out as one of Oscar's dog sitters, she's quickly become his favorite. Maybe he can sense that she has allergies, so she stays back a little, and that's what makes him more attached to her. Whatever it is, Oscar loves Micayla, and when he's around, Micayla doesn't even really mind sneezing so much.

We have the same routine every day. We walk down to the boardwalk and then head over to Dog Beach, where Oscar plays with his friends, usually dogs that are much smaller than he is.

When we first started bringing him to the beach, he usually ignored Snowball and Marshmallow, but now they get along really well. They always chase each other at the beginning, and then when it seems like they need a break, they lie down in a circle with their paws in the middle facing each other.

They're a little crew who seem to pretty much ignore all the other dogs around them. Marshmallow and Snowball are smaller and daintier, kind of like Micayla and me. Oscar is bigger and more outgoing, like Bennett.

I watch them from across the sand, and I swear they're

even starting to look like us. I've heard that people can start to look like their dogs, but this may be taking it a bit too far—they're not even our dogs!

"Oscar is so kind," Micayla says. "Don't you see how he's always looking out for the other dogs? That black Lab just fell down and Oscar went to check on him."

"He's awesome," Bennett adds. "He seems like the camp counselor at the dog park, always going around to make sure the other dogs are having fun."

Just then Amber rushes up to us and taps me on the shoulder. "Hi, Remy, so sorry to barge in on you, but your mom said you were here. Would you mind keeping an eye on Marilyn Monroe for a second?" She smiles at me and then turns to face Micayla. "I'm not sure who is more inquisitive, my dog or my toddler! I guess my toddler, because he's running away!" She says the last part as she chases Hudson down the beach.

I'm so happy to see Marilyn Monroe on a day other than Monday or Wednesday that I bend down and scoop her up into my arms and give her a million kisses. Today, she has a purple bow in her hair, and the light brown part of her fur is looking extra light, almost like she's been tanning.

It's my first time seeing Marilyn Monroe at Dog Beach, and she runs around wildly, faster than any of the other dogs, stopping every five seconds to smell a section of sand or to study the dog closest to her. At Dog Beach, Marilyn Monroe has a constant expression of contentment. It seems like she's about to say, "This is nice. I'll take it," every time she stops moving.

I guess Oscar notices me by another dog, so he runs over and sits at our feet.

"Hi, Oscie," I say. "Are you jealous?"

He stands up on his back legs and scratches his paw against the top of my jean shorts. I pet him for a little while, and Bennett gives Marilyn Monroe some attention. Soon, Micayla comes over with the Maltese twins, and before I realize what's going on, we're in a circle surrounded by dogs.

We look like a magazine advertisement for dog food.

"Guys, look at us!" I yell. "We are surrounded by dogs." I'm not really a yeller, but between the barking and the sounds of the ocean, I'm forced to raise my voice.

"We must look crazy," Micayla shouts.

"We should start a doggie day camp," Bennett suggests. "Like Seagate Day Camp, but for dogs! Look, they love us!"

First Mr. Brookfield said it, and now Bennett, and the more we talk about it, the more I wish it was a real idea and not just a funny thing to think about.

We start coming up with all the activities we could do in our doggie day camp—totally in a joking way—but even discussing it is so much fun. We decide we could even safely offer instructional swim in the ocean, since dogs are already good swimmers. And we could serve lunch on Dog Beach.

"It'll be better than the Seagate Day Camp lunch," Bennett says. "We were practically eating dog food to begin with!"

Seagate Day Camp used to have a cook named Trey Fischer, and my mom said he was some musician back in the day. He loved cooking—he just wasn't very good at it. His lunches were pretty terrible. He somehow found a way to ruin grilled cheese. Eventually he retired, and now kids bring their lunches from home. It's much better that way.

"Thank you guys so much," Amber says, now pushing Hudson in a jogging stroller as he shoves Cheerios into his mouth. All parents have jogging strollers on Seagate—they're the only ones tough enough to maneuver on the sand. "Come on, Mari," Amber says. But Marilyn Monroe just stays where she is, lying on the sand, with Micayla rubbing her belly.

"Well, this is the happiest I've seen her since we've gotten to Seagate, except when she's with you, Remy," Amber admits. "Normally she has a dog walker in the city, since I have my hands full with this one." She points to the stroller. "I think she's felt neglected."

Wow. There really is a need for a doggie support group. All these dog owners admit that their dogs aren't getting the attention they need.

"Everyone loves Dog Beach," I admit. "Even humans."

Amber attempts to put Marilyn Monroe in the second seat in the stroller, and Bennett bursts out laughing. I elbow him to get him to stop, but in all fairness, it's just so funny. Soon Micayla is laughing too, and once two of us are cracking up, the third one can't help but laugh.

"It's crazy, I know." Amber is laughing along with us now.

"I should let her walk, but I need to get home quickly."

She puts Marilyn Monroe in the seat, only for her to hop back out. This happens three or four times, and then Amber turns to us. "Hey, I have a wacky idea. You guys can totally say no. I know this isn't in your set hours, but, Remy, you are so good with her. And you're here anyway. Do you have any interest in keeping an eye on her for a little while longer? And then walking her home?" She raises her eyebrows. "I'd pay you extra, of course."

The three of us look at each other, moving our eyebrows up and down, doing weird blinking patterns, trying to communicate with our eyes.

"Sure!" we all say at the same time.

"Thank you." Amber smiles. "I had a feeling Remy would have awesome friends."

We spend another hour at Dog Beach, playing with the dogs, running around with them, and joking that we're on the path to really running a doggie day camp.

After that, we return Oscar to Dawn, and Marilyn Monroe to Amber, and we tell them that we're available for walks in the afternoon if they need us.

"So you're making all this dog-watching money," Bennett says to me as we're walking home. "Are you saving up for something?"

I shrug. "I haven't thought about it really."

"Well, there's a new iPhone coming out in September; you can always get that," Micayla suggests.

"Maybe." It does sound cool, but I feel weird taking these people's money, since I enjoy watching the dogs and spending time with them so much. In some ways, I feel like I should be paying *them*. Spending time with these pups has helped me so much when I'm sad and missing Danish. It's not like he's been replaced, but spending time with other dogs is better than spending time without any dogs at all. In the back of my mind, I've already decided that I'm going to donate the money to an animal shelter in Manhattan when we get home.

We're all so tired after the morning of dog-sitting that we head down to the pool and get side-by-side lounge chairs and decide to pull a Mr. Brookfield and take an afternoon nap right out in the open.

"Psst," I hear Micayla say, from the lounge chair next to me.

"I'm sleeping," I mumble, even though I know that won't stop Micayla from talking. We made a pact at a sleepover when we were eight that we could always wake each other up if we had something to say. And we've never broken that pact.

"Do you think it's weird that people trust us so much with their dogs?" she whispers.

"No, they can tell we're dog people," I assure her. "Dog people can sense other dog people. It's kind of like how moms can tell if another woman is a mom too."

"Is that true?" Micayla asks.

"I think so."

"Okay," Micayla says, and closes her eyes again.

But after that, I'm pretty convinced my afternoon nap is over. I've never been much of a napper. My mom says that getting me to nap even as a baby was pretty difficult, that the only place I'd really nap was in the stroller on the boardwalk. Obviously this only worked in the summer months, so winter in New York City was kind of hard.

I look over at my two friends, sleeping peacefully on the beautiful royal blue lounge chairs, and I realize that though things may be different this summer—it's strange without Danish, and we didn't expect to be dog-sitting—maybe different is okay. Maybe I can get used to different.

After the pool, I'm home, sitting on the front porch with my mom, when Mr. Brookfield walks over and asks to talk to her. That's something about Seagate that's probably the most different thing of all—people rarely use the phone; they'll just walk to someone's house to talk to them. It's kind of like we're living in olden times, in a tiny village.

My mom walks with Mr. Brookfield over to the garden at the side of the house. I twist my head a little to move my ear as close to the conversation as possible.

"Their mother would like them to be more social," I hear Mr. Brookfield say. "I am doing what I can. Would Remy like to come over for pizza later?"

I can't help but smile. Mr. Brookfield is making plans for Calvin and Claire like they're little kids. I bet back in Westchester, they're super popular and always busy. But on

Seagate, if you're not happy, you're a little bit weird.

"It's fine with me, but maybe you'll just want to ask Remy on your way out?" I hear my mom say. I don't know what to do. I don't want to say yes if I don't know if Micayla and Bennett are going. I don't know Calvin and Claire that well, and they don't really seem to like me, so I wouldn't want to go alone. But I can't tell Mr. Brookfield that.

"Remy, my dear." Mr. Brookfield looks around for me. He pretty much calls everyone his dear, but it's still a nice thing to say. "Would you care to dine at Casa Brookfield this evening? We will be eating Seagate's finest pizza."

I smile. "I accept your invitation, Mr. Brookfield."

"She's so polite," he tells my mom, and then turns to me. "See you at six."

When we can't see Mr. Brookfield anymore, my mom says, "That was nice of you, Remy. He's hoping his grandchildren can make the most of their summer here."

"It doesn't seem like they try very hard," I grumble. "And Seagate isn't a place you have to make the most of. It's a place where you relish every second."

"That may be true for you, but what's true for you isn't true for everyone."

It is as far as I can see.

A few minutes later, Micayla and Bennett text that they're going over to Mr. Brookfield's too, and I immediately feel better. It won't be that bad. If you're eating slices from Seagate Pizzeria, you don't really have much to complain about.

★ ★ ★

At six, we all meet over there. I'm the first one to arrive, so Claire takes me up to her room and shows me some of the new jeans she got when she was home.

"These are called the Five-Pocket Rocket," she tells me. "I hope I'm the only one to have them when we start school."

"They're really nice," I say, not because I notice anything that special about them, but because she seems so happy and proud.

She puts that pair on her bed and takes another pair out of the pale pink shopping bag. "And these are the Toile Stamp. They're brand-new, but the lady at the jeans store said they're definitely the next big thing."

"I like the stitching on the pockets." It was all I could come up with. To me, jeans are jeans. I can't ever tell the difference.

"That's exactly why they're going to be such a big deal," Claire says, holding the jeans up in front of us. "The stitching is all hand-done, and each pair is a tiny bit different."

"I could tell," I say, feeling proud I noticed something special. Then, a second later, it feels weird to be proud of noticing something I don't care about, like jeans.

We hear the doorbell, and for a moment I'm disappointed. Claire and I were finally connecting. Sure, it was about something totally superficial, but I still felt good about it.

"My man! Bennett!" I hear Calvin say. I look over the second-floor railing as they greet each other. They slap a high five so loud that I'm sure it made their hands sting.

"Calvin!" Bennett yells, and they do this weird chest-bump thing. I've never seen Bennett like this. It's almost as if he's acting in a play.

As soon as he sees me, he straightens his shirt a little and starts talking in his normal voice again. Soon Micayla arrives, and we sit in Mr. Brookfield's backyard drinking lemonade and eating cookies.

"Here we eat dessert before dinner," Mr. Brookfield tells us. "It's kind of a house rule."

"My kind of rule," I add.

Bennett and Calvin play paddleball against the back of Mr. Brookfield's house, and Claire, Micayla, and I sit around, still talking about Claire's new jeans. It seems that if we're talking about what she wants to talk about, she's happy. That's probably not a good quality, but it's better than having her rain on everyone else's fun.

"Pizza delivery!" Mr. Brookfield walks into the backyard carrying five pizzas. I'm pretty sure he over-ordered. Bennett jumps up to help him, and I feel proud again, prouder than Claire was about her new jeans.

Bennett is a good person. So what if he talked in that crazy voice before? He's good. He always does the right thing. I watch him talking to Mr. Brookfield as they set up the pizza, and I realize something. It doesn't matter who you are—if Bennett is talking to you, you feel like you're the only person in the world.

We sit and eat our pizza on Mr. Brookfield's Adirondack chairs.

"Would anyone care for some nice music while you eat your dinner?" Mr. Brookfield asks.

"Put on that scream recording," I tell him.

"Yeah!" Micayla says.

"Seriously, guys." Claire makes a face at us. "No one wants to listen to someone screaming over and over again."

"We do," I say.

Bennett looks at Calvin. It seems like he's waiting to see what Calvin does before he says anything. Maybe they're not paying attention, though, because they both stand up for another slice. They've already finished a whole pizza, just the two of them.

Mr. Brookfield puts on the scream recording loud enough for us to hear it in the backyard but not so loud that those awful Spitzes hear it next door. Although maybe it would stop their bickering and bring a smile to their always-disgruntled faces.

"Tell us the story again," I say to Mr. Brookfield, and everyone groans, except Bennett. I know most people don't like to hear the same story over and over again, so I don't mind when the rest of them go inside to play some video game on the computer, and I stay outside with Mr. Brookfield.

"Mrs. Pursuit said that maybe next summer your scream could be the signal for the start of the Sandcastle Contest," I tell him.

"Ah, never thought of that," he says.

"We can find other ways to make your scream a part of the Seagate tradition," I say. "It doesn't just have to live in the recording forever."

He replies, "I don't mind it. Sometimes things stay in the past and that's okay."

"Really?"

"Sometimes, Remy." He pats me on the shoulder. "Now go on inside with everyone else. Calvin has been playing this video game nonstop. Maybe you can explain to me what the big deal is."

"I'll try."

Bennett and Calvin play the game for hours—or at least it seems that way—so Claire, Micayla, and I go back upstairs to look through Claire's closet.

"I'm glad you guys are so into fashion," she says, which makes me realize that maybe she's not all that into fashion herself. If she were, she'd probably be able to tell that we pretty much wear the same jean shorts every single day.

We're going through Claire's hooded sweatshirt collection (so far we've counted fifteen) when we hear stomping up the stairs. The boys come barging in.

I hear my phone beep three times, telling me I have a voice mail. I can't believe what it says.

"You guys," I say, a little out of breath. "I just got a call. Marilyn Monroe's mother recommended us to another dog owner."

"Marilyn Monroe's mother!" Claire yelps, and bursts out laughing.

"She's a dog," I explain.

"She's, like, a really famous, beautiful actress, Remy," Claire replies.

"Duh. I know that. But Marilyn Monroe is also the name of a dog on Seagate." I glare at her. "I watch her two mornings a week. She's my pal."

"When? What kind of dog?" Micayla asks, ignoring Claire.

Claire looks at us like we've all lost our minds and goes back to her closet. I wonder if she has any clothes left at home, or if she brought everything she owns to Seagate.

"A Newfoundland named Rascal," I tell them. "I don't know when. We have to call her back."

I look at my phone to make sure I save the message and see another missed call and a voice mail. A man needs help with his German shepherd named Atticus.

"Wow, are you guys, like, running a dog-sitting business or something?" Claire asks, folding what seems like her fifth gray hoodie.

"I guess so," the three of us reply at the same time.

Sometimes something that starts out small becomes another thing entirely. Watching one dog turned into watching many dogs. And maybe that's how Mr. Brookfield feels about his scream. To him, it's just a loud scream, but to movie watchers, it's a huge part of the experience.

Micayla, Bennett, and I agreed to meet at the Dollhouse Café for breakfast at eight in the morning. We want to beat the brunch crowd and be able to sit and talk about our plans for this dog-sitting business. When we first discussed a doggie day camp, we were kidding, but now that we're starting to get more requests, it really seems like it's happening.

Although I'm usually the latest sleeper of us all, I get to the Dollhouse Café before they do, which is great because it gives me a few minutes to look around and see if Fatima has added any new dollhouses to the place. She collects dollhouses, but she keeps them all at the restaurant so that everyone can see them. She even lets the kids play with them before their meal arrives or when they're done and waiting for their parents to finish. She has every kind of dollhouse—

old wooden ones, modern plastic ones, steep dollhouses like brownstones in Brooklyn, and sprawling mansions like you'd find in Victorian England.

The scrambled eggs here are the best in the world, and you get some time to play with a dollhouse—what could be better?

Fatima greets me with her famous "How are things?" and I tell her I'm meeting Micayla and Bennett here. She brings a basket of fresh muffins and scones and a hot chocolate.

"Sorry we're late," Bennett says when they get to the table.

We all order the same thing: scrambled eggs with cheddar and chives (Fatima's specialty), as well as buttered biscuits and home fries.

"Calvin was really intrigued by our business," Bennett tells us.

"Let's not declare it a business yet," Micayla adds. "We haven't even called the new clients back."

Micayla's usually a morning person, but she seems really grumpy today. She's slumped over in her chair, and her eyes are puffy, almost like she's been crying.

"Let's vote on a name first," Bennett says. "Things become real when they have a name, I think."

I take a second to ponder that, and I think he may be on to something. Maybe Mr. Brookfield's scream never became known because it didn't have a name. I wonder what would happen if we named it now.

"Sure," I say. "How about the Seagate Dog Sitters Service?"

"What about Seagate Pooch Pals?" Micayla suggests.

"Or Seagate Doggie Day Camp, like we said originally?" Bennett starts writing down the names on the place mat. I like how organized he is.

I sip my hot chocolate and say, "Y'know what? Let's think about it while we discuss all the other stuff first." If we're going to name it, it has to be the right name. And I'm just not sure we can come up with it on the spot.

They agree, and I go through all the other stuff that we need to discuss: calling back the people who have called us, making up a schedule of who handles what dog and when, putting up posters so we can get other customers, and making sure we always have bags to carry any supplies the dogs need and also to clean up after them.

"This is kind of a lot of work," Micayla admits.

"It'll be fine, Mic." I rub her shoulder. "We're in this together."

"What about me? I have to take care of Asher, and Calvin's trying to convince me to take this lifeguarding class with him at the pool. It starts in a few days." Bennett's phone starts ringing and he answers it right here, even though his mom hates it when people take calls in restaurants. "Yo, dude," he says. "Yeah, okay, I'll call you."

"Calvin?" I ask.

Bennett nods and goes back to his eggs. We divide up the customer calls and agree to meet at Oscar's around ten, when we always pick him up. The other dog owners can bring their pets to Dog Beach around ten thirty, and we can figure out their needs.

Bennett leaves early so he can go check out the sign-up sheet for the lifeguarding class. Then it's just Micayla and me, finishing our breakfast. Micayla keeps saying how overwhelming this dog-sitting thing is and how she didn't expect to have a job this summer. I need to change the topic, because she's starting to make me feel stressed. The thing is, I don't understand why she's suddenly so crazed with all of it.

Everyone was so excited yesterday. I don't understand what happened.

"So what else is new?" I ask her. I realize this sounds so dumb, since I spend pretty much all day with her, every day, but I wanted to change the topic.

"Huh?"

"I mean, like, I dunno, have you heard from your home friends? Did you get your last report card? Who are your teachers going to be next year?" I look down at my plate. It suddenly feels strange to make eye contact with her.

She moves her chair back from the table a little bit. "My stomach is starting to hurt." She takes a sip of water. "You're asking me too many questions."

We're the kind of friends who can always be honest with each other, but I wish she hadn't said that. No one likes someone who's pushy and makes them nervous. Maybe I did ask too many questions.

I stay quiet and finish my muffin and try to think of something funny to say, but nothing comes to me. When you're friends like Micayla and I are friends, you can usually read each other's mind. But I guess I messed up.

I look into Micayla's hot chocolate mug. "Yours looks creamier than mine."

"I think I got an extra marshmallow."

Micayla and I used to do this all the time when we were little—compare our hot chocolates, count the marshmallows in each mug, see how the color changed as we drank it. I don't know why we did it, or how it started, or why it was even a game, but somehow it made drinking the hot chocolate even tastier.

That's pretty much how everything is with Micayla—she makes every game more fun, every meal more delicious.

I think back to what Mr. Brookfield said about thinking about the past too much, and how it's important to also focus on the present and the future. But the past is comforting, and the future seems overwhelming.

Focusing on the present is probably most important anyway. And that's good, because we have a lot to focus on with this new dog-sitting business. It may not have a name yet, but it has a ton of potential.

"You guys might want to hand out a form," Mason Redmond tells us. We're all standing around Dog Beach, watching Oscar and waiting for our other clients to show up. It sounds silly to refer to dogs as clients, but I'm not sure what else to call them.

"Like for the owners to fill out, with the dog's name, their owner's number, any special information you might need to know," he continues. "Or I guess you could put it all in your phones."

"That's a genius idea!" Micayla yelps. "Save paper, and we'll have it handy! With a folder, we could forget it or lose it or something, but we guard our phones with our lives." I'm glad to hear her enthusiastic again, after our awkward breakfast at the Dollhouse Café. Maybe she was just having a bad morning.

Bennett laughs. "That's kind of embarrassing to admit, Mic."

"It's just society these days," Mason adds, like he's some old grandfather and not a kid who is exactly our age. "We're so focused on technology and disconnected from—"

"Well, thanks for the advice, Mason," I interrupt him, because he'll go on and on about something for hours, and I see Marilyn Monroe coming.

"From now on, can you please pick her up?" Amber asks us, looking exhausted. "I'll pay extra; I just can't schlep her here and then schlep Hudson to music class."

I want to remind her that the whole island is only five miles long and seven miles wide, but I don't think that would really help her much. Plus, I'm used to her frazzled state of mind. I feel really good when I can calm her down and make her feel better.

"Amber, we're going to be taking on some new clients, so we're reorganizing our schedule," I tell her. "We should be able to pick up Marilyn Monroe. By the time we return her to you, we'll let you know how the rest of the week will go."

She smiles and looks down at her stroller to see her sleeping toddler. "Thank you for being so organized." She sighs. "Guess we missed Seagate Toddler Jam. But at least I can sit outside and enjoy my coffee in peace."

Amber leaves and Marilyn Monroe runs around happily, her red bow in her hair just perfectly. Oscar comes over to greet her, and they bark at each other for a few minutes.

I'm starting to get the sense that Oscar may have a crush on Marilyn Monroe—it's the way he follows her around but doesn't get too close, and the way he looks for her all the time, even when he's not with her.

It's like Micayla and Mason Redmond.

Rascal and Atticus arrive a few minutes later, even though the owners don't seem to know each other. The woman who brings Rascal is wearing yoga pants and a tank top and keeps running in place even as she talks to us. "I'm Andi, nice to meet you." She smiles. "Rascal is my mother's dog, but she's recovering from a hip replacement and can't walk much now," Andi says, panting in a similar fashion to Rascal. I notice this and cover my mouth to stop myself from cracking up. "So, if you could pick him up and watch him for a few hours, and then bring him back to 328 Seashell Place, that would be great. I teach yoga and have a very busy schedule."

"We can handle that," Micayla says, petting Rascal's head.

"Great. Thanks."

Micayla puts Andi's information into her phone while I introduce myself to Rascal. His fur is so smooth and silky and as black as can be—it looks like velvet. He's happy digging in the sand, but before we know it, he's off and running and swimming in the water. We get a little freaked out at first, but Mason assures us that Newfoundlands are good swimmers.

Atticus's owner stays around for a little while and plays with him, and then he tells us that Atticus appears lonely at home and needs to make some friends. "I don't know what it is," the man tells us. "I just get the vibe that he's bored."

We turn around and watch Atticus sprinting across the sand and into the water and playing with Rascal. It almost looks like they're purposely splashing each other.

"Are you on Seagate all summer?" I ask. "What's his life like at home?"

Bennett cracks up and elbows me. "You sound like my mom, Rem! You can be a doggie psychiatrist."

I start laughing too, and even Atticus's owner chuckles a bit.

"I'm a literature professor, and we rented a house for the summer, just Atticus and me, but I'm busy working on my new book," he tells us. "I'm Paul, by the way."

We all introduce ourselves, and I start to wonder—is Atticus lonely? Or is Paul the lonely one?

Are all owners' problems reflected in their dogs?

I'm too embarrassed to say any of this out loud, but maybe Paul should be bringing Atticus here to meet other dog owners, and they'd both make friends.

"How'd you find out about us, Paul?"

"My neighbor is Amber, Marilyn Monroe's owner."

We nod.

"She mentioned some kids who were watching dogs, and I figured it would be good for Atti."

Atticus and Rascal hit it off right away, almost as if they've been waiting their whole lives to meet and be friends. I start to wonder if the yoga lady and Paul would make good friends too.

Bennett, Micayla, and I finish putting the dogs' names and owners' contact information into our phones, and we spend the next few hours running and playing with them.

Marilyn Monroe usually sits and waits for other dogs to come to her. She likes to hang with me, and sometimes I think she's asking me to go to Daisy's, just the two of us, like we did that one time. I get that sad, missing-Danish feeling, but I don't have much time to feel bad. I'm hanging out with four dogs right now, and my best friends.

I'll always miss Danish, but I can't think about it all the time.

Oscar is the kind of dog who hangs out with everyone, checking on Marilyn Monroe every few minutes, visiting the Maltese duo, swimming with Atticus and Rascal every now and then.

It's only been a few hours, but all the doggie personalities are coming through.

I sit back on the bench for a few minutes and take it all in. We actually have a dog-sitting business. We still have to set our prices, but I almost don't care if we get paid.

It seems so strange and so amazing, I don't even know what to really think about it.

Off to one side, I see Micayla talking to Mason Redmond. They're actually chatting and she's not running away. I see Oscar going up to Marilyn Monroe every few minutes, and it's seriously cute, but I wonder if she's starting to get annoyed. She turns away from him every now and again.

I look around for Bennett and see him throwing a Frisbee to Rascal, while Atticus tries to get into the game too.

Bennett talks to them like they're people, not dogs. "Atticus, hold up a minute, pal."

I'm watching them and Bennett doesn't notice, so I keep watching and laughing as Rascal brings the Frisbee back over and over again, and Atticus jumps up on Bennett's legs to get it out of his hand.

Bennett's cargo shorts are hanging low, and he keeps pulling them up. He's wearing the T-shirt from last year's Seagate Sandcastle Contest, and I don't know what it is exactly, or why it's happening now, but I feel like I'm seeing Bennett, my Bennett, my best friend for life, in this whole new way. Like all the times I saw him before, it was a blur, or I didn't look closely enough, or I didn't notice him at all.

It's like the narrow wooden table in the foyer of our Seagate house. It's been there forever, and I never paid any attention to it. But the other day I lost my keys and I was searching everywhere. I discovered they had fallen and were underneath that wooden table.

I was so grateful to find the keys that I looked at the table more closely and realized it has all these pretty designs on it. My mom told me that Grandma and Grandpa found it lying on the sidewalk one day. They brought it in, cleaned it up, and then carved their initials in the bottom—MB + SB.

It had been in our house all this time, and I never knew that.

Bennett feels like that table right now, only better and more special and more lovable.

I want to run up to him and tell him that, tell him the whole thing about the table, because I really think he'd understand. But I can't. I'm worried the words would come out weird, and I wouldn't make any sense.

So I stay back on the bench and continue to take it all in.

It doesn't take long for us to settle into a schedule.

I go pick up Marilyn Monroe and Atticus, since they live on the same street and they're the closest to me. Micayla picks up Rascal, and Bennett picks up Oscar, and we all meet at Daisy's before we walk over to Dog Beach.

On the days that I watch Hudson and hang with Marilyn Monroe in the mornings, Micayla and Bennett take care of the other dogs and then we meet them there.

Sometimes we get pancakes at Daisy's, and the dogs spend time together, drinking water and eating treats. Sometimes we just pick up lemonades to go.

Either way, it's a routine. And I like routine.

The days speed by, taking care of the dogs—we're with them every weekday morning and sometimes afternoons too. We also have a few new clients.

Buttercup, the yellow Lab, is here for the next two weeks. She's part of a family with two parents and two kids, and they're always taking day trips. They go to explore the lighthouses on all the islands and also take ferry trips to Connecticut and Massachusetts. So when they're on a day trip, we get Buttercup for the whole day. She's sweet and playful and is just the friend Marilyn Monroe needed.

When Buttercup's not with us, we can all tell that Marilyn Monroe misses her. She'll wander around aimlessly, looking forlorn. We give her extra treats on those days.

We also watch a Shar-Pei named Lucky every now and again. He's only on Seagate for another week, but his owners like to spend all day sunbathing and reading on the beach. Lucky pretty much keeps to himself, but Bennett's trying to get him to come out of his shell.

Every time I see Bennett, I get this excited, energetic feeling. It's so weird. I was always excited to see him, but now it's different, and I can't even really explain it or understand it. I keep thinking it's going to disappear, but it's almost the end of July and it's still here. A month from now, we'll be leaving Seagate, and I have no idea what I'll do with this feeling when I won't see Bennett every day.

We're so busy taking care of the dogs, but we still have time for fun. The Seagate Knowbodies Trivia Competition is tomorrow, and I can't wait. It's definitely on my list of top five favorite nights of the summer.

Micayla, Bennett, and I are always a team, and we compete against other teams of three. The teams can be all kids or all adults, and everyone is treated fairly. Some people think it's weird for kids to compete against adults, but when it comes to Seagate Trivia, sometimes the kids know more.

We've won the past two years in a row, and I think we can win this year too.

Mr. Brookfield invites us over for pizza again, and I hope we'll have time to go over our trivia after dinner. I don't want to talk about it too much in front of Calvin and Claire, though, because I don't want to make them feel bad about not being on our team.

We've been to Mr. Brookfield's for pizza once a week for the last three weeks. He always orders too much, puts dessert out first, and pretends he doesn't want to play his scream recording, when I know he really does.

Calvin and Claire seem to have warmed up to life on Seagate, even though they don't really do much except lie by the pool and eat ice cream. They haven't asked to help with the dogs, and we haven't offered.

The way things are going, business could get really crazy in August, though, and we may need to ask for their help. We'll see. I'm getting along with Claire a little better now, but I wouldn't want her to say something mean and ruin the dog-sitting.

We're all sitting around eating our pizza, listening to the Scream, when I overhear Bennett and Calvin talking.

"Did you tell them yet?" Calvin whispers to Bennett, and

then looks up. He sees me looking at them, and I guess he knows I overheard.

I can't help it. I look at Bennett way more than I used to.

"No, man." Bennett bites into his slice. "I will. Don't worry."

Calvin nudges Bennett, and then they both look up at me, and now they both know I was listening. I look down at my plate and pretend to be really involved in whatever Micayla and Claire are discussing.

"Yeah, my mom says I have to wait until eighth grade to wear makeup to school," Claire says. "But no one really wears it yet where I live anyway. Just, like, a little lip gloss."

"Same with me," Micayla adds.

"What are you guys talking about?" I ask.

"Shh," Micayla says to Claire, not to me, and I can't figure out what's going on. What's so secret about wearing makeup?

I decide not to ask questions, but it bothers me the whole rest of the night. We end up staying at Mr. Brookfield's really late, and we don't have time to practice our trivia.

"Don't worry. We know everything there is to know about Seagate," Micayla tells me as we're walking home. "They don't change the questions much."

I shrug. "I guess so."

"I have to tell you guys something," Bennett says, following a few steps behind us out of Mr. Brookfield's house.

I had almost forgotten about Bennett and Calvin's secret conversation. What with Micayla and Claire's weird makeup talk, there are too many secrets and strange whispers to keep track of.

"What?" I ask.

"Promise you won't be mad," Bennett says. He smiles a little in his goofy, cheerful Bennett way, and I feel like I could never be mad at him, no matter what. But I'd never tell him that.

"What is it?" Micayla asks, impatient.

"I'll be here for Seagate Knowbodies, but I have to bail on the next few days of dog-sitting," he tells us. It's a short sentence, but it feels like a knife in my chest, and I'm not sure why. "Calvin invited me to go on his dad's boat for a few days, and I feel like I should go."

"Well, don't go just because you feel like you should," I say, and then instantly regret it. I sound angry and I don't like it.

"No, um, I mean . . ." Bennett waits a few seconds before talking again. "I want to go. I think it'll be cool. Just us guys."

I don't know what to say to that.

"It's okay for me to have other friends, you know." He jabs me a little with his elbow, like he's joking. But sometimes jokes can be truths in disguise. I think this is one of those times.

"No biggie," Micayla says, like none of what Bennett said was a big deal or even a little bit surprising. "Rem and I can handle the pooches."

We get to her house, and she says good night and blows

us kisses, the way she always does. Through the window, we see her mom sitting in the big armchair, reading.

Maybe Micayla doesn't think it's a big deal that Bennett's leaving for a few days, but I do. I know I can't say that, though. I know I need to play it cool and act like it's fine. I mean, of course it's fine. Bennett can have other friends.

I just don't know why it feels so sad. It's not like he's going on the boat trip and never coming back.

"We'll be fine with the dogs," I say. I realize that we passed by Bennett's house, and he kept walking with us until he finished talking, and now he's walking me home, totally out of his way.

"You'll be more than fine," Bennett says. "You're awesome with those dogs, Rem."

"Thanks. But you are too." I smile. "Imagine, if you never found Oscar, we might not even have this business."

He shakes his head. "Imagine if you never started sitting at Amber's house while Hudson napped. And you were the one who cared about finding Oscar in the first place." He high-fives me, and I walk down the stone path to my house.

When I get to the door, I can't resist looking back at him. "Get psyched for trivia," I say. He's just standing there, at the end of the path, watching me walk inside. I wonder what that means. I've never seen him do that before.

"You know it," he replies.

The next day is really busy. We meet at Dog Beach earlier than usual because Oscar's mom has to take the babies to their pediatrician. I get worried that he'll be lonely without Marilyn Monroe and the others, so all the dogs get picked up early.

Then we take them for lunch at Daisy's—she serves up a full doggie menu on weekdays, when she's not so busy—and we entertain them for most of the afternoon.

I can tell that Marilyn Monroe wishes it was just the two of us at Daisy's, the way she sits on my lap at the table and then leaves a few dog treats by my feet, as if she thinks I'd enjoy the treats too.

It's a great day, but by the end, we're so tired that I'm worried we won't have enough energy for trivia.

"Let's meet there," Micayla tells me as we're walking home

from Sundae Best. After such a tiring day, we deserve ice cream and we need the sugar to energize ourselves. "Six o'clock, right?"

I nod. Bennett's already back home, since he needed to meet Asher after camp. I don't know why they wouldn't pick me up on the way, but I'm too tired to ask.

I rush inside, shower, put on a pair of skinny jeans and a tank top—and even though I only planned to lie down for five minutes, I fall sound asleep on my bed.

When I wake up and look at my clock, it's five thirty.

I rush out of bed, tie my hair back in a ponytail, since it's such a mess from my falling asleep with it wet, and hurry downstairs.

"Rem, no dinner?" my mom asks. She grilled some hot dogs, and they're on a platter in the middle of the kitchen table.

"I can't. Seagate Knowbodies tonight."

"Take a hot dog for the walk," my mom says. "We'll meet you there."

I quickly put a hot dog on a paper plate, squirt some ketchup on it, and hurry out the door.

I get there in ten minutes, and I'm pretty impressed with my ability to walk and eat. Micayla and Bennett are already sitting up on the stage, and they're testing out the buzzers. The best part of Seagate Knowbodies (aside from winning) is that we get to use actual buzzers like in a real game show.

"Sorry I'm late, guys," I say, a little out of breath.

Micayla motions to me that I have something on my face, and I quickly wipe away the drop of ketchup from the corner of my mouth. Maybe I'm not as good at walking and eating as I thought I was.

I sit between Micayla and Bennett. They saved me the middle seat. It was nice of them to do that, but that wasn't the reason they did it. They did it because we always sit in this order, and we're a little superstitious. We've won the past two years sitting in this exact formation.

Up on the stage, I can see everything. All the people who came to watch, Sundae Best's ice cream cone sign, the one-dollar-books cart in front of Novel Ideas Book Shop, and even the path all the way to the ocean.

They only put up the stage a few times a year: for Seagate Knowbodies, for the Fourth of July concert, and for the judges of the Seagate Halloween Costume Contest.

I feel lucky that I get to sit here, because the view is one of the best in the world.

Unfortunately, I also see Claire and Calvin in the front row. Yes, they have grown on me, but it doesn't feel right to see them at such a Seagate-y event. Also, Calvin is sitting there making faces at Bennett, doing those armpit farts and then pretending to faint from the imaginary smell. He's going to distract Bennett, and we're going to lose. I don't think that's what any of us want. And Claire looks ridiculously bored, staring at her phone and rolling her eyes.

"Welcome to the fifteenth annual Seagate Knowbodies

Trivia Competition!" Mr. Aprone yells out into his megaphone. He's the head of the Seagate Community Association, and he also owns the Novel Ideas Book Shop. He lives in Rhode Island but comes to Seagate every weekend of the year. "That's K-N-O-W, people! Our reigning champions, Team RemBenMic, are back, and we also have a few newcomers, Team Sunny Days and Team No Sugar Added."

We're allowed to keep coming back to the contest because we keep winning, but the newcomers have to go through a rigorous selection process. They have to submit a proposal about why they want to participate, and they have to score high enough on Mr. Aprone's entrance exam. He takes this whole thing very seriously, obviously, which only makes it more fun.

"Team No Sugar Added is a group of ladies from the diabetes support group," Micayla whispers to me. Her mom is a nurse and she volunteers with that group during the summer, helping answer questions and stuff. "They look so excited, don't they?"

"Yeah." I look over at them again after I hear the loud slaps from their high fives. "I guess they're not Sundae Best's best customers." I laugh.

"They have sugar-free flavors," Micayla reminds me, all serious-sounding. Maybe my joke wasn't really that funny.

"So, teams, hands off the buzzers!" Mr. Aprone says. "We're ready to begin."

He pauses for applause, and I see Calvin standing up,

clapping furiously, the only one who has decided to give us a standing ovation before the contest has even started.

Bennett cracks up but stops when I glare at him.

"First question: How many gazebos are there on Seagate?"

My hand hits the buzzer first. Mr. Aprone always starts with an easy one, and this one is almost too easy.

"Yes, RemBenMic has hit the buzzer first," he says. He has a screen that shows which team's buzzer buzzes first, so there's really no debating it.

"Six," I answer.

"That is correct," Mr. Aprone says. "Bonus question goes to RemBenMic first and then will be opened to the other teams if they answer incorrectly. It is: Where are the gazebos located?"

I don't have to hit the buzzer since it's our question, but I do offer it up to Micayla and Bennett to see if they want to answer. They shake their heads. Maybe I'm imagining it, but I start to feel like I'm the only one fired up about the contest.

"On the grassy lawn by the stadium, by the entryway to West Beach, one in front of Sundae Best, one by the entrance to Dog Beach, one behind High Tide Bar & Grill, and one at the end of Ocean Walk."

"That is correct!"

Everyone claps after I answer, and even Claire looks a little bit proud, but Bennett and Micayla have sort of a delayed reaction. They don't look as excited as they should be. I want to nudge them with my elbow and get them to perk up. I wonder if it's the long day with the dogs that exhausted them, or if it's something else. I can't interrupt the contest to ask.

I also can't be the only one on the team to answer the questions. That's a Seagate Knowbodies rule—one team member can answer a maximum of three questions in a row.

"Next question," Mr. Aprone says after he adjusts his microphone. It was making a terrible screeching sound, and we all had to cover our ears. "When was Seagate founded?"

I attempt to hit the buzzer, but No Sugar Added gets to it first. I guess I delayed a little bit because I was hoping Micayla or Bennett would take the chance.

"1932," one of the women answers.

The bonus question is who was the first person to come to Seagate, and of course I know the answer is Melvin Jasper, but they get the first chance to answer and they get it right.

The next question goes to Sunny Days, but I didn't know the answer. It was some geographic question about what it's called when an ocean experiences two equal high tides and two equal low tides in a day. The answer is *semidiurnal*, and I always forget that.

We each get a few more questions, and then the score is tied.

"Come on, guys," I say, finally. Micayla did get the answer right about the number of kids in Seagate Schoolhouse's first graduating class, so I high-fived her for that. "We need to perk up! Bennett, you haven't answered a single question."

"Okay, okay." He does this weird finger signal to Calvin and then bursts out laughing. It seems like Bennett would much rather be in the audience watching with Calvin instead of participating with us. "The next one is all me."

So when Mr. Aprone asks, "Name the famous actor who once had a summer home on Seagate," and Bennett hits the buzzer, I get all excited because he obviously knows this one.

Except that when Bennett's ready to answer, Calvin does some awkward fist-bump thing and Bennett starts laughing and then says, "Alec Baldwin."

"Unfortunately, that's incorrect," Mr. Aprone says.

Then No Sugar Added hits the buzzer because I'm not allowed to answer, since my teammate got it wrong.

"George Clooney," one of the ladies says, and that team takes the lead.

"That is correct!" Mr. Aprone yells. "We will now take a five-minute break."

"Bennett!" I say. "Don't you remember our moms telling us the story over and over again?"

He looks at me, confused.

"Remember? When we were little babies, I was crying so loud that George Clooney came over from his table at Picnic to our table and picked me up and got me to quiet down?"

"Why were you eating at Picnic when you were so little?" he asks me.

"My parents' anniversary." I glare at him. That's so not the important part of the story. What is wrong with him? "Duh."

"Sorry, Rem." He hits the buzzer accidentally and gets everyone's attention. "Sorry, folks, technical difficulties." He's not even making sense. That wasn't a technical difficulty; that was him being stupid, but Calvin laughs anyway.

It seems Calvin will laugh at whatever Bennett does.

He's ruining our chances at winning for the third year in a row, and yet he's just laughing. I turn my head to whisper something to Micayla, and I notice that she's not sitting next to me anymore.

I look around, shocked that I didn't even notice her leaving. Maybe she was sick and had to leave in a hurry. I wonder if I should go check on her. Then I look out into the audience and I see her sitting next to Avery Sanders, whispering something in her ear.

Mr. Aprone announces that the break is over, and Micayla runs back onto the stage.

"What was that all about?" I ask her.

"Nothing." She looks at me weirdly, like it's a bizarre question. I don't have time to say anything else, because Mr. Aprone tells us it's now round two.

"Name three of Sundae Best's retired flavors," he says.

Bennett whispers, "I got this one," and hits the buzzer. He answers, "Peach pistachio, caramel apple, and s'more explosion!"

"Yes!" Mr. Aprone matches Bennett's enthusiasm, and then everyone starts cheering. It's silly, but the fact that Bennett answered this question right immediately makes me feel better. Of course he knows the answer. He knows the Sundae Best flavors better than anyone.

But after that, things go downhill again. Sunny Days gets a question right about the consistency of sand, and No Sugar Added correctly answers a question about some old folk-singer who performed on Seagate more than two hundred times. Then we get an answer right about the Seagate Book Club, since all our moms are in it.

But the final question is about the price of a summer home on Seagate in 1950, and we have absolutely no idea.

We lose.

The RemBenMic victory streak is over.

Bennett's leaving tomorrow for a four-day boat trip, and Micayla was whispering with Avery Sanders.

Maybe I'm being dramatic, but it feels like it's not just the Seagate Knowbodies contest that's over. It feels like Seagate life as I know it, and have always known it, is over too.

At least I have the dogs. That's what I keep telling myself. When everything else feels out of control, the dogs are reliable. In a way, dogs are better than people. They don't take their bad moods out on you, if they even get in bad moods. They don't let you down, and they're always pretty much the same.

Bennett plans to leave at ten in the morning. He told us last night to meet him at Mornings at nine. When I asked him why, he replied, "I want to say good-bye, duh," in this weird voice that made me wonder if he was kidding.

Micayla picks me up on the way, but she's not her usual cheery, morning-person self. Instead she's dragging her feet and rubbing her eyes and complaining.

"I want a day off from dog-sitting," she grumbles.

"Well, we got the morning off," I remind her. "So we could go meet Bennett for who knows what reason."

"Rem, he just wanted to say good-bye," she says, sounding exasperated. "You're overthinking it as usual."

After that, I stay quiet. It seems like I'm always saying the wrong thing, and it feels so bad that it makes me want to say nothing at all.

We get to Mornings, and Bennett is at the table with three chocolate croissants and three fresh-squeezed orange juices.

I get excited that it's just the three of us about to eat this amazingly yummy breakfast—but when I see Calvin come out of the bathroom, I feel out of sorts again.

"No croissant for you, Cal?" I ask.

"Cal?" Micayla says, and everyone laughs like it's totally strange that I called him that. It's just a nickname. Sheesh.

"I already had one," he says. Then there's an awkward silence, and I take a bite of mine just to have something to do.

Calvin's phone pings. He looks down and then says, "My dad wants us to meet at the main dock in twenty minutes. He got here early."

So Bennett shoves the whole croissant into his mouth and chugs his fresh-squeezed orange juice and burps as loud as I've ever heard anyone burp. No joke.

"Sorry to run out," he says, "but I have to go pick up my bag first."

"Yeah, and my dad gets really annoyed when people are late," Calvin tells us.

"Bye," I say quickly, not looking at either of them. "Have fun."

"Yeah, enjoy your bromance," Micayla teases, and I start laughing along with her.

"Ha-ha." Bennett gets up from the table and throws away his trash, and just like that he's off with Calvin, leaving Seagate, and us, behind.

"So we should probably go get the dogs, right?" Micayla asks me, looking down at her phone.

"Yeah," I reply.

We walk to Oscar's first and then to Marilyn Monroe's. Atticus and Rascal will meet us there. I wonder if we'll be okay handling two dogs each without Bennett to help with Frisbee and treats.

I count off how many days Bennett will be gone.

I've always missed him and been excited to see him, but this is different. This feels like a tiny part of my world is missing, like things won't be normal again until he's back. And the thing is, he was acting like a total doofus at the Seagate Knowbodies competition and even this morning, with the burping and running out like we didn't matter at all.

He wasn't acting like the Bennett I know. But I miss him anyway.

Rascal, Atticus, and Oscar are involved in a fierce game of chase-each-other-around-the-beach, and Micayla and I are sitting on the bench with Marilyn Monroe at our feet. We haven't said much to each other since breakfast, and I'm not sure why. Probably because I'm sad about Bennett leaving, but I think it could be more than that.

Micayla didn't really put much into the Seagate Knowbodies competition either, and after it was over, she seemed more relieved than anything else.

"Are you okay, Mic?" I have to ask. She's not herself, and

waiting around for someone to go back to being herself never works for me. I'm too impatient.

"Yeah. Fine. Why?" She looks down at the sand and not at me.

I continue to pet Marilyn Monroe, who is so happy to just be sitting between Micayla and me on this bench. She has no interest in being with the other dogs today. Maybe she could sense that we'd be feeling a little lonely without Bennett.

"You just don't seem like yourself," I say, because it's true.

"I'm fine, I said." She looks at me finally. "You're not acting like yourself either. I'm going to talk to Mason."

She gets up from the bench before I have a chance to say anything else and leaves me alone with Marilyn Monroe.

"Do you notice anything strange about her?" I ask Marilyn Monroe. She looks up at me and lets out a little whimper, then lies back down so I can rub her head.

I know that whimper. It means she agrees with me.

Across the beach I see Micayla talking to Mason Red-mond. That's one thing that's changed. She doesn't run away from him anymore. Now she stands there, waving her arms, laughing. I wonder what they're talking about.

So I sit there on the bench and continue to feel sorry for myself. Marilyn Monroe doesn't mind it, and every few minutes I'll tell her how I'm feeling, and she'll whimper and look up at me, and it really makes me feel like she understands.

She's not Danish, but I never imagined I'd feel this close to a new dog so soon. Dogs can't be replaced. I think everyone knows that. But I'm realizing that it's possible to find an empty spot in your heart for a new one.

At the end of the day, Micayla and I round up Marilyn Monroe, Atticus, Oscar, and Rascal. We also offered to bring Palm home, because his owners were going for an early dinner at Picnic. We'll just let him in through the doggie door. They left food out for him and everything.

So Micayla walks with Oscar, Marilyn Monroe, and Atticus, and I have Palm and Rascal. The dogs are being good and not trying to run away or go off leash, but I can't wait to get them home and be done for the day. I'm feeling anxious about what's going on with Micayla. I don't know what it is, but things just don't seem quite right.

"So what are you doing tonight?" I ask Micayla after we drop off Oscar and Atticus.

"Hanging out with Avery," she says like it's no big deal. But they never hang out one-on-one.

"Really?" I ask.

"Yeah, really." Micayla crinkles her cheeks at me. "What's the big deal? She's our friend. And anyway, she's really fun this summer. You never even gave her a chance."

"That's not true." I smile, trying to make it seem like she's wrong and I don't care that she just said that. "Well. Have fun doing whatever you're doing."

"She's taking me on a tour of Seagate Schoolhouse."

"Um, okay," I reply, not knowing what to say to that. I didn't even know the schoolhouse was open during the summer.

"I'm becoming a year-rounder, Remy," Micayla says so quickly that I almost miss it.

"Oh." I'm so surprised, I lose my grip on the leashes I'm carrying, and the dogs start to run away. Thankfully, I get them back before they've gone too far.

Dogs, just behave right now. Please. I just got some huge news, and I can't focus on so much at once.

"I can't believe it," I say. "Did you just find out?"

"I'll explain after we've dropped off the dogs," she says, like she doesn't really want to talk about it but she's being forced to.

How could she have waited to tell me something so big?

We don't stay and chat with the dogs' owners as long as we usually do, and I feel a little bit bad about that. But when your best friend tells you huge news, you just don't have room for any other conversations.

After all the dogs are returned to their homes, we sit down on the Adirondack chairs by the stadium so we can talk without any interruptions.

"So did you just find out?" I ask again, looking down at my feet. My hot pink toenail polish is now chipped and baby pink from being exposed to so much sun.

"No." She doesn't look at me. "I've known since the end of the school year."

I nod and finally look up at her, and she's all slumped over her knees in the chair, instead of sitting back comfortably— the whole purpose of an Adirondack chair.

We sit there quietly, not talking, even though I have a million questions. Then I ask, "How come you didn't tell me?"

"Remy, you were so depressed about Danish, and then so busy with the dogs, and basically, I just didn't feel like you'd care that much." She finally leans back in the chair.

"Not care? Hello? Micayla, you're my best friend, and Seagate is my favorite place in the universe. How could I not care?" I feel myself yelling, and I don't want to yell. I don't want to be mad. I just can't understand this at all.

She's been keeping this from me for weeks. She's never kept a secret like this before—not that I know about, at least.

"I just wanted to enjoy the summer like we've always done," she tells me. "If you knew from the beginning, you'd be obsessing about it, telling me about which places stay open all year, who I should be friends with, y'know."

It's getting chilly, and I wish I had my hooded sweatshirt with me. I fold my arms across my chest to stay warm. "Well, I guess you don't want my opinions," I say. "Fine. Now I know."

"How about not thinking about yourself for one minute?" Micayla asks. "Okay? I'm telling you something big, and you're just focusing on how it affects you."

"I'm focusing on how I could have helped you. That's what friends do." I don't know what else to say, but words keep coming out of my mouth. "And I don't know why you're even stepping into a school in the summer. Summer is the one time when you can put school totally out of your head." Clearly,

I'm not only thinking about myself. I'm thinking about how I could've been a much better friend if I'd only known.

"Thanks for being so supportive," Micayala says, getting up from the chair. "I have to pick up a loaf of bread for my mom on the way home, so I'll just see you soon."

Micayla leaves me sitting there. I take the back way home, through the neighborhood, not on the main road. I don't want to see anyone. My hope is that stopping by my favorite house with the colored beach pails will cheer me up, but it doesn't.

Bennett's away, Micayla's mad at me, and all the dogs are at home for the night.

It feels like the time I got separated from my parents at the Museum of Modern Art. It only lasted a few minutes, but they were a dreadful few minutes. I was completely lost. I feel like that now. Lost and totally alone.

Later that evening, I decide to sit on the back porch and try to clear my thoughts. Our backyard has a perfect view of the ocean. I could sit out here for hours and hours doing nothing but staring at the sea. But I usually don't do that, because I'm always so busy.

I bring a book in case I need a break from sea gazing, but I don't get very far. I read a few words and then my mind wanders, and I can't seem to get it to pay attention to the book again. I don't know where things went wrong with Micayla. Maybe I should have responded differently, but I don't know what I should have said. Maybe if Bennett were home, he'd be able to help me make sense of things. I wonder if he knows already, and if he's been keeping it from me too.

Just as I'm about to ask my mom what's for dinner, I get a text from Claire:

Just my mom and me tonight. Going to F's Fish. Want 2 come?

On the one hand, it's surprising (and a little exciting) that Claire invited me to do something with her. I always thought she hated me. And maybe it will be good to get out and get my mind off things. On the other hand, it's Claire, and I'm never sure how she's going to act. She can invite me to dinner and be all nice about it and then act totally mean when I get there. But her mom's coming. And most people aren't mean in front of their moms.

I go inside and ask my parents if I can go, and then I remember that my dad had to go back to the city for a few days. That'll leave my mom home all alone for dinner, and I get lonely just thinking about it.

Well, if Claire's going with her mom, I can always ask if I can bring my mom along too. That's not weird, I don't think. Or maybe it is. But on Seagate, weird things are considered acceptable, sometimes even quirky and fun.

Can my mom come too? I text back.

A few seconds later, I get *TOTES* back from Claire and feel better already. Sometimes when you're feeling really down, a little invitation to do something makes everything feel better.

Claire kind of scares me. But right now going out to dinner with her and our moms feels like a scoop of ice cream on the hottest day of the summer.

"So you and Claire are friends now?" my mom asks me

as we're walking over to Frederick's Fish.

"I guess." I've been kicking a pebble down the path since we left our house, and I can tell it's driving my mom crazy. But I've gotten it so far, I can't stop now.

"You seem awfully quiet, Rem." She says it like a question, and I know she wants me to tell her what's on my mind. It's kind of strange how people use the word *awfully* to just mean *very* or *extremely*. That never really made sense to me.

I just shrug and don't really say anything. I'm upset about my conversation with Micayla, but I don't know how to tell my mom about it. Partly because I don't know if I'm right or Micayla's right. Maybe I *was* thinking about myself too much. But it wasn't like I did it to be mean. She didn't tell me what was going on.

We'll be at Frederick's Fish soon, and I'm sure Claire will talk about her jeans the whole time and save me from having to say much of anything at all. That's a good thing about someone like Claire—she'll talk and talk and talk, and you can just stay quiet if you want to.

I think I like being the quiet one. It's easier to listen to someone else than to talk about myself.

We get to Frederick's Fish, and Claire and her mom are sitting on the bench out front.

"Hello, I'm Iris, Claire's mom. Nice to meet you."

"I'm Abby," my mom replies.

They talk for a few minutes about Seagate life and remark on how odd it is that they don't remember each other as young girls spending summers on Seagate. I don't under-stand that at all. I know I'll remember everyone on Seagate when I'm my mom's age. I'll remember Mason Redmond and Avery Sanders and even people I'm not really friends with.

"Do you miss your brother?" I ask Claire, because I can't think of anything else to say.

"Not at all." She takes a lip gloss out of her cross-body bag and smears some on her lips. "He's gross. I wish I had a girl twin. Or a plain old sister."

"At least you have a sibling." I pick up the pebble that I kicked all the way here and put it in my pocket. It's so child-ish and superstitious, but something about that pebble feels lucky to me.

"You're not suffering that much, Remy." She rolls her eyes. That's the Claire I'm used to, but it doesn't seem to bother me as much today. She's being honest.

After a few minutes of awkward silence, Claire asks, "Where's Micayla tonight anyway? I was going to invite her too, but my mom said I could only invite one friend."

"Touring the school here." I force myself to say it without any commentary. I'll let Claire form her own opinion. Truth is, I wonder if Claire already knows about Micayla becoming a year-rounder. Maybe I was the last to find out. That might make me feel even worse than I do now.

"School?" Claire scoffs. "In July?"

I nod.

"That is just depressing."

"I agree! Thank you!" I'm immediately guilty for how excited I am about gossiping about Micayla. This isn't right. I know I'm doing the wrong thing, and yet I'm doing it anyway.

Luckily, the hostess at Frederick's Fish tells us that our table is ready, and she walks us to the back deck of the restaurant.

"Outside okay?"

"Of course!" my mom says. "The best view on Seagate!"

The hostess smiles and leaves us our menus. I'm not sure I agree about the view—there's the view from high up on the stage that's pretty awesome, and of course the one from the tippity-top of the lighthouse. But there are so many good views, it's hard to pick the best one.

"Where's Micayla tonight?" my mom asks me after we order our appetizers and our meals. So I explain the whole thing all over again.

"I see," my mom replies. She doesn't seem that surprised. Maybe she already knows. She probably does. She's pretty close with Micayla's mom.

Another person who knew before me.

"We're not attached at the hip, you know."

"Yeah you are," Claire says.

The waitress brings over a plate of fried zucchini sticks and a vegetable platter.

After she dips a zucchini stick into Frederick's secret sauce, Claire's mom says, "I was a year-rounder once." Which makes it sound like Claire already does know, or at least her mom already knows. Or maybe she's just bringing it up to make conversation.

"You were?" I ask.

Claire doesn't say anything, so I guess she already knows this story.

"For a year. My mom thought we needed a break from city life. My dad was depressed about the whole movie career bust, even though it had happened years and years before. We just sort of stepped out of regular society for a little while." She dips another zucchini stick. "And it was great. It was a chance to really spend time together and slow down our pace."

I nod. I wonder if she'd want to do that now, if she'd want to move here with Calvin and Claire for a year.

"It's not so bad, is all I'm saying." She smiles.

"Mom. Please don't tell me this is your way of breaking the news to me. I have Phoebe and Jenna at home. I can't just leave my best friends behind."

I wonder what "Home Claire" is like. I imagine her all popular, always invited to everything, the kind of girl other girls secretly hate but desperately want to be friends with at the same time.

Here on Seagate, it almost seems like she might like me. But at home, she probably wouldn't talk to me at all.

"Well, I don't know if Grandpa would be pleased with all of us just descending on his home for an entire year," Claire's mom says. "But it's something to think about. I hate that there's so much pressure on you in Westchester."

"I hate that too," my mom admits. "It's so tough, but I have come to accept that there is no perfect place to live."

The moms go on and on about this—suburbs versus the city, living on Seagate year-round, all of that. Claire and I stare at each other for a few seconds before she starts to tell me this story about her friends Jenna and Phoebe and how they got in trouble for skipping band last year.

"So what was the punishment?" I ask.

"We had to go five minutes late to lunch," Claire says. "I was totally freaked out that we wouldn't get our usual table, but we did. And there wasn't even a long line for food by the time we got there. So it ended up being not that bad."

"That's good," I say. My stomach grumbles so loudly that Claire and I both start cracking up.

"What are you like at home?" Claire asks. "Are you, like, friends with everybody? Just a small group? Or what?"

I dip a zucchini stick, partly because I'm hungry and partly because I want the time to think of the right answer. She wants to know if I'm popular.

"I don't know what I am. I guess I'm somewhere in the middle."

Thankfully, Claire doesn't press it further. I want to tell her I liked it better when we never used to think about these things. We were just ourselves, and that was good enough. But maybe she knows that. Maybe she didn't used to think about these things either.

Our fish sandwiches come, and we dig into the deliciousness that is Frederick's Fish. Nothing else really matters when you're eating a Frederick's Fish Sandwich. It's pretty much perfection in a sandwich.

After dinner, we all walk home together, and we find Mr. Brookfield sitting on the front porch. "Hope you ladies enjoyed dinner," he says. "We played three games of canasta, and my team won every time."

We all congratulate him and his teammate Mr. Mayer, from around the corner.

"And I heard from the boys," Mr. Brookfield tells us. "They're having a blast."

I'm glad that Bennett's having fun, but I also hate it. I hate that he's having a blast without me, without Seagate. What if he comes home and he's better friends with Calvin than he'll ever be with me again?

I never used to think about these things. Like popularity, they never used to matter. But they matter now, and as much as I tell myself that they don't and that things are exactly the same, I know it's not true.

24

*It seems like a million dogs have descended on Sea-*gate—right when Bennett is away and Micayla and I are fighting. Micayla and I still see each other, but she hasn't asked me to go swimming or go to Sundae Best since our fight. When we're with the dogs, she hangs out more with them than with me, and we haven't said more than five words to each other in the last few days.

One morning I get a call from a woman named Betty. She's an artist and she was just commissioned to paint a mural in one of the biggest houses on Seagate. She'll be gone for most of the day, and she's heartbroken about leaving her beagle, Tabby, home by herself. Of course I agreed to take on another dog, and I'm happy to do it.

But that isn't the only call I get. We also need to look after a collie named Potato Salad (and I thought Marilyn Monroe was a weird name for a dog!) for a few hours this week while his owner goes for physical therapy off-island. And then there's a new family with a cocker spaniel, Lester. The only thing is, the house they're renting doesn't really allow dogs, so they're trying to keep him outside as much as possible.

That brings the dog tally to seven: Oscar, Rascal, Atticus, Marilyn Monroe, Tabby, Potato Salad, and Lester. And only Micayla and me around to work.

I sit at the kitchen table and make a list of all the dogs and their needs, carefully writing down who needs to be picked up and returned and who will be dropped off. Thankfully, Bennett will be coming back in two days. I hope he'll be excited to hear about the new dogs, and happy to see me too.

I'm all ready to go get Oscar and Atticus for the morning shift when my phone rings. It's Micayla. Strange that she's calling instead of just coming over.

"Hi, Mic," I say, as cheerful as can be, hoping if I'm friendly, we can just pretend we never had a fight at all.

"Don't kill me, Remy. Okay?"

When people say *Don't kill me*, they're pretty much warning you that they're about to say or do something really annoying and you should be ready. Also, they're saying that they know they're doing something wrong, but they're going to do it anyway, and you just have to accept it.

"What?"

I can hear her taking a deep breath through the phone. "I need a day off."

I know she's talking about the doggie day care business, but it occurs to me that maybe she means a day off from our friendship. I'm mad and worried at the same time.

"Why?"

"You're going to think this is lame, but Avery Sanders just found out that there's another new girl on Seagate. She just moved here, and she's going to be a year-rounder too. And I feel like I should meet her so I know another new person."

I want to be understanding. I want to say that it's totally fine and that I would want to do the same thing if I were her. I know Micayla has to do this. But it still hurts. It still feels like I am being left behind.

Maybe it wasn't just that she waited so long to tell me. Maybe I also feel like I'm being replaced by Avery Sanders.

"Fine. Whatever. I have to get the dogs." I wait for her to say something else, but she doesn't. I don't know if I should tell her about our three new clients. I doubt she'd even care.

"I'll call you later," Micayla says.

"Don't bother. You're obviously not carrying your weight in this business. You have other things to focus on right now. Go hang out with Avery Sanders and the new girl." I end the call and feel even worse than I did yesterday.

Bennett's away, and he has a new BFF anyway. Micayla's moving on and staying in the same place at the same time. And I'm just here, same as I ever was. Things are changing all around me, and I can't do anything about it.

But I don't have time to think about any of it now. I'm late to get Oscar and Atticus, and I have to be at Dog Beach in twenty minutes to meet the others. I hate being late!

When I get to my first stop, Dawn is already waiting outside with Oscar. He's running in circles on the lawn as Dawn holds one baby over her shoulder and the other two whimper in their stroller. I quickly attach Oscar's leash and run to get Atticus. Paul is waiting outside too, and Atticus is sitting next to him. I get the sense that Paul wants to chat, but there's no time for that now. I can't be late for the others.

I run and try to get to the beach before any of the other dogs. But Lester is already there waiting with his family.

"We needed him out of the house bright and early," the dad says. "The owners of the house apparently live on Seagate too! We're totally going to get busted."

He doesn't seem nervous, so I laugh, thinking that he's making some kind of joke. Lester joins Oscar and Atticus and they all start playing, and soon after, Marilyn Monroe arrives unexpectedly.

Amber goes on and on about how Hudson used to sleep through the night and now he's not, and she really needs a babysitter so she can find time to work out. She's always stressed about something, and I just don't have the time or energy to deal with it today.

"I guess you don't have time for more babysitting with all your dog-sitting, Remy," she says. "Any other suggestions?"

"I don't know. I'll think about it," I tell her. I hate to be short with her, but this woman basically needs me to be her full-time child and dog nanny, and I can't. I have enough problems of my own.

When it's just Oscar, Atticus, Lester, and Marilyn Monroe, everything feels easy and smooth. But then Rascal arrives, and he's all out of sorts today—rambunctious, barking, tormenting the other dogs. It's so unlike him. I wonder if he woke up on the wrong side of the crate. Even his velvety fur doesn't look as smooth today.

In a way, he's acting how I feel—totally out of control. And the more I try to control him, the crazier he gets. Maybe dogs are kind of like people and they don't like to be told what to do or bossed around.

I try to introduce all the regular dogs to the newcomers, but almost all of them seem a little shy and not so eager to make new friends. Except for Lester. He runs around, paying attention to all the other dogs. In a way, he feels like my assistant today in trying to keep everyone happy. Maybe I should just keep him with me for the rest of the time his family is here.

I keep encouraging all the dogs to play together, but they just turn away and go back to the dogs that they know. They seem as resistant to change as I am, and from the outside, it's frustrating.

"You're here alone today?" Mason Redmond asks. I didn't even see him walking over. I notice he's wearing a whistle, and I wonder if it's at all effective when the dogs swim out too far.

"Yeah. Unfortunately." Rascal comes over for a treat, and then Potato Salad wants one, and soon all the dogs are at my feet waiting for their morning snack.

"You're handling it pretty well." He gives me two thumbs up, and I notice his nails are dirty. It's pretty gross. A "forward thinker" should have clean nails.

"Thanks." Tabby's the last to get a treat, and she licks my arm after she gets it. I think that's her way of saying thank you. Her ears flop back and forth as she runs toward the ocean. Beagles are such happy-go-lucky dogs—I wish I could borrow her attitude. "We'll see."

"Well, if you need any help, I'll be over there on the old lifeguard's chair." He points to the tall wooden chair a few feet away from the water. Usually it cracks me up that he sits there for most of the day, just watching, not really interacting with the dogs. He's more of a dog lifeguard than a volunteer at Dog Beach. But today it only makes me sad. Everything is bothering me, and this is just one more thing to add to the list.

"Thanks, Mason."

"And you'll probably be really hungry when this day's over, after working so hard and everything." He pauses and starts twirling the string of his whistle around his fingers, the way real lifeguards always do. "So if you want to go to Sundae Best, I'll totally go with you. I think today's the day they're unveiling their latest signature flavor."

"Oh, I think it's mango something," I start to say, and then

I get a funny feeling. Mason Redmond is asking me to go to Sundae Best with him. Just the two of us?

"Yeah, I heard mango too, but that could be a rumor." He turns around when he notices one of the dogs is too far out. He blows his whistle and motions for the dog to come back, but I'm not even sure the dog can see or hear him, and I'm certain the dog's owner is here somewhere watching anyway.

"I'd better run," he says. "But let me know if you, um, want to go. We can discuss the dogs, and ideas for the business and stuff."

Mason sprints across the sand, tripping a few times and losing a flip-flop along the way. I wonder what Micayla sees in him. Still, it was nice of him to ask me and offer ideas for the business. On a day when I was feeling like the biggest loser in the world, it was nice for someone, even Mason Redmond, to ask me to go to Sundae Best with him.

The day goes downhill after that. Potato Salad gets completely tangled in seaweed, and it takes three people (me, Mason, and a stranger) to untangle her. Then Atticus seems to have a stomachache, because he poops about five times and it's very difficult to clean up. And Marilyn Monroe just wants to sit by my side and be petted. She keeps putting her paw on my leg and then barking when I don't go back to petting her.

Luckily, Rascal's mood has improved and he seems to be bonding with Lester. Oscar is happy because he found a kid to play Frisbee with.

But when it's time to take everyone home, all the leashes get tangled up with one another, and it takes me fifteen minutes to untangle them.

Everything is totally out of control. Micayla bailed on me, Bennett is away, and now even the dogs are going nuts. Dog-sitting was supposed to be fun and low-key, not super stressful. And I was supposed to be doing it with my friends, not all alone.

And just as I'm walking out of Dog Beach, I see Micayla walking with Avery Sanders and the mysterious new year-rounder girl. The new girl has those fancy jean shorts on. I only recognize them because Claire has a pair.

"So no Sundae Best with me?" Mason yells as I'm half-way out the gate. I totally forgot about his offer, but it would have been too weird to go anyway, especially dragging along seven dogs.

"Sorry." I shrug. "Next time. Okay?"

He nods reluctantly and blows his whistle for the millionth time.

I'm finally out the gate and onto the pavement with all seven dogs following behind me, and there's Micayla, standing right in front of me.

"You and Mason? Sundae Best?"

"Don't even ask," I mumble.

"I won't. You know I like him, Remy." She turns away, walking again with Avery and fancy-shorts year-rounder girl.

It takes me the whole walk to Oscar's house to understand what just happened. Micayla thinks I like Mason now. She thinks I tried to get him to ask me to go to Sundae Best. No way. No way at all.

I'll have to explain. I have to make her listen.

I may have said some mean things the past few days, but I'd never steal her crush. That's against all the best-friend codes of conduct in the world. I may only be eleven, but even I know that.

When all the dogs are returned to their homes, I decide to go for a walk. Alone. It's rare that I want to be alone on Seagate, but I'm exhausted from such a busy day taking care of the dogs, and I need to figure out what to say to Micayla. I want to make it right and explain what happened with Mason, but I'm also still upset that she kept a secret from me. I'm not the only one who needs to apologize.

I text my mom to tell her I'm going for a walk, so she won't worry. I walk to the beach and then across the boardwalk, down the path to the main part of Seagate, past Sundae Best—there's a line all the way down the street waiting for the unveiling of its new flavor—and I keep walking, past Picnic and Mornings and the Dollhouse Café, past Novel Ideas Book Shop and Frederick's Fish and the art gallery. I walk the whole perimeter of the island. I see Bennett's mom picking Asher up from day camp, but I look away before she sees me. I don't want to say hi to anyone, because I'd have to pretend I was fine and I'm not. I keep walking, not even stopping to see who's playing Ping-Pong.

Finally I decide to sit down on one of the benches at the far end of the island, near the lighthouse. I look under the bench to see if any of our chalk drawings from last summer are still there. I know they're gone, but I look anyway, just to see if maybe the tiniest bit of chalk didn't get washed away by rain.

I wish I could be one of those people who can roll with the punches, who jumps into any new situation with open arms and an open mind. That's Bennett. Nothing fazes him. He can be thrown into a roomful of strangers and be totally fine. His mom could tell him tomorrow that they were becoming year-rounders, and he wouldn't even stress about it. He'd find a year-rounder friend and play Ping-Pong and be as happy as can be.

I'm the opposite, and I hate that about myself.

But maybe I just need to accept myself and how I react. And maybe I just need to accept the chaos and not try too hard to tame it. Maybe I just need to accept my weird feelings about Bennett, and that Micayla is making new friends. Maybe worrying is just making the problems seem bigger and making me feel worse.

I see Mr. Brookfield walking toward me out of the corner of my eye, and I try to look away, look down at my feet or gaze at the ocean, so he doesn't see me. I like him, but I just don't feel like talking to him right now.

"Funny meeting you here," he says.

I guess there was no way of avoiding saying hi.

"Hi."

"I thought this was my bench," he says, sitting down. "Usually I'm all alone when I come here."

"I was alone until you got here."

"A penny for your thoughts, Remy," he says. He even hands me a penny, and I hold it in my hand, planning to save it for later when I'll throw it into the wishing well.

"Well, I gave you the penny," he reminds me after we're quiet for a few seconds. "So start talking."

"I don't know what to say," I admit. "I'm just feeling a little blue."

"Still about that dog of yours?"

It takes me a minute to understand what he's talking about. Of course—he's thinking of Danish. It surprises me, because I actually haven't missed Danish as much lately.

"No." I shake my head. "Just a really tiring day." I tell him how I'm so tired from watching the dogs today and how it was hard to do it alone, and I tell him about the whole tangled seaweed incident and the other stuff. I explain that the more I try to control the dogs' behavior, the crazier they act.

He half smiles. "I think there's more going on inside that head of yours."

"I guess it's everything, really." I shrug.

He folds his arms behind his head. "Go on."

I don't know if I even want to unload all of this right now, but I guess it's better than keeping it locked up in my thoughts.

"Well, everything feels so different than it was last summer and all the summers before. My friends don't want to do the same things we always did before. And I guess I just don't know what to do. I don't know how to make things go back to the way they used to be." I can't look at him. I can't look at anyone right now. Eye contact with another human would only make me start to cry. A dog would be okay, maybe. But a human, no.

"Things don't always go back to the way they used to be," Mr. Brookfield says. His legs are stretched out in front of him, and his tube socks are pulled up to his knees. At least the way he dresses always stays the same. "Believe me. I know that personally."

I hand him the penny. "Now your turn."

He chuckles a little. "I spent years wishing things could go back to the way they were when I was in the movies, when I was auditioning, when my scream was a big deal." He sighs, and I worry that he'll start to cry. "And the years I spent wishing that things would be back to the way they used to be were years that I wasted. Years that I didn't pay as much attention to my children and my wife, years that I didn't pursue new hobbies and learn new things."

I swallow hard. I'm a different kind of sad now—sad for him and not for me.

"And I still long for the old days, believe me. The old days of the movies, sure. But other old days—when my children were young." He smiles and hands the penny back to me.

"But the new days are good days too. And if we spend too long thinking about how to get the old days back, we miss the new days. The new days are the important ones."

I nod. "But what do you do when the new days seem so strange? And everything changes so fast, before you even have time to prepare for it or to see it coming?"

"It's hard," he says. "I'm not going to tell you that it's easy."

"But you'll tell me that everything will be okay?" I look at him, finally. He has bright blue eyes, and I never noticed. I guess that's where Calvin and Claire get their blue eyes.

He readjusts a tube sock, and I wonder if this is a good time to suggest sandals. Wearing sneakers and socks on Seagate is practically a crime. "I promise you that everything will be okay . . . eventually," he says. "And things will be okay before you even realize that they're okay. So make sure you pay attention."

"I'll try to believe you."

He looks at his watch. "It's almost six! And it's pizza night in the Brookfield home. You're coming, right?"

"I wouldn't miss it."

"Too bad the boys are coming back tomorrow," Claire says, putting on the Scream recording. I'm surprised that she does that, because Bennett's always the one to put it on, and Claire's always the one to complain about it. "It's been so quiet and un-gross without them. Right?"

"I guess." *Un-gross* is a funny way to describe it. I grab a mushroom slice from the box. "Maybe it's been too quiet?"

"Well, it's just you and me tonight. I texted Micayla to come, but she asked if you were coming, and when I said yes, she said she was busy." Claire narrows her eyes at me. "What's that all about?"

I take my slice and a glass of lemonade to the green Adirondack chair and hope I can find a way to change the topic.

"Come on, what's going on with you guys?" Claire asks, sitting in the blue Adirondack chair next to me. "I thought you guys didn't fight all the time. I thought you were different from Phoebe, Jenna, and me."

"I thought so too."

"So?" she asks.

"So, I don't know." It comes out more harshly than I'd meant it to.

"Okay. Sheesh."

I sit farther back in my chair and we eat our pizza quietly. Even though Claire has grown on me, I wish these weekly pizza dates hadn't become a tradition. Mr. Brookfield thinks I'm some kind of crazy person now, and Claire thinks I'm a mean friend.

I keep counting the minutes until Bennett gets back, but even when he does, it's not like I can expect him to make everything better all on his own.

"Do you think Micayla has a crush on my brother?" Claire asks, totally out of the blue. Maybe she was tired of the silence. Or maybe she really has been wondering.

"What?" I ask, not able to hide my shock. "Um, no."

"Hey! Don't say it like that."

"Say it like what?" I turn to look at her and notice she has some pizza sauce in the corner of her mouth. "You said yourself he's gross."

"I'm allowed to say it." She glares at me. "He's my brother. You're not allowed to say it."

"Okay." I'm confused but don't want to admit it. "I'm sorry."

Claire gets up to grab another slice. When she comes back, she asks, "So does she?"

"Honestly, I don't think so. She likes Mason Redmond." I sip my lemonade and debate saying anything more about how he invited me to Sundae Best and how Micayla thought I was interested in him. Maybe I shouldn't have even told Claire about the whole Micayla and Mason thing. Is this another thing she'll be mad at me for?

"Oh, Mason—the kid who helps at Dog Beach?" she asks.

I nod. "Yeah, I don't really get what she sees in him. He's kind of nerdy."

Claire cracks up. "Hello? Remy? You started a day camp for dogs. That's a little bit nerdy too."

I should probably shrug off her comment, but it stings. It seemed like Claire and I were finally becoming friends, and now she's making fun of me.

"Aw, don't go cry about it." She nudges me with her shoulder. "You want brownies? I made some earlier."

We go inside and have brownies, but I keep thinking about what she said. And I wonder about Micayla. Maybe she really does like Calvin but hasn't told me. She's kept other secrets. I want to know why Claire asked, but I feel too uncomfortable.

"You didn't need to say my business idea was nerdy." I finally get the courage to say it when we're up in Claire's room and she's going through her jean collection for the millionth time.

"I was kidding, Remy." She throws a T-shirt at me. It still

has the tags on, and it cost more than fifty dollars. "I still think you're cool, even with your nerdy business. Don't be so sensitive."

Claire thinks I'm cool. Really? I mean, I know she wouldn't say it unless she meant it. That's the thing about Claire. She says what she thinks—whether it's appropriate or not, whether it's nice or not. It's kind of helpful to have a friend like that.

A little while later, Claire and Mr. Brookfield offer to walk me home, but I tell them that I'm fine on my own.

The truth is, I just want some time to clear my head.

I thought I was feeling so much better after the talk with Mr. Brookfield and after that dinner with Claire and her mom, but I'm just as confused as ever. The dog-sitting business is going well, but Micayla and I are in our first real fight, and I have all these feelings about Bennett that I don't know what to do with.

It's like a mosquito bite that just keeps itching and itching. The more I scratch it, the worse it gets.

I can't fall asleep that night, so I text Micayla at
eleven thirty. I wouldn't normally do that, but it's summer
and people stay up late. And I'm not sure I can go another
day being in this fight with Micayla. It's too painful.

Come to my house for breakfast tomorrow before dogs.
We need to talk.

I wait and wait and wait for a response. Finally, an hour
later, she writes.

Will let u know in AM

But when morning rolls around, I still haven't heard from
her. I assume that she's coming and that she just forgot to
text me back. I decide to scramble some eggs and toast some
rye bread. I'll even cut up strawberries and bananas and put
some grapefruit juice in a pitcher.

My mom comes in, frazzled because she's late for a meeting with the Seagate Community Association. "Ooh, maybe I'll take some fruit to go," she says. "Wait. Did you make this for me?"

I shake my head. "No. For Micayla. I hope she's coming."

"Is everything okay, Rem? I'm starting to worry."

"It's okay. Go to your meeting. You're going to be late."

She nods reluctantly and gives me a kiss on the cheek. "I'll see you this afternoon. You and I have a date. We're splitting a banana split. No arguing!"

"Deal." I smile. Then I start digging through the pots and pans for the little omelet pan. I can't make an omelet in any pan but this one.

I know it's a little bit weird to have so many feelings about an omelet pan, but there's a good reason for it. It's so small and perfect for making eggs for one or two people. On the other hand, I also hate it. I hate it because I imagine Grandma making eggs in it, all by herself. She never had people over for breakfast, so when she was using this pan, she was all alone. I hate to think about her all alone on Seagate during the year, without us. But then I get happy using this pan because it makes me think of Grandma, and I like thinking about her.

It's confusing how I can really think this much about a tiny frying pan.

I continue with the breakfast even though I'm not sure if Micayla is coming or not. Luckily, the doorbell rings at nine thirty, so all this food will not go to waste.

"Smells good," Micayla says, not really looking at me. She comes right in and takes a seat at the kitchen table. She pours herself a glass of grapefruit juice and butters her toast before I've even sat down.

I'm glad that she still feels comfortable here. Sure, it's only been a few days of awkwardness between us, but it feels much longer.

"I guess this is your way of apologizing?" Micayla asks me, after spooning some eggs onto her plate.

I pour myself some juice and try to figure out what to say. "Well, I just wanted to talk to you."

"Talk to me about how you're stealing Mason Redmond? And have become a totally mean friend?"

"Huh?"

"He asked you to go to Sundae Best. I heard it."

"I don't like him like that."

"Why? What's so bad about him that you don't like him?"

"Well, he only wanted to go to Sundae Best to discuss the dog-sitting business. That's what I mean. It wasn't, like, a date. If that's what you were thinking."

I take a small bite of eggs. I'm not really sure what's happening right now, but it's not the way I wanted the conversation to go. "But anyway, I wanted to talk to you about other stuff. I wasn't only thinking about the Mason thing."

"Of course you weren't," Micayla says. "You always think about yourself. That's the problem. When you were sad about Danish, I did everything to cheer you up. And when you wanted to do the doggie day care, I did everything I could to help. But now that I'm going to be a year-rounder on Seagate, you don't care. And even the whole Mason thing, you don't care about that either."

"Micayla, that's not true."

"It is true, Remy." She pushes her chair back from the table, and it makes a terrible screeching sound. "I have to give up all my friends and my whole life, and you don't even want to talk about it. For one second, think about somebody other than yourself."

Micayla walks out of my house without saying anything else. That wasn't at all how I expected this breakfast to go, and I don't have time to get upset about it. I have to clean up all the dishes and go get the dogs. But when I look at today's schedule, there's a huge problem. I am watching all of our usuals: Oscar, Atticus, Rascal, Marilyn Monroe, plus Tabby and Potato Salad. But I also said I could keep an eye on Palm and the pair of Malteses. That's nine dogs. And one me.

There's no way I can handle that.

And now that Micayla wants nothing to do with me, there's only one person I can call to help.

"Claire," I say as soon as she picks up the phone.

"Yeah," Claire answers.

"It's Remy."

"I know." She pauses. "What's up?"

I take a deep breath and pray that this works. I have ten minutes before I need to be at Oscar's. "I need your help. I know you said that the dog-sitting thing was nerdy. And I know you think I'm too sensitive. But I'm begging you. Can you please help me with the dogs today?"

"Really?" she asks, and I'm expecting her to tell me she's busy ironing her jeans again or she has to go to the pool and work on her tan.

"Yeah."

"I thought you'd never ask!"

"Huh?"

"Remy, I've been waiting for you to ask me to work with the dogs all summer. But I figured you didn't like me and didn't want me around, so I never asked."

"I had no idea," I admit.

"I'll meet you at Oscar's in five minutes," she tells me.

"You know where Oscar lives?"

"Yeah." I hear the creak of her closet door in the background. "I pay attention, Remy."

It turns out Claire is awesome with the dogs. Marilyn Monroe loves her instantly, and I swear they're sitting on the bench together talking about jeans. Even though Marilyn doesn't wear them, she seems like she'd be very into fashion. Marilyn Monroe barks and Claire turns around to show her the stitching on her jean shorts. It's very funny to watch. But it's not only Marilyn Monroe who Claire's great with—she's also great at rubbing Potato Salad's tummy in just the right spot, and Rascal has a good time splashing with her in the waves.

I wonder why I've waited so long to ask Claire to hang out with the dogs. And when I think about that, I start to feel bad. You really don't know what goes on inside someone's head until she chooses to tell you—or you choose to ask. I don't think I've been doing enough asking.

"We still need to go to Sundae Best together," Mason says, catching me totally off guard when I'm at the water fountain filling up the dogs' bowls. "I think I have more good ideas for your business. Whenever you have time."

"Okay, hopefully we will find some time."

I look over at Claire, who's playing Frisbee with Atticus and Rascal while Marilyn Monroe watches from a few feet away. She's throwing the Frisbee and chatting with Marilyn Monroe, and I swear I've never seen her happier. Not even when she's talking about her jeans.

Maybe I could borrow her honesty and say something important.

"Mason, I have to tell you something," I say.

"Yeah?" He perks up and then looks out into the ocean to make sure all the swimming dogs are okay.

"You should ask Micayla to go to Sundae Best."

"Huh?" He blows his whistle for no real reason, but I can tell he feels most comfortable when he's in charge.

"I mean, not just to discuss dog-sitting. I just think she'd like it if you asked her," I say. "I'm just telling you, because, um, in case you didn't know."

He nods. "Okay, Remy. I'd better get back to the lifeguard's chair. The water can be dangerous for these little guys." He pets Marilyn Monroe, who has just run over to us and is now sitting at Mason's feet. I pet her too. I wonder if she can see the difference in me—how honest and open I'm being.

At the end of the day, Claire and I walk the dogs home and I tell her how great she was. "Seriously, you're amazing with dogs."

"Thanks." She smiles. "They're awesome. I think I might want to be a dog groomer one day. But more like a dog stylist. Or maybe I could just come up with an upscale fashion line for dogs. Doggie Couture or something."

"All good ideas."

After all the dogs are dropped off, I ask her if she wants to come over for dinner. "I think it's taco night," I tell her. "My dad is back in the city, and my mom is really into tacos. She makes all kinds of fillings—fish, tofu, chicken, beef. She brings everything over to the table, and we can make our own combinations."

I feel silly getting so excited about taco night, but I can't help it.

"Sounds delish. I'll ask Grandpa," she says. "Oh wait, but Calvin and my dad are back. I'll probably have to see them. Boring."

"I understand." I hadn't thought about Bennett coming back for most of the day. Now I'm nervous all over again. I can't keep my feelings a secret anymore. I don't even know what the feelings are, but Claire inspired me today. You have to speak up. And when you do, amazing things can happen.

"You told Mason about Micayla, didn't you?" she asks. We're standing outside Mr. Brookfield's house, and part of me wants to run home but part of me wants to stay so that I can see Bennett.

"How did you know?"

"He asked me about it," she says. "He was like 'what do you know about Micayla Walcott?'"

"And?"

"And I said I didn't really know much, and then he said you told her that he should ask her to go to Sundae Best, and the whole thing was so funny to me that I just started cracking up."

"Why?" Now I'm laughing, though I'm not really sure why.

"He's just so weird!" Now we're both cracking up, not really about Mason and not really about Micayla. I'm not even sure what we're laughing about. But in the middle of the full-out laughing session, two things occur to me:

1. Claire and I are real friends now. Only real friends have this kind of cracking-up moment.
2. Bennett and Calvin are watching this whole thing.

"We're baaaaack," Calvin says. "Miss us?"

"Yeah, right." Claire looks at me. "On second thought, Remy, maybe I will come for those tacos. And then maybe I will move in with you too?"

"Tacos? Abby Boltuck's famous taco night?" Bennett asks, and my heart immediately feels warm and happy, the way it does after I've had a bowl of lobster bisque at Frederick's Fish.

Bennett remembers everything.

"Yup" is all I can manage to say. I want to invite him over, but there's too much that I have to say. I wouldn't be able to eat the tacos, and I can't do that to my mom. Our conversation will have to wait. At least until after taco night.

"So what were you guys laughing about?" Calvin asks, zooming me back into the conversation.

I look at Claire and Claire looks at me.

"Just girl stuff," she says.

It's been almost a week and Micayla's still not talking to me. Bennett stopped by her house the other day to say hi, and he said she was kind of cold to him too. We don't really know what to do about it. We've never seen her like this.

Thankfully, Claire loves helping with the dogs. And Calvin seems pretty into it too. He really only pays attention to Rascal, but it's okay. I think Rascal needs some one-on-one time.

"So. Two questions," Claire starts when we're on our way to Dog Beach. We've picked up Oscar, Marilyn Monroe, and Palm. The boys are getting the others.

"Yeah?" I ask, admiring the rhinestone bow Marilyn Monroe is wearing today. I've been searching online for doggie hair bows, so I can send her one for the holidays. I kind of want to make sure she remembers me during the rest of the year.

"When are you going to admit that you're in love with Bennett? And when are you going to make up with Micayla?"

That's another thing that's changed since Claire and I have become friends. She'll just ask really bold questions like it's no big deal at all. Basically, whatever's on her mind will come out of her mouth.

It took her pretty much all summer to say that she loved dogs and wanted to help out with the business. And now she'll say anything.

It's kind of crazy how someone can change so much in such a short amount of time. Or maybe Claire didn't really change—I was just willing to look at her in a different way.

Claire's personality is part awesome and part scary. I never know what she's going to say, and in a way I'm always worried that she'll embarrass me. But the good part is that she brings hard-to-talk-about things out into the open, and that can be really helpful.

"I guess my answer is the same for both questions," I reply. "I don't know."

"Oh." Claire looks at me, but I don't make eye contact with her. I feel exposed, like she just walked in on me changing out of a bathing suit. "I need to tell you one thing, though. About Micayla. You're being kind of selfish, you know. She's the one going through this whole big change. All you need to do is be understanding. So what if she didn't tell you right away? Maybe it was hard for her. Anyway, it's boring to talk about this, so that's all I'm going to say."

Her honesty stings the way it usually does, but maybe she's right. She probably is.

"Thanks. I'll think about it." I can't look at her. "But how did you know? About the Bennett thing, I mean. Did your grandfather tell you?" I look at her, finally.

"What? My grandfather?" She laughs. "Why would he know?"

"No reason." I guess she doesn't know about our conversation, and now I feel weird talking about it. But it's pretty clear that Mr. Brookfield isn't very gossipy. He kept his scream a secret for all these years.

"I know about your crush because it's crazy obvious," Claire says. "The way you act when he's around—all nervous but chatty. The way you look at him. They way you bring him up in conversations when we're not even talking about him at all."

"Oh." I look down at my feet, and at the dogs, basically anywhere but at Claire. I feel even more exposed now, like I'm walking to Dog Beach totally naked.

I wait for her to say something about Bennett. Maybe that he acts the same way around me. Or that she's overheard him talking to Calvin about me. Or anything, really. But she doesn't. The conversation ends there, and I'm not sure if we'll ever talk about it again. I'm not sure if I ever want to talk about it again.

The dogs are all thrilled to be at Dog Beach, and they're behaving themselves, so there's not much for me to do.

They're all playing happily. The boys are keeping some of them busy with a wild game of Frisbee. Potato Salad and Tabby are sunbathing together. They're the oldest dogs of the bunch and they love to lie around, but they love to lie around together. Whenever one's there without the other, they just roam around gloomily. Lester continues to be the social butterfly, spending a little time with each dog.

After all the dogs are settled, I decide to walk around the beach a little bit and check on them individually. I always focus on them as a group, but they're all a little like Rascal: They need their one-on-one time.

As I'm walking around, I notice that Mason Redmond isn't here. He's been here every single day this summer, and he never mentioned that he was going off-island or anything. I wonder if he's sick.

Claire and I are sitting on the bench mapping out a plan for the rest of the day. Most of the dog owners wanted a full day of care today, so we had to plan it all out. We collected bowls and plastic bags of food from all the owners this morning so everyone will have something to eat. Sometimes Tabby and Potato Salad like to nap after lunch, so they can just do that on the beach. Marilyn Monroe spends most of the day lounging anyway, and she's happy to be outside.

When it comes to Rascal, Atticus, and Oscar, they're happy as long as they're playing and they're fed. Lester just likes to keep busy. And Palm is being picked up at noon, so we didn't need to worry about his lunch.

"Ooh, your boyfriend is coming over." I look up, expecting to see Mason, since Claire likes to make fun of the whole "let's go to Sundae Best together" thing, even though he only wanted to discuss the dogs. But it's Bennett walking over to us. I hope he didn't hear her say that.

"Weird that Mason's not here, right?" He looks at me. It's like he just read my mind. "Is it safe for the dogs to be swimming unsupervised?" He laughs and I do too, and then I feel bad for making fun of Mason. It's true that he's not really a dog lifeguard, but he takes his pretend job seriously.

"Maybe he's sick," I say.

"Sickly in love with Remy!" Calvin yells, and then Bennett and Calvin high-five. Claire gives them a "come on" kind of look, and my face feels like it's resting on a campfire.

"Maybe that's why Micayla's so mad at you," Bennett says. "You stole her man."

"Ugh, my man? Seriously? And I didn't steal anyone." I don't know how I manage to get the words out, but I do. "I need to go fill up Atticus's water bowl. He looks parched."

I get up and walk away, but I hear them whispering behind me. I plan to take a very long time filling up Atticus's bowl. I should have brought all the dogs' bowls over and filled each of them one by one.

As I'm walking back, trying carefully not to spill all the water, I see Claire running over to me. Immediately I assume something is wrong with one of the dogs, and my heart starts pounding. Maybe we took on too many clients. Maybe we weren't ready. Maybe Calvin doesn't take this seriously enough.

"What's wrong?" I ask.

"You're going to kill me."

"What did you do to Marilyn Monroe's hair?" I ask. Claire has been threatening to style it in some wacky way, and I have forbidden her to do it.

"It's not that," she says tentatively. "It's worse."

"What did you do?" I ask, even though I already know the answer. I see Bennett and Calvin out of the corner of my eye. Marilyn Monroe is sitting all alone on the bench, and I need to go over there but I'm scared to.

"I'm sorry. It's just they were saying that you loved Mason or that Mason loved you and it was so untrue, and I knew you were never going to admit your feelings to Bennett and I couldn't help myself. So *I* had to." She's digging a hole in the sand with the toe of her sparkly flip-flop, and all I want right now is for that hole to be big enough for me to fit inside it.

"What do I do now?" I ask. I don't know if I will ever be able to talk to Bennett again. The secret is out and things will never go back to normal. I'm too afraid to ask what he said in response.

I expect Claire to have an answer. She seems like the

kind of girl who could write a guidebook to navigating life at eleven years old. It could be called *Claire's Guide to Cool* or something. She seems confident enough. She tried to get away with not playing tennis at tennis camp. She always says what she thinks.

Though I wish she hadn't said what she thought to Bennett just now.

"I don't know," she says. "I'm sorry. But I think this is for the best."

"Claire." I grab her arm as she's walking away. "I can't go back over there. I'm scared."

"Well, we have dogs to take care of, Remy." She links her arm with mine. "Business is business, babe."

That makes me laugh, and as soon as I'm laughing I can walk back over to them. But when we get to the bench, the giggling stops. Bennett looks at me. And I look at him. We look down at our feet. And no one says anything.

"Do you guys want to take the dogs over to Daisy's for some treats?" Bennett asks after the world's longest pause. "I think they need a change of scenery. We've been here all morning."

"That never bothered them before," I say, more defensively than I'd meant to.

"Well, our boys are bored," Calvin says. He's calling them his boys? He's only been helping out for a few days. "We're gonna take Rascal, Lester, Atticus, and Oscar to Daisy's, and then we'll take them home later."

I look at him, annoyed that he's making this decision.

"That's okay with you, Rem?" Bennett asks. He's smart enough to ask me that. It's my business, not Calvin's.

I nod. "Sure. Fine. Whatever."

They gather the dogs' belongings and head out. I can't help but wonder if Claire's comment made them want to leave. And I can't tell if I'm sad that they're gone or sad that Calvin called those dogs his boys.

I feel cloudy again.

"Well, that wasn't good," Claire says. Tabby, Potato Salad, and Marilyn Monroe are all sunbathing at our feet. It's going to be a very relaxed afternoon.

"What wasn't good?" I ask. I'm only half paying attention.

"The way you acted." She looks at me, and when I don't turn to face her, she puts her hands on the sides of my face and literally turns my head. "If you like him, then just go with it. Don't act all weird and like you don't care. I mean, it's Bennett. You've known him your whole life. Just be who you are."

"I don't know who I am," I say. "It's all so confusing. One of my best friends isn't talking to me. And I think I'm in love with my other one."

"Don't be so dramatic, Remy." She rolls her eyes—something I haven't seen her do in at least a day. "Get out of your head for a few minutes and just be normal."

I know Claire's trying to help, in her way, but this whole debacle has made me exhausted. I just need some quiet time.

The dogs are resting, and I want to rest too. I get up and pull over one of the Dog Beach lounge chairs. Thankfully, there isn't too much fur on it. I decide to lie down for a few minutes.

But I can't really relax. I won't close my eyes, because I need to pay attention to the dogs.

Tabby and Potato Salad get picked up early, and then it's just Claire, Marilyn Monroe, and me.

"Psst," I say to Claire, who's dozing off on the bench.

"What?" she asks.

"I have an idea. Since it's just the three of us, let's do a special trip." She uh-huhs me with her eyes closed. "Let's take her to Mornings."

"What? No! That place is too fancy for dogs." She opens her eyes and raises her eyebrows. "That lady Beverly seriously scares me, and no one scares me. Did you hear she wouldn't even allow her own cousin into the store because he wasn't dressed well enough?"

I glare at her. "She's really mean, but Mornings was Danish's favorite place," I say. "He'd wait outside on their front porch, and I'd bring him a croissant. That's what we'll do. I figured out how to work the system and get around Beverly every time."

"For real?"

"Totally. Just trust me."

"All right, let's do it." Claire smiles.

"You're gonna love this, Mari," I whisper to her as we're

walking over. "It can be our special thing. I wouldn't take just any dog there, but you're different."

She barks softly and wags her tail with her ears perked up. She's excited. She must know something's up.

When we get there, I tell Claire and Marilyn Monroe to wait on the side of the porch so Beverly won't see them. I'll go in and get some croissants and some fresh-squeezed orange juice and be right back.

We have the plan all figured out.

I walk inside and it's crowded, but not as crowded as it is in the morning. The place is called Mornings, so that does make sense.

"Hello, Remy," Beverly says in a not-so-pleased-to-see-me tone. That's kind of how she is with everyone, but especially kids. I think she'd prefer it if Mornings was an adults-only place, but Seagate isn't like that. She's, like, the only mean person on the whole island, but her chocolate croissants are the best in the world. It doesn't make any sense.

"How are you, Beverly?" I ask, all polite, the way my parents taught me.

"Doing well, thanks." She takes my order: I tell her two chocolate croissants and one plain (dogs shouldn't have chocolate), and two fresh-squeezed orange juices and a cup of water. It's all going according to plan, but she does seem to be moving more slowly than usual, and I start to worry. Marilyn Monroe isn't the most patient dog, and I'm pretty sure Claire is even less patient than she is.

Just as I'm digging through my pocket for some money, calculating the total in my head so I can be ready to pay as soon as Beverly comes back to the counter, I hear Claire's raised voice.

Oh no. Hopefully, she tied Marilyn Monroe outside carefully so she can't run away.

And then I hear barking. Marilyn Monroe's unmistakable, high-pitched barking. That bark means that she wants what she wants and she's going to get it and nothing can get in her way. Not even Mornings. Not even mean Beverly. I stand on my tiptoes to look out the window.

Uh-oh.

"Remy! Help!" Claire yells, reaching out for the leash in front of her, but it's too late. Marilyn Monroe is off and running, all around the restaurant, her sea-green hair bow bobbing up and down as she goes. Claire runs into the restaurant and grabs my hand. "She kept looking for you and sniffing around, and maybe she smelled the croissants? Or maybe she missed you. She just took off. Someone opened the door and she took that as her moment and she stormed in, ran through the door, and oh—" She makes a horrified face.

"What?"

"She's sitting on that woman's lap!"

We both look back and see Marilyn Monroe sitting on some fancy lady's lap. The woman doesn't look pleased.

"Remy!" Beverly is yelling now. "Get that dog out of here!"

"Sorry, Beverly. So sorry."

"We do not allow dogs. How many times have I told you that? Think twice before coming back."

I scoop Marilyn Monroe off the woman's lap and apologize a million times. But I don't realize that her right paw is stuck under the tablecloth, so when I lift her up, I get the whole tablecloth at the same time. Iced coffee spills everywhere. Water spreads all over the floor. Eggs end up in laps, pancakes fly in the air, and the beautiful variety croissant basket flops off the table and lands at an angry man's feet.

"Sorry. So sorry."

Claire's just standing there, holding her head with one hand and grabbing my arm with the other. It feels like five hundred years pass before we make it outside. And when we're finally out there, I realize that the croissants we came to get are still on the counter. I guess we'll never get them now.

"Oh my goodness, that was the most horrible few minutes of my whole life," Claire says. "That was so embarrassing."

"We should tell Amber what happened, in case she tries to go there with Marilyn Monroe again."

"Oh my God, Remy, no! It totally wasn't our fault, and it's over now anyway. Let's just take Marilyn Monroe home and forget about it."

I'm speechless.

Claire goes on and on about how the place is dumb, and Beverly is too uptight, and why did we go there? And how it was the stupidest idea ever.

"Claire!" I finally interrupt her. "How could you let her escape?"

"Let her escape? I was using all my power to hold her back." She glares at me and does her signature Claire eye roll, but then I see that she really does feel bad. "I'm sorry, Remy. It was an accident."

I look at Marilyn Monroe. "Any apologies from you, my dear?"

She lets out her little whimper and tries to jump up my leg. I guess she wants me to pick her up. She needs me to comfort her—even though she's the one who acted poorly. Oh well. I can't say no to that face.

On our way back, we see Mason Redmond and Micayla on the bench outside Sundae Best, and Marilyn Monroe tries to break away from us as soon as we see them. She is pretty strong when she sets her mind to something, I'll admit that.

When we get closer, Marilyn Monroe hops up onto Micayla's lap.

Micayla says, "She must've smelled me. I guess she's been missing me as much as I've been missing her." I'm not sure if Micayla is talking to me or to Claire, but I nod anyway.

We tell her and Mason the whole story about the debacle of Marilyn Monroe breaking into Mornings. They don't seem as shocked or amused as they should be.

"You didn't come to Dog Beach today." I look at Mason and notice that he and Micayla are sharing a cherry chip sundae in one cup with two spoons. I wonder if that's his favorite flavor too. If it is, they're meant for each other. I don't know anyone else who likes cherry chip besides Micayla.

"I took the day off," he says. "My boss said it's okay."

"I see." Mason is pretty much his own boss, and he finds this joke very funny.

Claire's just standing next to me, not saying anything— for once.

"Well, I guess we'd better get Marilyn Monroe home," I say. "We're pretty tired from all the stress."

"Okay. Well, bye!" Micayla says, all cheery. I have no idea what she's thinking. All these days have passed, and we haven't talked. I never found out about the tour of Seagate Schoolhouse or the new girl Avery Sanders knew who's also going to school there. I haven't heard how the Mason Sundae Best thing happened. Maybe it was because he took my suggestion. Maybe not. I want to tell Micayla about Bennett and me, and what Claire said, and how I feel about him in general, but clearly now is not the time. We leave Micayla and Mason and take Marilyn Monroe home.

"Well, today has certainly not been boring!" Claire says. She's carrying Marilyn Monroe in her arms. We can't trust her to walk alone anymore today. "Most exciting day on Seagate all summer!"

"Yeah. For you."

"What does that mean?" she asks.

"You're not the one with all these emotional obstacles to

overcome," I say. "And now I'll never be allowed a chocolate croissant from Mornings ever again!"

"First of all, rein it in, Drama Queen Remy. And second of all, I'm sure Beverly will forget by next summer."

"You think?"

"Totally," Claire says.

After we bring Marilyn Monroe back to her house, I walk home quietly, thinking about the day. Tonight's my mom's August book club meeting, and Dad is back from the city, so I'm excited for a quiet night with him.

I realize I was at Sundae Best today but didn't even take the time to get ice cream. I must've been really distracted to forget about ice cream.

I sit down on the rocking chair on our front porch before heading inside for dinner. Maybe Claire's right. I wish we hadn't trashed Mornings, but it was actually kind of funny. It distracted me from the Bennett embarrassment. It was an exciting day, and a little excitement never hurt anyone.

"Funny seeing you here," Mr. Brookfield says, zapping me out of my thoughts. I look around and wonder what he means. I'm on my own front porch. Dad and I had a nice dinner together, but all I could think about was getting outside again.

"Huh?"

"I'm kidding, Remy." He winks. "How are things?"

I shrug. "Fine, I guess." I don't feel like getting into any major discussions right now. "Going for an evening stroll?"

He nods. "Of course."

Mr. Brookfield comes to join me on the porch. He starts to tell me all about his Seagate routine—a walk in the morning and a walk at night, with all sorts of things in between—when I start to feel uneasy again.

As exciting as it was, I'm starting to feel guilty about all the trouble Marilyn Monroe caused. I should have stayed back with her, not Claire. And maybe I shouldn't have brought her there in the first place. Marilyn Monroe is awesome, but she's not Danish. She's her own dog, and maybe she's just not Mornings-ready yet.

I don't care what Claire says: I have to tell Amber. I can't keep this huge thing from her and let her find out the hard way, when she's craving a chocolate croissant and a fresh-squeezed OJ and she's turned away without even knowing why. Beverly will probably scream at her and embarrass her, and Amber hates to be embarrassed. She'll be forced to sell her Seagate house and she'll be miserable for the rest of her life.

I guess there I go being Drama Queen Remy again, as Claire would say.

"Doggie Day Camp going well?" Mr. Brookfield asks. He always calls it that, even though I'm not totally sure that's what it is. We should have picked a name right away. If you go too long without naming something, it just goes unnamed. Or people call it what they want to call it.

I nod my head yes. I don't feel like talking. Everything that might come out of my mouth will sound sad or frustrated.

"I heard someone talking about you the other day," Mr. Brookfield says. "I was on my morning walk and two of the ladies from the Seagate Singers were sitting on a bench after practice, gabbing about the group of kids who take care of the Seagate dogs. It was very sweet."

I nod again.

"I'm awfully proud of you, Remy. For all the work with the dogs, and the way you've welcomed my Calvin and my Claire." He looks at me. I try to smile. But then the tears just start pouring out of my eyes.

"Don't be proud of me," I say. "Marilyn Monroe broke into Mornings today and pulled a whole covered tablecloth off. And Micayla's mad at me. And nothing is really as great as it seems."

"What are you talking about?" he asks in his jokey voice, like I'm overreacting.

I tell him the whole story about making Claire and Marilyn Monroe waiting outside Mornings and how Marilyn Monroe just couldn't wait anymore.

"I see" is all he says after that. He's not joking anymore. He's not saying anything at all. Maybe he's waiting for me to continue.

"And I was mean to Micayla. She waited so long to tell me they were becoming year-rounders, and I got so upset that she didn't tell me that I didn't even pay attention to how she was feeling about it. And now things are just strange and angry between us."

Mr. Brookfield sighs and sits back in his chair, like he's about to say something wise. "It happens. My best friend Morris and I once went a whole year without speaking."

"Really? Why?"

"It's hard to remember, Remy. Something about a poker

match and a beef stew and being late for a fortieth birthday party." He smiles. "Eventually we made up. If a friendship is meant to stand the test of time, it will."

"I guess it's like anything else," I start. "An everything-happens-for-a-reason kind of thing."

When I don't say anything else for a few seconds, Mr. Brookfield asks, "And what about Bennett? I haven't seen you two together much lately."

I think hard about how I'm going to answer that, but in the end I just say, "I can't talk about it."

"I understand," he replies. "You don't need to say anything else." I should give him more credit for understanding the way an eleven-year-old thinks. I'm pretty sure he gets it.

I'm glad he doesn't think I need to say anything else, but all of a sudden, I feel so much lighter. I feel relieved. Maybe that's why Claire always says what's on her mind. It's better that way. You don't have to carry these heavy thoughts around with you all the time.

"Things will work out, Remy," Mr. Brookfield says, tying his shoelace. "They always do."

"Thanks. I think I feel a little bit better." I smile.

"Good. I'm glad." He stands up. "Now I must be finishing my evening walk before it's time for my morning one! Good talking to you."

I sit outside for a few more minutes and then realize that I was on cleanup duty for dinner. I only planned to be outside for a minute or two, but then Mr. Brookfield came by, and now those dishes have been sitting in the sink for a little too long.

I go back inside and load the dishwasher, and then I hear a knock on the door. I'm having déjà vu from last month's book club night, when Mom was out and Bennett found Oscar. I put down the stack of dishes and go to the door. And it's not actually déjà vu, but it does seem to be a repeat of last month.

Bennett's at the door.

"Can I talk to you?" he asks.

My heart starts flipping around like a fish desperately trying to get back into the water. I peer back into the kitchen and yell, "Dad, I'll be on the front porch for a minute."

"Again?" he asks from the living room. He gets up and sees Bennett in the doorway. "Oh, um, okay."

"Did you find another lost dog?" I ask Bennett when we're alone on the front porch.

It takes him a second to get what I'm talking about, but then he laughs.

"No. I just feel like we haven't hung out that much since I went on that trip with Calvin. And I'm kind of worried— what's up with you and Micayla?"

I look at him to make sure he's being serious. He usually makes jokes out of "girl fights." But tonight he came over here all on his own. That makes me think that this fight with Micayla is more serious—if even Bennett noticed it, it must be bad.

"I've been hanging out with Claire. And Micayla is hanging out with some year-rounders, I guess. And Mason Redmond." I pause and wonder if I should say what I'm about to say. "You said it yourself that it's okay to have other friends. Didn't you?"

"Remy. Come on."

"What?" I ask, not looking at him.

He sits down on the little bench on the porch. I stay standing, because I don't know if I can handle sitting that close to him right now. I'm too nervous. "Obviously it's okay to have other friends, but you don't just get into fights with your best friends and not make up," he says. "That's really not like you, Remy."

I don't know what to say, so I just keep quiet.

"I told Micayla I was coming here. I told her the same things I told you," he says. "It's freakin' annoying that you two are being babies, so I had to stop it."

"Mediator Bennett!" I say, trying to lighten the tone of this conversation. I finally sit on the edge of the bench with him.

"Well, yeah, and also I have to bail on dog-sitting in two days. Calvin and I signed up for the tennis tournament."

"You finally have a tennis partner," I say. Bennett loves tennis, but Micayla and I never got into it. He's been trying to find a partner for the tournament for years now. I guess I'm happy for him. About that, at least.

"So I need Micayla to get back into the business. We can't both bail on you."

"Well, that's true."

I wonder if I should say anything else, about how he knows that I have all these mixed-up feelings for him. Or maybe he's already forgotten about that, or he doesn't want to talk about it because he doesn't think of me like that.

But I can't bring it up. It doesn't feel like the right time, and I'm way too nervous to talk about that kind of thing. When I can't think of anything else to say, I bring up Mr. Brookfield's scream and how we're still obsessed with it, and also about the other teams participating in the tennis tournament. Just average Seagate stuff. But it feels like there's a cloud hanging in the air between us, not allowing us to have a comfortable conversation. And also, one minute I want to give Bennett a hug, and the next minute I want to push him off the porch.

I'm disappointed about Bennett bailing on dog-sitting, but I'm happy for him about the tournament. And I'm happy that he came over to talk to me.

I decide not to bring up what Claire told him. I think back to what Mr. Brookfield said before about that fight he had with Morris about beef stew and how it lingered on for a whole year. I can't let that happen with Micayla. I have to fix things with her before I tackle anything else.

The next morning, everything seems clearer. I'm not sure why. It's one of those rare mornings when I hop out of bed feeling refreshed and rejuvenated.

I step outside the way I always do first thing in the morning. In the city, you can't just go outside for a second. It's a whole process—going down the hallway, into the elevator, down to the lobby, and outside.

But here I can walk straight out the back door and breathe in the ocean air, still in my pajamas. I never take that for granted. Today, though, the air seems fresher than usual. Maybe it was the talk with Mr. Brookfield, or maybe it was that Bennett stopped by and seemed to actually care about what was happening with Micayla and me. But the combination of everything has given me a whole new outlook.

My mom is in the kitchen making pancakes, and my dad

used our juicer for fresh-squeezed orange juice. I'm not sure what it is, but everything seems delightful.

And as I'm sitting down at the table, eating my mom's famous made-from-scratch pancakes with maple butter on the side, it occurs to me. It's like an epiphany, but an epiphany that's been there the whole time, just waiting for me to realize it.

It's so simple, really. But I know why I've been so mixed up about everything. Because I've been keeping all these confusing feelings to myself. The same way that Mr. Brookfield never really told anyone how much he missed the movies, how he never told anyone that the Scream was a big part of his life.

I need to tell Micayla that the whole year-rounder thing feels like a big change. But the person the change will affect the most is Micayla, not me. And that I'll always be here for her if she wants to talk. And if she doesn't want to talk, that's okay too.

I need to get up the courage and tell Bennett myself how I'm feeling.

And probably the first thing I need to do is be honest with Amber about Marilyn Monroe and Mornings. I'll never feel okay with everything until I fess up about what happened.

After I finish my pancakes, I run upstairs to change into shorts and a T-shirt. But I pack a bathing suit and a towel just in case I find time for a swim later in the day. I really doubt it will happen, since I still have to make up with Micayla, and that could take a while. But on Seagate you should never leave home without a bathing suit. Micayla and I used to swim at least once a day. And then things got busy with the dogs and weird between us. And everything felt different.

Different isn't always bad, though. It's comfortable when things stay the same, but comfortable can also mean boring, and different can also mean exciting. It's all in the way you look at it. Plus, it's not all black and white. Different doesn't have to be totally different; it can be just a little bit different. Like with Calvin and Claire coming this summer. It was still Seagate, just Seagate with a couple additions.

The new days can still be a little bit like the old days, I think, as long as you make room for new traditions too.

I stop at Claire's first to tell her about my plan to talk to Amber. I'm not going to force her to come too, but I want to let her know what I'm doing.

I knock on the door a few times, but no one answers. Finally I decide just to go in. It makes sense that they didn't hear the knocking, because Claire and Mr. Brookfield are sitting on the living room couch listening to the Scream.

"Good morning!" Mr. Brookfield says, all cheerful. "Are you hungry? We have fresh-baked muffins."

"I just had pancakes," I tell them. "But thank you."

Claire pats the couch, so I sit down next to her, and for the next few minutes we just keep listening to the Scream over and over, like we do at our pizza parties. Only this time, there's no talking over it. We're just sitting here quietly.

Mr. Brookfield stops the recording. "Now you're awake, right, Claire?"

She nods. "We started a new morning tradition," she tells me. "We listen to the Scream together. It really wakes us up."

"Yeah. I can imagine."

"It's like a wake-up call to get up from sleeping, and also a wake-up call to start the day and do something extreme," Claire says. "I can't really explain it. So we listen to the Scream, and then we scream!"

"I like it. I think that's really cool."

"Thank you," Mr. Brookfield says. "It's a way to appreciate something old and make it new at the same time." He winks at me.

If I knew how to wink, I would wink back. I hope he knows how much our conversations have changed the way I think about things.

"We have to go tell Amber what happened," I say to Claire. "I can't live with the guilt."

"But MM is fine." Claire widens her eyes at me like I'm a crazy person, and I get the sense that she wants me to keep quiet and not talk about the incident anymore in front of her grandfather. "It wasn't that big of a deal. And Beverly is old; she'll forget about it."

"You know how you just say what's on your mind?" I remind Claire. "Well, I'm trying to be more like that."

There's a moment where we just look at each other. Then Claire nods slowly, all proud of herself. "Well, when you say it like that, I guess I'm in. I'll be down in a minute."

She runs up the stairs, and I sit on Mr. Brookfield's couch and look at his collection of tiny director's chairs.

"Feeling any better about things?" he asks me, picking up his mug of steaming coffee.

I shrug. "Maybe a little bit. I'm going to think about the Scream wake-up call. Maybe I need something like that in my life too."

"You can join us anytime," he says. "It's done wonders for my little Claire."

He's right about that. When I think about Claire at the beginning of the summer and of her now, she seems like a completely different person. Her surly, angry personality has been washed away.

She's still honest—she says whatever's on her mind, even if it's rude or embarrassing. But her attitude has changed.

Maybe the Seagate air was a remedy for her grumpiness, or maybe it was quality time with her grandfather. I'm not sure. But the new Claire is way better than the old Claire. I guess that's an example of change being a really good thing.

Claire and I walk over to Marilyn Monroe's house totally silently. I wonder if she's as nervous as I am.

"Hi, girls, you here to get Mari?" Amber asks, greeting us at the door. She's in yoga pants, with some kind of workout video on the TV behind her. "You're early. Didn't we say noon?"

"Yeah. We, um, I mean, I wanted to talk to you for a second," I tell her.

"Sure. Come in."

Amber turns off the workout DVD and sits with us on the couch. Hudson's toys are thrown all around the room. Marilyn Monroe is sleeping under the kitchen table, and I know how much she values her naps. It would be nice to pet her right now, but I don't want to wake her up.

"I'm sorry I didn't tell you this last night," I start. "But Marilyn Monroe sort of broke into Mornings yesterday, and Beverly's really mad about it, and you probably can't ever go back there with Marilyn Monroe again. We probably shouldn't have taken her there, but we thought it would be a special treat. I used to do it all the time with my dog, Danish. Anyway, I guess she was so excited, she just stormed in and hopped up onto an old lady's lap and then ripped the tablecloth off. Well, maybe that was my fault, because it happened when I tried to take her off the lady's lap. Actually, maybe it's all my fault, because I shouldn't have taken her there in the first place."

"I see." Amber pauses to think for a minute, looking a little bit confused. But then after a long moment she starts laughing. Really laughing. Claire cracks up next. And then I start laughing too. When one of us laughs, we both laugh. Usually uncontrollably.

"My Mari wants what she wants. She's an independent woman," Amber says. "I'm disappointed she stormed in, but I'm glad you told me."

"I'm really sorry," I say again.

"Me too," Claire adds.

"I know, and I appreciate that." Amber smiles. "We all make mistakes. Once, I left my son behind at the yoga studio. He was napping in the back room, and I just left without him." She shakes her head like she can't believe how dumb she was. "I never told my husband," she whispers.

"I'm trying to be more honest," I tell her. "And not hide my feelings so much."

Claire nudges me with her arm and gives me a look that says I'm talking too much and Amber doesn't want to hear this.

I guess there's a balance, and I haven't found it yet.

But we sit and talk with Amber for a little while longer, and she tells us that she still gets in fights with her friends. I'm not sure if that's supposed to make us feel better or worse, but it's interesting to hear about.

We end up taking Marilyn Monroe a little early and then going to pick up Oscar and Atticus. Bennett and Calvin are picking up the others today.

"That was easier than I thought," Claire says.

"You didn't say anything!"

"Yeah, I mean, easier for you." She grins. "So your next project is . . . ?"

"Micayla. I have to fix things with Micayla," I say. "Let's take the dogs and stop at her house. You can wait outside. I can't have you laughing and distracting me."

"Fair enough," Claire says. "My laugh is pretty powerful."

She bursts into some weird Wicked Witch of the West laugh, and we both crack up again.

Maybe Claire changed. Or maybe I changed. Or maybe we both did. Regardless, I don't know how it's possible that I ever hated her.

On the walk to Micayla's, my head is full of ideas.
Ideas about what I'm going to say to her to make things right,
ideas about how I'll eventually talk to Bennett. And an idea
for Mr. Brookfield too. Claire and Mr. Brookfield's new morning Scream tradition made me think of it, and I want to tell
Claire, but I'm worried she'll think it's dumb. And she's not
afraid to tell me when she thinks something's dumb.

We're friends now, but I'm still a little scared of her. That
makes sense, though. I don't think people could ever change
completely, if we'd even want them to.

"I just timed it," she says, breaking me out of my thoughts.

"Timed what?"

Claire looks at me, but I don't meet her gaze. "The amount
of time you've been silent. One minute, eight seconds. Something must be on your mind. So spill."

I don't say anything right away.

"Oh Lordy," she groans. "Not again. I thought you were done with being keep-things-to-yourself Remy. I thought you were going to speak your mind now!"

I laugh. "Okay. Promise you'll have an open mind?"

"Suuuuure," she says, sounding reluctant.

"Well, do you know about Seagate Halloween?" I ask.

"Remy, it's only August."

I nod. "Yeah, I know. But Seagate Halloween is Labor Day weekend. It's a huge tradition. There's a big parade and people dress up and then we eat all the candy we can. That's it. No trick-or-treating or anything."

"So it's basically a big costume party?" Claire asks.

"Yeah. But the best costume party you've ever been to."

Claire bends down to clean up after Oscar. "So what's your idea?"

"Well, here's the thing. For all the past years, we did Seagate Halloween exactly the same. Same costumes, same traditions, everything the same. And that was kind of what made it so awesome."

"Uh-huh."

"Well, I've realized that things can't always stay the same. We're forced to change. And I think we can make a new addition to Seagate Halloween!"

"Oh-kay." Claire looks nearly ready to roll her eyes. I need to get to the point.

"Here's the idea: Your grandpa starts the parade with

his scream. We make a little introduction and tell everyone who he is, and then he screams! I thought about adding the Scream to the Sandcastle Contest, but this makes way more sense."

"Go on."

"He and I had this whole talk about bringing your past into your present but not too much and not dwelling on it and all that." I start speed-talking, a little afraid Claire will shoot down my idea before I say it all. "And I think this is exactly in that spirit! Old things and new traditions! And it's Halloween, so a scream fits!"

I hold my breath and wait to hear what she'll say.

"I like it," Claire says. "It'll be like he's a celebrity finally."

"Good. As long as you're on board, we can make it happen!"

"Well, I don't know about that. But okay." She pauses for a second. "I have an idea to add to your idea. Ready?"

I nod.

"Y'know how every Sunday on Seagate they show movies on the lawn behind the stadium?"

"Uh-huh."

"So maybe in the weeks leading up to Seagate Halloween, they can show scary movies, the ones with my grandpa's scream." She looks at me, and I swear this must be the most excited I've seen her since the day she showed me her new jeans. "And then people can hear it, and they'll recognize it at the parade. And then they'll realize that he really is famous!"

"I love it. I love it. I love it!" I jump up and down and grab Claire's hands, and soon we're jumping up and down together like people who have just won the lottery.

We get to Micayla's house, and I feel like I'm bursting apart with excitement. I'm going to make things right with Micayla and Bennett. And then Claire and I are going to make Mr. Brookfield the star of Seagate, which he is already, even though nobody knows. Everyone's going to hear his scream in those movies, and everyone is going to know how amazing he is.

Claire tells me she's going to take the dogs and meet Bennett and Calvin at Dog Beach, and that Micayla and I should come when we're done.

"Hi, Rem," Micayla's mom says when she opens the door. "I've missed you."

"Same," I say. "I have to talk to Micayla. Is she here?"

"Yup. Go on up."

Micayla's sister, Ivy, is sitting on their living room couch looking at the computer. She does one of those backward waves, not turning around. I wave back, even though she can't see me.

Micayla has her door open, and before she even sees me, I peer in and notice that her room looks completely different. For one thing, she has a desk in it now. She never needed a desk before, but I guess some of the furniture from their house was moved here already.

She's sitting on her bed looking at magazines. I don't want to startle her, so I knock gently.

"Remy!" she yelps. I guess I startled her anyway. Maybe there was no way of avoiding it.

"Micayla, I'm so sorry." I say it right away. I need her to know that's why I'm here. "I should have been more support-ive and understanding of this whole big change in your life. I should have been a better friend."

"Well, thanks. But you're not good with change." She smiles her soft Micayla smile. "You're always talking about tradition and wanting everything to be the same, year after year. I guess maybe that's why I didn't want to tell you. I felt like if my life changed, it would let you down."

"But it's your life, not mine." I sit down on the edge of her bed. I realize we haven't had a sleepover all summer. Are we too old for sleepovers? I hope not. I don't think that you can ever really get too old for sleepovers. I mean, even when you're married, it's pretty much like a sleepover every night.

"That's true," Micayla says.

"It hurt my feelings that you'd keep a big secret from me. And then I guess I just got worried that I was being replaced by Avery Sanders. She's nice and everything, but . . . you know."

Micayla shakes her head. "You're not being replaced. I promise."

"Good." I smile.

"Anyway, I forgive you. I miss you too much to not forgive you."

"I missed you so much too." I reach across and give her a

hug. "Why did your parents decide to become year-rounders? I never even asked you that."

She sighs. "You mean aside from the fact that Seagate Island is the best place on earth?"

I laugh. "Yeah. Aside from that."

"Well, we just don't need the big house in New Jersey anymore, since Zane and Ivy are away at college. It feels really empty when they're away. And my parents started wondering why they were paying for two places when they'd rather just be here." She shrugs. "I don't know. That's what they said. And we're all so happy on Seagate, it just made sense."

"I bet it's going to be great," I tell her, because it seems like the right thing to say. And then I feel even guiltier for not being more supportive before. This was likely a big decision for them, not something they just decided in a few minutes. And it probably will be great—just because it's not the Seagate I know doesn't mean it's not still Seagate.

"Oh! I still have to tell you about Mason Redmond," Micayla says.

"Oh yeah!"

"I think we, like, *like* each other," she says.

"*Like* like?" I giggle. "Really? How do you know?"

She twists a few braids around her finger. "We had fun at Sundae Best. And his favorite flavor is also cherry chip. And we had a lot to talk about." She pauses. "He's not always thinking about his future, you know. I mean, he is, in that he signed up to play lacrosse this year, but that's it."

"That's good. So what happens now?"

"No clue." She gets up and grabs the hoodie off her desk chair. "But it's fun. Do I look okay?" She turns around and poses. "We're going to Dog Beach now, right?"

"Yeah." I smile. "You look beautiful."

On our walk over to Dog Beach, I tell Micayla about my idea for Mr. Brookfield's scream and Seagate Halloween.

"I love it!" She high-fives me. "So smart. Halloween is all about screaming!"

"I know, right?" I throw up my hands. "It just came to me. And hey, there's something else we need to talk about."

Micayla looks at me sideways. "Bennett, right?"

"How did you know?"

"Come on, Rem. You totally like him. It's, like, the oldest story in the world—girls fall in love with their best friends all the time."

"They do?" I ask. "How do you know?"

She gives me an are-you-serious look. "I just know. And also, Ivy told me she was in love with her best friend from home for three years."

"I don't know what to say," I admit. "I don't know exactly what happened. I just know that things changed. He's not just plain old Bennett anymore with the ratty T-shirts and the untied shoelaces who always burns the top of his mouth when eating pizza."

"Well, he still is that Bennett, but maybe you just see something else too?" Micayla asks.

"Yeah. I guess that's it. He's still the same, but there's kind of more to him, or more underneath that only I can see. I can't explain it."

Micayla nods. "I get what you're saying."

"So what do I do?"

"*That* I don't know."

"That's exactly what Claire said," I tell her.

"Claire gives you advice now?" she asks, raising an eyebrow.

"Sometimes. But don't worry, you haven't been replaced or anything."

"I know I can't be replaced. I'm not worried."

"We didn't even talk about Seagate Schoolhouse and Avery Sanders and all that," I say. "We got off track. Tonight: you and me, sleepover and s'mores. Sound good?"

"Sounds perfect."

The rest of the day at Dog Beach goes well. Everyone's happy to be there. Calvin and Bennett keep a game of Frisbee going for more than an hour. Marilyn Monroe is happy traipsing around from Micayla to Claire to me to all the other dogs.

Tabby and Potato Salad are lazy as usual, but they push a ball back and forth with their noses, and it's so cute that I take a video of it with my phone. I'm convinced it's going to be the next YouTube sensation.

It feels weird without Lester here, but they were only doing a short-term rental. Maybe he'll be back next summer.

If I were to give out awards, I think I'd give him "most social dog."

I keep watching Mason and Micayla to see what it's like when two people like each other. I don't really notice anything that crazy. They laugh often and smile all the time and have tons to say to each other, but that's it as far as I can tell.

"Things are okay with you guys?" Claire asks me when Micayla's at the lifeguard's chair.

"Really okay," I say. I almost tell her about the sleepover, but I don't want to make her feel left out, and I also don't know if I should include her. Perhaps Micayla and I need some one-on-one time. "Now I just have one more big idea. We need to finish our day here so I can talk to your grandpa and then I can talk to Mrs. Paisley tomorrow, the one who handles all the planning for Seagate Halloween."

"So come over after we drop the dogs off," Claire says. "I think your boyfriend and my brother are going out for burgers with my dad."

"Oh, your dad's back?" I ask.

"Yeah, my mom leaves and he comes back. I don't know what that's all about."

Suddenly the tone of the conversation goes cloudy, and I don't know if I should ask any more questions.

"Probably just schedules," Claire says. "They're confusing. I try not to think about it too much."

"Aren't grown-ups mysterious?" I ask, trying to make a joke. "They can drive and they have jobs and bank accounts and stuff. But then sometimes you'll ask them the reason for something and they'll just say because they said so. And then you realize they don't have anything figured out at all."

"Exactly." Claire shakes her head. "They're all cuckoo."

"Mr. Brookfield, I have the best idea!" I yell, running into the house. Claire and I find him sitting in his armchair reading a thick book with a dark, spooky cover.

"Yes, Remy?"

"You will be the voice of Seagate Halloween! You know how everyone dresses up and we have the parade and everything?"

"Of course!"

"Well, your scream will start the whole thing. Kind of like a fanfare on a trumpet or a whistle." I put my hands on my hips. "What do you think?"

"I'm in!" He winks. "Isn't that what all the young people say these days?"

Claire and I crack up, and Bennett and Calvin do too. They're hanging over the railing listening to our whole conversation. It's surprising that Mr. Brookfield didn't need much convincing, but maybe he's been waiting for this all along.

Claire tells him all about her idea to show scary movies during the Seagate Sunday night movies.

"I'll talk to Mrs. Paisley," I tell him.

"We'll go together," Mr. Brookfield says. "I've known her for years."

"She's always at Breakfast by the Boardwalk in the morning," I say, even though he probably already knows that. "Let's meet her there tomorrow. Claire, you come too."

"I'm in," she says, laughing.

In the end, I don't invite Claire to the sleepover, but I think it's okay, because she said she was excited for a Claire-Grandpa date. They were going to Frederick's Fish and then seeing a movie at Seagate Cinema after. I think Claire likes time alone with her grandfather. She hasn't really said it out loud, but I can tell.

I walk home more quickly than I think I've ever walked on Seagate. It's as if my excitement is carrying me and making me walk faster. I can't wait for Seagate Halloween. I can't wait for Mr. Brookfield to scream and for all of Seagate to hear it. Everyone will want to know his story. And he'll be so happy to tell it. His past will become a part of his present and his future, and he'll finally be the celebrity he was meant to be.

The only thing I am still trying to figure out is Bennett.

What should I say to him? On the one hand, I think he already knows. I mean, I know he knows, because Claire told him, but I don't know what he thinks about it. And things are still okay with us. And maybe I shouldn't make anything muddy, since I don't even know what my feelings really mean. But on the other hand, I feel like I'm bursting with feelings, like I'm carrying balloons under my shirt and I have to let them out.

I run through the door and say, "Mom, Micayla's sleeping over!"

My mom comes out from the kitchen and smiles, unsurprised, and I realize she already knows. I guess Micayla's mom told her. And my mom seems so happy, and I'm relieved that this fight—the longest one of our friendship—is over.

"Do you think you're going to want pizza? Or should I make baked ziti? Or what?" my mom asks. She has her painting apron on, and there's a speck of purple paint on her cheek.

"Let's see when Micayla gets here. She just went home to grab her stuff."

I run up to my room and straighten up. Even though Micayla has been here a million times, I feel like tonight is different. It's the beginning of our friendship after the Fight. We have so much to talk about—Seagate Schoolhouse and Mason and Bennett and the dogs.

I look around my room, and for the first time in my whole life, I want to change the decor. I want to take down my old posters, the ones of sunsets and puppies and old-fashioned ice cream parlors. I want to spruce things up. Maybe Mom and I can redecorate—paint over this lavender and make the room a cool sea green or something. Or maybe Mom and I can paint a mural. Mom will have to do all the hard painting, but I can help a little bit.

I want to take out my old gingham beanbag chairs and put in something cool—a director's chair like Mr. Brookfield has, or maybe even some kind of indoor chaise longue.

I don't know what's come over me. Maybe it's that I'm so excited for the future that I want to get it started right away. I'm looking forward to all the possibilities, and I want to be ready for them. I don't want to hang on to old pieces of the past just because they're comfortable and they've always been there.

I want to start fresh and embrace what's coming.

"Remy!" I hear someone yelling from downstairs, so I throw the last of my dirty laundry into the hamper and run down. Micayla's on the porch, grinning.

"Let's get sandwiches at Pastrami on Rye and then have a picnic on the beach behind your house," Micayla says. "We haven't been to the deli since June!"

"I can't believe it," I say, grabbing my bag from the foyer table. "Mom, do you want anything from the deli?"

"Ooh," Mom says, walking in, this time with some yellow paint above her eyebrow. When I say she gets into a painting, I really mean it. "I'd love turkey with coleslaw and Russian dressing."

"You got it." She hands me money and I give her a hug, and soon Micayla and I are off on our walk—like the old days, but even better.

"You're never going to believe who my teacher is," Micayla says.

"Who?"

"Paul. Atticus's owner."

"I thought he was a college professor?" I ask. "And that he's working on his dissertation, or whatever it's called."

"He was. He is. But he's taking a year off and staying on Seagate, and he got a job teaching sixth-grade English." She shakes her head. "But guess why he's staying."

"Um?" I look at her and try to think of the craziest reason ever. "He needs Sundae Best all year long?"

"He's dating Andi! Rascal's owner's daughter. Remember?"

I think back to earlier in the summer. We don't see the owners as much anymore, since one of us just runs into each house to pick up the dog. We never really stay to chat.

"Oh yeah, the yoga one? And her mom had hip surgery?" It's all coming back to me now.

"Yeah, they started talking when they picked up their dogs from us on Dog Beach. The dogs brought them together!" Micayla says, all excited. "Or I guess *we* brought them together!"

"Andi's staying all year too? To teach yoga?" I ask.

"And to help her mom," Micayla reminds me. "And because she's in loooove."

We both start laughing and decide that we're starving and we need to race to Pastrami on Rye.

This is going to be the best sleepover ever.

It's amazing what a sleepover with Micayla Wal-
cott can do. It's basically a miracle panacea—it can cure
anything. That's what Micayla is for me. We stayed up until
two in the morning, had a beach bonfire, played truth or
dare (mostly just truth, actually), and talked and talked and
talked.

So what if she's a year-rounder now? So she'll be on Seagate when I'm not. She's still Micayla and I'm still Remy. And
yeah, things change, but deeper things stay the same. That's
a relief.

We're on our way to Breakfast by the Boardwalk to meet
with Mrs. Paisley and Mr. Brookfield, and then we're going
to pick up the dogs. I can't wait to observe Paul and Andi in
action. Lovebirds in love because of their dogs. Can you get
a better story than that? I don't think so.

When Micayla and I get there, Claire, Mr. Brookfield, and Mrs. Paisley are already there.

"Don't worry, Bennett and Calvin are with the dogs," Claire says, running up to us. "Oscar's mom had to take the triplets for an early pediatrician appointment, so Bennett went to get him, and Calvin decided to pick up Marilyn Monroe on the way."

"Awesome." I smile. "Thanks, Claire."

"Just didn't want you to panic." She looks at Micayla and then back at me. "You two are okay again? Back to being BFFs?"

We nod.

"Thank goodness. That was getting so annoying," Claire adds, rolling her eyes.

We all join Mr. Brookfield and Mrs. Paisley at the table, and Callie, one of the waitresses, brings over hot chocolates and the bakery basket.

"So tell me about this mysterious scream," Mrs. Paisley says, leaning over, her hands folded on the table. "And how come I've never heard about it? Don, I've known you for thirty years."

"I know." Mr. Brookfield laughs, picking a croissant out of the basket. "I guess I always figured no one would care."

"I care, Don." Mrs. Paisley smiles, and it's funny that she keeps calling him Don. I never even knew his first name.

So Mr. Brookfield tells her the story, and she keeps saying "Wow" and "Incredible" and "You're famous."

As he's telling the story, I get a new idea, and it's genius.

I wanted Mr. Brookfield to be the voice and mascot and announcer of Seagate Halloween, but I don't think that's enough. I think everyone needs to scream!

"So what's your idea, Remy?" Mrs. Paisley asks. I quickly whisper to Claire that I just had a major epiphany and am making a slight change to the original idea. I want her to be prepared, because she's a major inspiration for my idea.

I tell them my old idea and they seem intrigued, so I know they'll love my new idea. "And the best part will be a Seagate Scream Contest!"

Claire looks at me and smiles, but it's actually more than a smile. It's more like she's beaming in this super proud way. Her face looks different from how I've ever seen it before, and I almost want to take a picture so that I can show her how happy she looks.

You don't really know what pride looks like until you see it on someone else.

She tells them her idea about the Sunday night scary movies, and Mr. Brookfield's eyes light up. I bet he'll just sit quietly in the back while people watch, not making a big deal out of it at all.

"Well, I love all of this. We'll start showing the Sunday night movies next week," Mrs. Paisley suggests.

"Great!" Micayla says. "We can make posters telling people about the Scream. And everyone will want to know more about it and get even more excited."

We spend the rest of breakfast going over how Mr. Brookfield should dress and where he should sit and who should introduce him and all these other exciting logistics.

To be honest, even though I love Seagate Halloween so much, it always made me a little bit sad because it's over Labor Day weekend, the last weekend of the summer, and that means the end of Seagate for me until next summer.

But this summer, it feels different. I'm excited about it. It almost makes the end of summer tolerable.

It's funny how you can want something to stay the same so, so badly, but then little changes happen, and you realize how great the new thing can be.

When we walk up to Rascal's house later that morning, we notice that Atticus is on the front lawn. Paul and Andi are sitting on the front porch, next to each other on a wicker love seat, while the dogs chase each other.

"Look at them," I say softly to Claire and Micayla.

"Totally in love," Claire says.

"Rascal and Atticus could be stepbrothers very soon!" Micayla laughs. "Stepdogs!"

We all start laughing, and that's when Andi and Paul notice us.

"They're ready for you," Paul says. "Can you watch them until about five today?"

"Sure," I say, putting their leashes on and making a note of the time change.

"Great." Andi smiles. "We're going on a day trip to the wineries in Ocean Edge."

"Sounds fun," Claire says, and when I look up, I notice that Andi and Paul are holding hands. Our little doggie day care is a matchmaker!

We spend the rest of the day with all our dogs—Marilyn Monroe, Oscar, Rascal, Atticus, Tabby, Potato Salad, and Palm.

Everyone's happy. Claire, Micayla, and I sit on the side and people-watch and dog-watch and take everything in. Bennett and Calvin engage in the longest game of Frisbee in Dog Beach history. Then we all go to Ping-Pong and watch a few games, the dogs happily sitting on the side and watching too. And then we get the biggest table at Daisy's and enjoy breakfast for dinner.

All of us together. It's hard to imagine things getting any better than this.

But every time I look at Bennett, I get a flickery feeling—like someone turning a light switch on and off really fast.

It's not exactly a bad feeling, just a new and strange one. But I've realized that sometimes great things come from new and different. Just look at Claire—she didn't want to be here, and I didn't want her here, and now we're friends. I never expected it, and I pretty much resisted it, but it happened, and now I can't imagine Seagate without her.

35

The next two weeks fly by. Either we're busy with the dogs or we're busy getting ready for Seagate Halloween. Micayla and I have sleepovers pretty much every other night, to make up for all the nights we missed this summer. Claire sometimes comes too.

In addition to getting Mr. Brookfield ready for his new role, we're in charge of getting costumes for all the dogs, and we'll be the ones walking them in the doggie part of the parade.

Rascal and Atticus are going as Ping-Pong players—we're strapping Ping-Pong paddles to their backs. Marilyn Monroe and Tabby are going as Superwoman and Princess Leia. Oscar and Potato Salad are wearing matching doggie tuxedos. Palm is going as a Frisbee, since he's so little. We're basically strapping a Frisbee to him and hoping people get it.

We're trying to get them all into their costumes now so

that we can do a run-through before the parade tomorrow. It's a tough job, but someone's gotta do it. We don't want them to be totally caught off guard tomorrow.

The tuxedos are my favorite of all the costumes, and I kind of wanted Rascal and Atticus to wear them too. But Calvin and Bennett were set on some of the dogs being Ping-Pong players.

"Come on, Rem," Bennett said. "They love to watch the games, and Ping-Pong is a Seagate tradition. It would be weird to leave it out."

I agreed but am kind of regretting it. The tuxedos are just so cute.

Finally, after wrangling and twisting and bribing the dogs with treats, we have them all in their costumes. They're running around Dog Beach that way, and it's pretty much the most adorable thing I've ever seen.

We return the dogs home later with their costumes and tell their owners to make sure they're ready to go at eleven tomorrow. We want to get them prepared for the parade before everyone else gets there at noon.

That night, Micayla, Claire, and I have a sleepover at Micayla's house. Her mom makes us bouyon, an amazing St. Lucian dish that's a sort of stew, and homemade peanut butter cookies. We all sleep in sleeping bags on Micayla's screened-in back porch, even though her room is cozy and nice.

We want to make the most of one of our last nights here and sleep by the sea.

"So what's going on with you and Mason?" Claire asks Micayla.

"I dunno." She laughs nervously. "He's leaving tonight."

"What?"

"Yeah. His sister is starting college. So they had to go back to Philadelphia to get her all settled," Micayla says. "I said good-bye. He said to say good-bye to you guys too."

"He's missing Seagate Halloween!" I yell. "And all the dogs."

"I know." Micayla sighs. "But it's okay. There's always next summer."

I look at Micayla and am amazed by her attitude. But she's right. One of the best things about summer on Seagate is that there's always a next summer to look forward to.

"And what about you?" Claire asks me. "Are you ever going to say anything to Bennett? Or no? And do you guys feel replaced by my brother?"

"A little," I say. "But it's okay. Bennett needed a guy friend."

"You're just going to let the summer end and not say anything?" Claire asks. She seems so serious and concerned, it's making me feel uneasy. I kind of like my friendship with Bennett the way it is. We're friends. And I have a little-more-than-friends feeling about him. But that's okay.

It makes me wonder about Claire, though. Maybe she has a secret, and she's worried about keeping it inside until next summer.

"I'm okay with waiting until next summer," I admit. "I don't want to mess anything up."

"You won't, Rem," Micayla says and puts her arm around me. "Honestly. It's Bennett. He'll love you forever, no matter what."

"Yeah." I go over to the table and take another cookie. "Love me like a friend, like his sister."

"Well, I'm not so sure about that," Claire says. Her eyes have this strange twinkle, and I get the feeling that she wants to tell me something but she's not totally sure that she should.

Micayla and Claire move closer together on the couch. It's getting chilly out here, the way it always does at the end of August. It feels like summer is tired and needs a rest and can't handle being so hot anymore. It's breezier and colder, and we spend most of our afternoons in sweatshirts.

"We need hot chocolate," Micayla tells us, and she hops up from the couch to go and get it. I sit on the back porch with Claire, who now has her sweatshirt hood covering her head and most of her face.

I want to ask her what she's hiding, but I'm also kind of happy to have stopped the Bennett discussion. I don't know how I feel, and sometimes it's okay to admit that you don't know. It feels better that way. It feels like it's protecting me from doing the wrong thing.

"Remy, we have to tell you something," Micayla says when she comes back from the kitchen with a tray of steamy mugs of hot chocolate. I guess Claire and Micayla had a secret conversation at some point and I didn't realize it.

My heart starts pounding. It's happening, and I can't believe I haven't realized it until now. What if Claire loves Bennett and Bennett loves Claire and this has been going on all summer and I didn't even notice? What if that's why Claire told Bennett, so she could figure out if he liked her?

I don't want to know. I don't want to know.

"Bennett likes you," Claire says. "Really, really likes you."

"What?" I ask.

"I mean, okay, he doesn't love you like he's going to propose or anything. I mean, you're eleven," Claire continues. "But he likes you in a different way than he likes us. He slept over the other night. And I was in the bathroom brushing my teeth. My loser brother and Bennett were in my grandpa's upstairs den, and they were playing some dumb video game where they have to get robots into hot-air balloons. My brother might need an intervention, given how obsessed he is with computers and video games. But anyway—"

"Yeah?" I ask. My heart is racing. I can't look at Claire and I can't look at Micayla. I stare at the fraying cushion on Micayla's outdoor chair. I pick at the threads.

"And Bennett goes, 'Remy loves hot-air balloons.' And then my dumb brother goes, 'You've mentioned Remy, like, a million times tonight, dude.'"

Micayla starts laughing. "Your brother has a way of saying things. Have you noticed that?"

"Yeah. Always." Claire rolls her eyes. "And then Bennett basically said that he hadn't mentioned you that much, but then Calvin said he had, and then Bennett said, 'I guess I did. I dunno. She's pretty awesome.'"

Claire sips her mug of hot chocolate. "And then they went back to playing their game."

I don't want to feel or act too excited, because all that means is that he thinks I'm awesome, but I have to admit that it makes me happy. My heart finally calms down, and I smile and sit back on the frayed outdoor chair.

"Thanks for telling me that, Claire," I say. "You didn't have to."

"Of course I didn't have to. Duh." Claire eats another cookie. "But I wanted to. I thought you should know. Because even if you don't say anything, you can go home and spend the year knowing that Bennett thinks you're awesome. And yeah, that's a nice thing to know."

We spend the rest of the night chatting and thinking about the parade tomorrow.

Instead of sleeping on the back porch like we'd planned, we bring our sleeping bags down to the beach and sleep on the sand.

"It's good to have the ocean at our sleepover," Claire tells us. "That's something I never thought I'd say. But it's really true."

Micayla's mom makes us waffles for breakfast, and then we all head home to shower and get ready for Seagate Halloween. Micayla and Bennett came up with this awesome idea that all of us—Micayla, Claire, Calvin, Bennett, and I—should dress up as what Danish and I used to be for Seagate Halloween. So a few of us are beach pails and a few of us are shovels. Micayla's mom and my mom are both super crafty, so they were able to make the costumes for us out of cardboard boxes, papier-mâché, and paint.

I couldn't believe they thought of it, and that Claire and Calvin were excited about it too. Sometimes people will surprise you and do something so nice that it almost seems magical. Sometimes you don't even realize that people care that much about you, even though they've been caring all along.

"Is your grandpa nervous?" I ask Claire when Micayla and I get to her house. We walked over to pick up Claire and Calvin and then we'll all get Bennett together. "I mean, it's pretty much his first performance in—what? Fifty years?"

"I think so," Claire says. "He doesn't seem nervous. More like excited."

"What's his costume?"

"He dressed as Calvin!" She laughs. "I helped him order a pair of trendy jeans online, and he popped the collar of his polo shirt. He's even trying to spike his hair! And he's going to carry an iPad Mini! It's so funny."

Micayla and I crack up. "Calvin hasn't seen him getting ready?" I ask.

"No. He's totally oblivious."

Calvin comes out, barely able to walk in his red beach pail costume, and he high-fives us. "We look awesome," he says.

I look at Claire and Calvin, and I truly can't believe how different they are from how they were at the beginning of the summer. I wonder if they realize how different they are, and if they will always stay this way.

Are they going to be Seagate summer folk forever now? Or will they go home and forget about this summer and how amazing it was? I hope they always remember, and I really think they will. I know I will.

I'm pretty sure that once you're a Seagater, you stay that way for life. And all my life, I was convinced that every Seagate summer had to be exactly like the one before it—with all the same traditions and foods and routines. Now I know that's not true. Businesses can be formed, new people can join the group, anything can happen. Who knows—maybe I'll even pick a new favorite Sundae Best flavor next summer. Crazier things have happened.

Bennett is already waiting for us outside his house. He's playing catch with Asher, who is dressed as a baseball player.

"We're all going as baseball players," Asher tells us. "My whole bunk from camp. Even the girls!"

"Wow," I say. I've barely seen Asher all summer, and he suddenly seems taller and chattier and more mature. He's going over to the parade with the rest of his bunk from camp, so we say good-bye and our group of shovels and pails walks (or hobbles) down there together.

We must look so silly, but it doesn't even bother me. People say that cliques are bad, and they are in many ways, but sometimes it just feels so good to be part of a group. Earlier in the summer, I had no interest in Calvin and Claire joining our trio, but now it feels like they really belong, like they've been here since the beginning.

Bennett taps me on the shoulder. He and Calvin were walking a few feet behind us. "Are you sad about Danish today?"

"Not really. I'm excited to see all our dogs in the parade. And the fact that we're all wearing his costume kind of makes it feel like he's here with us." I adjust the cardboard on my back. "Thanks for asking, though," I say, because it really was sweet that Bennett was concerned about me missing Danish.

I know people say that no one is perfect, but maybe Bennett is. I mean, sure, he said that thing about needing to have more than two friends, and some space from us, and stuff. But most of the time, he's so nice and caring. He notices things about me and remembers them later. That's pretty amazing.

We get to the boardwalk right in front of Dog Beach, and all the dogs are waiting for us. They look great in their costumes.

"I am so excited for this," Dawn, Oscar's mom, says, pushing her superpowered triplet stroller back and forth. "You guys are seriously the best."

"They're superstars," Amber, Marilyn Monroe's mom, says. "Remy, may I please speak with you for a moment?"

"Um, sure," I reply.

We walk over to one of the benches and Amber says, "Listen, Remy, you and Mari developed quite a bond this summer. We're moving to a new apartment this year, and it was a huge decision that I really struggled with, but the building doesn't allow dogs. It's getting harder and harder for me to watch both Hudson and Mari, and we were going to give her to my mom, but now that I'm thinking about it . . ."

Her voice trails off, and I wonder what's going to come next.

"Would you consider adopting her? I mean, if your parents say it's okay? We could still visit. We both live in Manhattan and we're both on Seagate every summer. I just figured, y'know, because she really loves you, and you're dogless now, and . . . you know."

It seems like it's hard for her to say this, so I just keep nodding and saying, "Yeah," and nodding again. I need to ask my parents, but of course! It's Marilyn Monroe! "Of course, I'd love to. More than anything!"

We walk together for a few minutes, talking it over. I'll ask my parents as soon as the parade is over. I hope they say yes!

Andi and Paul are sitting next to each other on the bench that Mr. Brookfield usually sits on. They're sipping coffees and holding hands, and the dogs are at their feet. It's almost too cute to handle.

We round up all the dogs and head over to the stage, where the parade will be starting. Mr. Brookfield is hiding backstage until two minutes before, because he doesn't want anyone to see him. He may also be doing this because he's nervous, but I'm not really sure.

I run over to him and whisper, "You're going to be great, Mr. Brookfield. I mean, you're already great!"

"Thanks, Remy." He pats me on the shoulder. "You're not so bad yourself."

We quickly high-five, and I rejoin the group.

The Pooch Parade is always the first part of Seagate Halloween. I think it's because dogs are such an important part of life here. And they're treated like real Seagate citizens too.

From a dog-friendly restaurant like Daisy's to their own beach, it's clear that they're valued here. Seagate life wouldn't be the same without dogs. Everyone knows it.

And that's what makes it even crazier that there was never a doggie day camp before this summer. It's like it's been on the tip of everyone's tongue for years. I guess I'm just so grateful that it happened. And that we were the ones to make it happen.

"You guys ready?" Mrs. Paisley asks us. We're all lined up with the dogs, and the parade is set to start in exactly two minutes. I'm still amazed that we managed to get all the dogs into their costumes and they're all sitting patiently. It's like they know that they're part of something awesome and they're excited to be here.

"Yup!" I say.

Mrs. Paisley gives me a thumbs-up, which means it's time for me to go to the megaphone. My stomach gets all rumbly, and I can't believe I'm going to speak in front of every person and dog on Seagate. But even though I'm nervous, I can't wait to do it. I can't wait for Mr. Brookfield's amazing talent to be known by every person on this island.

"I'll be right back," I tell Claire, Calvin, Bennett, and Micayla. Claire and Micayla know what's happening, of course, and as soon as I make the announcement about Mr. Brookfield, I'm going to hop off the stage and join them.

I follow Mrs. Paisley onto the stage and she whispers, "You know what you're going to say?"

I nod. I tried to write it down but nothing seemed right, so I just decided to memorize some thoughts and then speak from my heart. I think I can do it.

"Welcome to Seagate Halloween!" Mrs. Paisley yells into the megaphone. "This has been a tradition for fifty years, but traditions can always be improved upon, as you will soon see. So I'm turning this over to Remy Boltuck, a Seagater since birth!"

"Hello, everyone," I say softly, and then realize I need to get people pumped up. "Hello, Seagate Island! The best place on earth!" I yell, and everyone starts cheering. "I know you're all as excited as I am for Seagate Halloween, so I don't want to take up too much time. But sometimes people have a secret talent that's really, really awesome, but no one knows about it. And then when one person finds out, she feels the need to tell everyone.

"So, without further ado, I'd like to bring out Mr. Donald Brookfield. I'm sure you've all seen him around—sitting on the bench by Dog Beach, sipping coffee at Mornings, and always ordering the butter pecan sundae at Sundae Best. But you didn't know he had this super amazing skill and that he's been in hundreds of movies—or at least, his voice has. So sit back, relax, put on your best listening ears, and enjoy the show!"

After that, everyone starts cheering even louder, and I wish that I could see Bennett's and Calvin's faces. I hand the megaphone back to Mrs. Paisley, and then Mr. Brookfield comes out—dressed exactly like Calvin in fancy jeans, spiked hair, and a popped-collar polo. It's so funny.

I run off the stage and catch up to the group right at the beginning of the parade route.

"I can't believe you did this, Rem," Bennett says, squeezing my hand for a second and then letting it go. "Claire and Micayla said this was all your idea."

I shrug. "They helped." I look up at the stage and see Mr. Brookfield about to start. "Shh. Listen."

"Welcome, Seagaters," Mr. Brookfield says in his spooky voice. "I dressed as my grandson Calvin Reich. He'll probably kill me for embarrassing him, but he's one of the best guys I know—so I had to do it." And then he pauses for a minute. Everyone looks around, wondering what's about to happen. Maybe he's quiet for more than a minute—I'm not sure, because my heart is pounding and I'm too excited. I know what's coming. I wonder what's spookier: knowing what's coming or not knowing what's coming. I guess that's true when it comes to Seagate Halloween and Mr. Brookfield's scream and life in general.

Finally, he does it.

He screams.

Aaaaheeeeeoowwwww!

Mr. Brookfield's famous scream is broadcast all across Seagate. Everyone at the parade hears it, and I'm sure even latecomers on their way to the parade hear it.

Mr. Brookfield's scream is different from how it used to

be, different from the recording I'd heard so many times. It's scratchier, maybe. It sounds older. But that doesn't mean it sounds bad.

This scream is a link from Mr. Brookfield's past to his future and the start of the parade all at the same time. It's kind of like a link to my old life on Seagate and my new one too.

It takes people a few seconds to realize that they've heard that scream before. And that they've heard it recently. I watch the people in the crowd turn to one another and whisper, and I bet they're saying that it's the scream from the scary movies that have been shown the past few Sunday nights. They get so excited when they realize it—cheering and clapping—until finally all of Seagate is giving Mr. Brookfield a standing ovation.

"See?" I whisper to Claire. "He is a celebrity! A real-life celebrity!"

"I know! And it's the best thing ever!"

Our little doggie day care staff high-five one another, and then we all run to join Mr. Brookfield on the stage. Everyone is cheering, and one by one we approach the microphone and scream. Our own, individual screams. We try to mimic Mr. Brookfield's *Aaaaheeeeoowwwww*, but the screams are all our own.

Claire's is soft and high-pitched, with lots of laughter mixed in. Bennett's and Calvin's are loud and goofy. And Micayla's sounds more like a song than a scream. I don't know what mine is—nervous and excited sounding, I guess. It's almost shocking that this sound is coming out of my mouth.

There's more cheering and more screaming, and it feels like the whole island is a part of it. Everyone who is here now will remember it forever.

After the cheering dies down, I make my way to the microphone again.

"As if that wasn't awesome enough, we have something even more awesome for you! We're starting something new. The first annual Mr. Brookfield Seagate Scream Contest. After the Pooch Parade, everyone who wants to participate should find me on the stage and sign up. We'll have an hour to practice while everyone's enjoying their SGI Sweets, and then we'll have the contest."

Soon it's time for the Pooch Parade. This used to be everyone's favorite part of Seagate Halloween, but I have a feeling the Scream Contest will change that. And that's okay, I think. It's okay to have new favorites.

We make sure all the dogs are with us, and we start marching. We get so many cheers and hoots and "That's so cute" as we walk. The dogs are barking and strutting their stuff, and I can't tell who feels proudest right now—Calvin and Claire about Mr. Brookfield's awesome performance, the dogs for being such a fabulous part of the parade, or me for being surrounded by amazing dogs and amazing friends.

I've had so many perfect moments in all my years on Seagate Island. But this moment, right now, feels the most perfect.

It's not the past that matters so much, or even the future. It's right now.

Right now, the moment you're living, is really the most important.

The scream contest gets off to a chaotic start.
There's a line around the block of people who want to partic-ipate—mostly boys between the ages of eight and fourteen. But Calvin, Claire, Bennett, and Micayla help me collect the names. Next to us, Mr. Brookfield offers coaching, free of charge.

It feels like the whole island is milling about, everyone eating candy, chatting, and savoring the last days of summer on Seagate Island, the best place on earth.

I go up to the microphone one more time. I don't need everybody to pay attention, but I hope some people do. So all I say is, "Seagate Island, get ready to scream!" I tell all the contest participants to stay quiet while the others scream. I feel like a teacher, or maybe a camp counselor. I think these kids may be harder to control than the dogs!

Mr. Brookfield starts off the contest with his famous scream, and then one by one, the participants go to the microphone and say their name and then scream.

It's chaotic and crazy and hilarious and amazing all at the same time.

Mrs. Paisley looks like she has a headache, but she's smiling anyway.

Finally, after the last competitor screams, Mr. Brookfield announces that the judges will vote in the next few hours and the winners will be posted tomorrow.

And we get to be the judges!

Later that night, Mr. Brookfield invites us over for one last pizza party, and it's hard to believe that this is the last time we'll do this for a whole year. But tonight's pizza party is different. It's not just the six of us. There are seven others here: Oscar, Marilyn Monroe, Atticus, Rascal, Palm, Tabby, and Potato Salad.

The dog owners thought it was funny that their dogs were invited to Mr. Brookfield's house and they weren't. Mr. Brookfield's pretty famous now, so they're a little jealous. But the dogs are part of our crew. They can't be left out on our last night.

The dogs sit at our feet and run around the backyard as we eat our pizza. We chat, reminisce about the summer, and talk about what the coming year will be like. Micayla promises that she'll email us every day to tell us about year-round life on Seagate. Calvin and Claire promise that they'll be back next summer.

"I can't believe we waited so long to spend a summer here," Claire says.

Calvin adds, "Yeah, and we had to be forced to do it."

"And just think," I say, "if you had played tennis at tennis camp, you might never have come back, Claire." I smile at her, and she smiles back and then hits me on the arm.

"You're never going to let that go, huh?"

"Nope!"

"If only Mason Redmond were here," Bennett says, in his jokey way, looking at Micayla and rubbing Potato Salad's belly. "Then the summer would be complete. It's a shame he had to leave early. Was he taking the SATs or something?"

Micayla rolls her eyes, and at just that moment Marilyn Monroe hops up onto her lap.

"Oh, leave her alone," Claire says. "Maybe you should be—"

"Should be what?" Bennett asks.

Claire looks at me. I speak to her in blinks, urging her not to embarrass me, not to ruin this most perfect day. She giggles a little. I wait for her to say something else. I mentally plead with her to change the subject.

"Maybe you should be a forward thinker," she says, shrugging, like it's no big deal, like it's what she planned to say all along. "Mason's not so bad. Leave Micayla alone."

Phew! Good cover-up. For once she didn't say the most embarrassing thing she could think of.

"Wow. Claire Reich, suddenly the one who's looking out for everyone." Bennett nods like he totally approves. "Anyone who looks out for Micayla is a friend of mine." He high-fives her, and then slowly and nonchalantly Claire winks at me.

As we finish our pizza, I tell them that I have an announcement to make, and I grab Marilyn Monroe from Micayla. "Marilyn Monroe and I are becoming roommates soon," I say. "Actually, next week!"

"Huh?" Micayla asks.

So I tell them the whole story about Amber and Marilyn Monroe and the new apartment and everything.

"Will your parents say yes?" Claire asks.

"Yeah, I asked them, and they said yes right away. I couldn't believe it, but then they said how impressed they were with the dog-sitting business, and how responsible I have been."

"You didn't say anything to him, did you?" Claire asks me a few minutes later, when Bennett and Calvin are attempting to play Ping-Pong in the air, without a table.

"What?" I ask, confused, still thinking about what it will be like when Marilyn Monroe is my dog. Really and truly my dog.

"About how you feel," she whispers, talking through her teeth. "Bennett."

I shake my head.

"How come?"

"I didn't feel the need to. Things are so great right now. I know that things change, and pretty often it's great when they do," I tell her. "But in this moment, for now, I just want this one thing to stay the same. I'm happy now, and I'm scared to think about things with Bennett and me being that different. Know what I mean?"

Claire nods. "I do."

"And besides," I say and put my arm around her, "there's always next summer."

We sit around talking for a while longer, and as we're talking, I look around at my old friends and my new friends, my human friends and my dog friends, and I realize that this summer and especially Seagate Halloween were completely different from all the ones that came before. Different and sometimes scary and hard.

But they were also better. Better than I could have ever imagined.

ACKNOWLEDGMENTS

First and foremost, I owe an ocean of gratitude to Aleah Violet Rosenberg and her amazing napping skills. Without them, this book would have never been written.

Thanks to Dave for all of the ideas, love, and support. And thanks for indulging my beach house dreams. One day, it will happen.

Thank you, Mom and Dad, for finally getting me a dog when I was in ninth grade, and for everything else, too.

David and Max, thanks for taking Yoffi out all those times when I was feeling lazy. You're superhero brothers and two of my best friends.

Thanks to Bubbie and Zeyda for being dog lovers, for introducing me to my first dog love, Candy, and for being wonderful in every way.

To the Rosenberg family—Karen, Aaron, Elon, Justin, Ari,

Ezra, Maayan, Libby, Bruce, Debbie, Marty, and Donna—thanks for all the encouragement and enthusiasm and for being "dog people."

Many thanks to Arthur, the Franks, the Freels, the Hermans, the Rosensteins, and the Friedmans. I feel the love all the way from Indiana.

Oodles of thanks to the Sterns and the Lincers and all the dog stories you've shared.

Thanks to Tata, Beard, Sarah, Aaron, and Juju for sharing your magical Block Island house with me and for providing me with so much inspiration for this story.

Caroline, Jenny, and Siobhan, thanks for all the help, the writing retreats, and the laughter.

Hugs and kisses and so much appreciation for Rhonda, Melanie, Margaret Ann, and the whole BWL family.

Alyssa Eisner Henkin, I say this every time because it's true: You're the best agent in the world, and I owe you everything. You can come stay at my beach house anytime.

A whole sea of thanks goes to Howard, Steve, Susan, Jason, Chad, Maria, Jessie, Jen, Meagan, Nicole, Laura, Elisa, and everyone at Abrams and Amulet. Thank you, thank you, thank you!

Maggie Lehrman, thanks for believing in this book and for being as excited about it as I am. You've made every page better than I could have imagined. There will be an Adirondack chair on the front porch waiting for you.